CULTURAL
IMPERIALISM
AND THE
INDO-ENGLISH
NOVEL

# Fawzia Afzal-Khan

# CULTURAL IMPERIALISM AND THE INDO-ENGLISH NOVEL

Genre and Ideology in
R. K. Narayan, Anita Desai,
Kamala Markandaya, and Salman Rushdie

The Pennsylvania State University Press
University Park, Pennsylvania

Library of Congress Cataloging-in-Publication Data

Afzal-Khan, Fawzia, 1958–
    Cultural imperialism and the Indo-English novel : genre and
ideology in R. K. Narayan, Anita Desai, Kamala Markandaya, and Salman
Rushdie / Fawzia Afzal-Khan.

        p.        cm.
    Includes bibliographical references and index.
    ISBN 0-271-00912-8 — ISBN 0-271-01013-4 (pbk.)
    1. Indic fiction (English)—History and criticism.    2. Literature
and society—India—History—20th century.    3. Desai, Anita, 1937–
—Criticism and interpretation.    4. Narayan, R. K., 1906–
—Criticism and interpretation.    5. Markandaya, Kamala, 1924–
—Criticism and interpretation.    6. Rushdie, Salman—Criticism and
interpretation.    7. Imperialism in literature.    I. Title.
PR9492.2.A4    1993
823—dc20                                                     92-29782
                                                             CIP

Published by The Pennsylvania State University Press, Suite C, Barbara Building,
University Park, PA 16802-1003
Printed in the United States of America

It is the policy of The Pennsylvania State University Press to use acid-free paper for the first
printing of all clothbound books. Publications on uncoated stock satisfy the minimum
requirements of American National Standard for Information Sciences—Permanence of
Paper for Printed Library Materials, ANSI Z39.48–1984.

*To my first and forever family, the Afzals of Lahore*

# Contents

# *Preface and Acknowledgments*

This book seeks to provide an analysis of how binary categories of cultural classification such as Us/Them and East/West have worked in the production of knowledge and counter-knowledge within what has been a largely dominant Orientalist framework of literary and cultural study.

In such a context, the terms "authenticity" and "culture" take on a nonessentialized significance. What I mean to suggest here is that different versions of identity and authenticity are always being circulated within the realm of ideas and cultural politics, and that each version generates its own "truth-effects." If we acknowledge, with Foucault, that knowledge and power are inextricably linked, then certainly we must recognize that particular versions of in/authenticity and non/identity will gain more currency at a particular site, depending upon the nexus of power relationships. Thus, for example, it becomes possible to elevate at the site of Western discursive power Naipaul's critique of the "authentic native" to the point where it assumes a certain transparency in its truth-effect, while simultaneously devaluing those positionalities that seek to establish a politics-of-presence or "authenticity" as a way of correcting an imbalance of power. It is precisely to challenge the truth-claims of the former kind that the notion of "native authenticity" is deployed as a countermeasure; albeit it is a notion whose efficacy is contingent on constantly evolving class, race, and gender-based histories of self/other, margin/center relations.

I hope that this book will make some small contribution toward that evolution, and that it will prove to be a handy guide for those seeking pedagogical frameworks suitable for the teaching of postcolonial literatures in general and South Asian literature in particular.

My career as a scholar would not have been launched had it not been for the patience, love, and guidance I have received from many people: my thesis adviser, Martin Green, has always been inspirational; Elizabeth Ammons has offered so much support over the years that this book could not have seen the light of print without her; Amritjit Singh has been a dear friend and a sharp critic of my work; R. Radhakrishnan's solidarity and criticism have been invaluable; Feroza Jussawalla deserves special thanks for her professional support and generosity of spirit; and of course, my husband Babar's quiet encouragement as well as my daughter Faryal's delicious presence and tolerance of her mother's often absent presence has made this book finally possible.

I would also like to thank my editor, Philip Winsor at Penn State Press, for his faith in my book, and the staff for their patience with a first-time author. I would also like to acknowledge Gregory Waters, Deputy Provost at Montclair State College for his much-welcomed assistance.

Portions of my chapters on Anita Desai and Salman Rushdie were previously published in the following journals: "Anita Desai: Moral Realist or Myth-maker?" in *South Asian Review* (July 1988); "Myths De-bunked: Genre and Ideology in Salman Rushdie's *Midnight Children* and *Shame*," in *Journal of Indian Writing in English* (January 1986); and "Post-Modernist Strategies of Liberation in the Oeuvre of Salman Rushdie," in *Journal of South Asian Literature* 23 (1988). My thanks to the editors of these journals for granting me permission. My thanks also to Robert Ross, editor of *International Literature in English: The Major Writers* (New York: Garland, 1991), for first publishing my essay on *The Satanic Verses* (which appears here as a portion of my chapter on Salman Rushdie).

# Introduction

This book focuses on the novels of four major contemporary Indian novelists writing in English—R. K. Narayan, Anita Desai, Kamala Markandaya, and Salman Rushdie—and explores the tensions in these works between ideology and the generic fictive strategies that shape ideology or are shaped by it. An important question raised in this study is how far the usage of certain ideological strategies actually helps postcolonial writers deal effectively with the trauma of colonialism and its aftermath. A related question is whether or not the choice of a particular genre or mode by a postcolonial writer presupposes the extent to which that writer will be successful in challenging the ideological strategies of "containment" perpetrated by most Western "Orientalist" writers and their texts on "other" peoples and cultures. The main argument developed in this study is that despite reflecting competing and sometimes contradictory ideological tensions, the works of these writers all demonstrate the use of ideology ultimately as a "liberating" rather than a "containing" strategy. This revisioning of the definition of ideology in the context of nonhegemonic groups/cultures extends the parameters of the debate about ideological structures of containment begun by critics such as Fredric Jameson and Edward Said[1] and carried on by younger critics like Abdul JanMohammed and Rabia Kabbani.

Fredric Jameson, in his book *The Political Unconscious*, states that ideology consists of "strategies of containment." The writer, by unconsciously (or, often, consciously) attempting to validate himself and his group in the face of what he perceives as an antagonistic other, ends up confining himself to the limited, and limiting, economic and sociopolitical interests of his class or group. In a similar fashion, he confines the other to an antagonistic value system.[2] Certainly, this has been true in the case of many hegemonic Western writers, who have tried to contain the colonized other in their narrative frameworks in order then to justify their group's (or country's) imperialist activities. As Edward Said explains in *Orientalism:*

> The Oriental is depicted in Western political and literary texts as something one studies and depicts (as in a curriculum), as some-

1. Said's *Orientalism* (1978) is of course the "founding text" upon which much of "postcolonialist" discourse theory is based. Like my work here, much of the scholarship following Said's lead has sought to extend the implications of his analysis by uncovering or "unpacking" discourses of resistance to Orientalism. Said himself admits in the introduction to his latest book, *Culture and Imperialism* (1993), that

> "what I left out of *Orientalism* was that response to Western dominance which culminated in the great movement of decolonization all across the Third World. Along with armed resistance in places as diverse as nineteenth-century Algeria, Ireland, and Indonesia, there also went considerable efforts in cultural resistance almost everywhere, the assertions of nationalist identities, and, in the political realm, the creation of associations and parties whose common goal was self-determination and national independence. Never was it the case that the imperial encounter pitted an active Western intruder against a supine or inert non-Western native; there was always some form of active resistance, and in the overwhelming majority of cases, the resistance finally won out" (xii).

My book plots just such a path of resistance, albeit in the realm of culture rather than politics, through the modern Indo-English novel. But, as Said too points out, "culture *is* a sort of theatre where various political and ideological causes engage one another" (xiii, my emphasis). Thus, I treat the novel much as Said does, as a cultural form that embodies the very "attitudes, references, and experiences" at the heart both of Imperialism and decolonization. "The power to narrate," claims Said, "or to block other narratives from forming and emerging, is very important to culture and imperialism, and constitutes one of the main connections between them" (xiii). It is precisely to counter the narratives of cultural imperialism, I argue, that colonized people have come up with their own narrative stories and methods; or, as Said puts it, to "assert their *own* identity and the existence of their *own* history" (xii, my emphasis)—however intertwined these narratives/histories/identities are with each other.

2. Fredric Jameson, *The Political Unconscious: Narrative as a Socially Symbolic Act* (Ithaca: Cornell University Press, 1981), 70, 80.

thing one judges (as in a court of law), something one disciplines (as in a school or prison), something one illustrates (as in a zoological manual). The point is that in each of these cases, *the Oriental is contained and represented by dominating frameworks.*[3] (emphasis added)

These dominating frameworks arose, as Said makes clear, because the West had made an assumption during the nineteenth and twentieth centuries that the Orient and everything in it (and by analogy in every other colonized geographical area) was, if not definitively inferior to, then certainly in need of improvement by the West. Since the West's was the more powerful culture, Western writers possessed certain privileges: they could penetrate, wrestle with, give shape and meaning to the "great Asiatic mystery."

The hermeneutics practiced through such a policy of representation are essentially those of the Western historicism definitively enunciated in the theories of such post-Enlightenment philosophers as Jürgen Habermas and Hans-Georg Gadamer. In his central study, *Truth and Method* (1960), Gadamer, for instance, raises the questions that the writers herein analyzed all attempt to grapple with in their respective works: Can we hope to understand works (or cultures) that are historically and culturally alien to us, and is objective understanding possible, or is all understanding relative to our own historical situation?[4] Gadamer's own answer to these questions reveals the cultural biases inherent even in Western liberal humanism. Even though, for Gadamer, all interpretation is situational, shaped and constrained by the historically relative criteria of a particular culture, interpretation of an alien work from within one's own or from an alien culture is possible, either through dialogue between past and present (if the work happens to be from the same culture) or between self and other (if the work is from an alien culture). Confronted with such a work, we listen, according to Gadamer's paradigm, with wise Heideggerian passivity to its unfamiliar voice, tone, content. By allowing the unfamiliar to question the familiar, the past to question the present, we begin to interpret the work (hence also the "alien" culture) more fully.

The event of understanding comes about, according to Gadamer, when our own "horizon" of historical and cultural meanings fuses with the

3. Said, *Orientalism*, 40.

4. Hans-Georg Gadamer, *Truth and Method* (1960; reprint, New York: Seabury Press, 1975), 245–53. All subsequent references to this work will be cited parenthetically in the text as Gadamer.

horizon within which the work operates. "At such a moment, we enter the alien world of the artefact, but at the same time gather it into our own realm, reaching a more complete understanding of ourselves." Instead of "leaving home," Gadamer remarks, we "come home." "Understanding is not to be thought of so much as an action of one's subjectivity, but as the placing of oneself within a process of tradition, in which past and present [self and other] are constantly fused" (Gadamer, 258). Gadamer's assumption is that there is a "unifying tradition" underlying all of history and that it is the recognition and acceptance of this tradition, this bias, that will help us to understand literature and ourselves. The question to ask Gadamer, contends Terry Eagleton in his book *Literary Theory*—the question implicitly asked by postcolonial writers of their colonizing counterparts—is, Whose tradition is such a hermeneutics based on? For Gadamer's theory is based on the enormous assumption that there is indeed a single mainstream tradition that all valid works participate in; "that history forms an unbroken continuum free of rupture, conflict, contradiction; and that the prejudices we (we who?) have inherited from our tradition are to be cherished."[5] Such a hermeneutics assumes, in other words, that history defines a landscape where one can always and in all places be at home; that works about the past or about a different culture or history, about the other, will not confuse us, but will rather increase our self-understanding; in other words, that the alien is always secretly familiar, the other both inscrutable and always already known.

Thus, in "giving shape to the great Asiatic mystery," the Western writer, even when operating within a liberal humanist perspective, even with the loftiest of motives, perpetuates an ideology of containment by assuming that the alien is secretly familiar. Mcbryde's racial theories concerning the Indians in E. M. Forster's *A Passage to India* exhibit just such familiarity: "The darker races are always attracted to the fairer, but never vice versa."[6] Arguably, Mcbryde does not represent Forster's own views. Nevertheless, Forster himself, in his depiction of Dr. Aziz, an Indian character with whom he empathizes, is unable to create an Indian without stereotyping him. David Rubin, in his recent study of Indo-English fiction, concurs with my view:

5. Terry Eagleton, *Literary Theory* (Minneapolis: University of Minnesota Press, 1983), 72. All subsequent references to this work will be cited parenthetically in the text as Eagleton.
6. E. M. Forster, *A Passage To India* (1924; reprint, Harcourt Brace Jovanovich: New York, 1984), 219.

Forster, for all his real sympathy for Indians and his censure of the ignorance and heartlessness of colonial Englishmen, is not free from certain common prejudices. Consider first his Indian characters . . . : Aziz, both childlike and childish, sentimental, prone to tears . . . helpless in a crisis, capable of great vindictiveness and the most astonishing fantasies and lies, such as telling Adela that his wife is alive; mediocre, cowardly and silly Dr. Panna Lal; the fatuous Nawab; and Professor Godbole, who is not so much profoundly spiritual as merely absurdly irrational. In the long run, their India remains true to the convention of muddle and what the author himself terms "the celebrated Oriental confusion."[7]

The ideology of containment, of which a writer like E. M. Forster is a benign example, perpetuates misunderstanding of a historical and cultural other, especially when the self (of the writer, of the writer's culture) has the power to define that other. Yet, as Said has written, and as the ideological strategy of containment shows, the vocabulary and the vision of such a historicist "privilege" are constricting and limited. Consequently, the Orientalist and colonialist "reality" has been both antihuman and persistent.

Faced with an ideology of containment that has thus sought to represent the "alien" writer and his or her people as the dehumanized other, or object, what are the ideological paths open to the postcolonial writer? He or she can either accept this contained image as other by sharing the hermeneutic enterprise of historicism, resulting in a literature that is primarily self-hating, as in the case of Naipaul, or he or she can refute the ideology of containment with an ideology of liberation. The latter is an ideology that allows writers from colonized lands to transform their past, their culture, and their people, from being determinate objects to becoming living subjects, from constituting the antagonistic other to becoming a sympathetic self.

Before I look into the difficulties inherent in defining and adopting an ideology of liberation, it is important to examine, albeit briefly, the concept of "self-hatred" that is the ideological response most evident in much of V. S. Naipaul's work, most specifically in his "travel" narratives. Keeping

---

7. David Rubin, *After the Raj: British Novels of India Since 1947* (Hanover, N.H.: University Press of New England, 1986), 17. All subsequent references to this work will be cited parenthetically in the text as Rubin.

in mind Naipaul's formal strategies, it will become clear later, during my discussion of Rushdie's oeuvre, that such a concept does not apply to Rushdie. The distinction is important because Rushdie has been accused, especially of late, of being another Naipaul. Yet, a brief look at "The Crocodiles of Yamoussoukro" (a short narrative about Naipaul's trip to the Ivory Coast), and at some key passages in *An Area of Darkness* and *The Middle Passage*, reveals how Naipaul endorses the same Western Orientalist notions about Third World cultures and societies that Rushdie, in his novels, quite explicitly rejects.

Although Naipaul, in "The Crocodiles of Yamoussoukro," is not writing about his own West Indian culture and society, it is clear that he views the African society of the Ivory Coast as merely an extension of what he already knows about the postcolonial Third World whence he hails. He states:

> I travel to discover other states of mind, and if for this intellectual adventure I go to places where people live restricted lives, it is because my curiosity is still dictated in part by my colonial Trinidad background. I go to places which however alien, connect in some way with what I already know.[8]

What Naipaul "already knows," then, about the natives of the Ivory Coast is that they lead "restricted lives." They lead such circumscribed, "petrified" lives because, in Naipaul's opinion, they adhere to a culture that still stresses belief in the old mythic (primitive) traditions in tribal politics and in magic, which keeps them chained to a never-changing past—and this, despite the ostensible desire for "progress" and "modernity," for entering the "new world," exhibited through the various projects initiated by the president himself. For, as Naipaul sees it (and repeats as a constant refrain in his narrative), "The new world existed in the minds of other men. Remove those men [Europeans] and their ideas—which after all had no finality—would disappear. Skills could be taught. What was fragile—to men [i.e., Africans] whose complete real life lay in another realm of the spirit—was faith in the new world" ("Crocodiles," 141).

And, since "faith in the new world" is so sorely lacking, on the slightest pretext, Africans throw off the garb of civilization that they don in the presence of the "civilized" Frenchmen and other Europeans (who have

---

8. V. S. Naipaul, *Finding the Center: Two Narratives* (New York: Alfred A. Knopf, 1984), 90. All subsequent references to this work will be cited parenthetically in the text as Naipaul, "Crocodiles."

stayed on after "independence" to help them run their country) and return to their primitive ways. (These expatriate neocolonials, says Naipaul elsewhere in his narrative [83], "become genuinely good people" because they are performing "a disinterested exercise of virtue" by staying on!)

Naipaul's theory that Africans, at heart, are primitives living in a state of historical and cultural petrification is confirmed when a beach restaurant that normally is "worth the fare and the journey in the midday heat," because of the "French style of the place," is found not to be so on one particular day. From this "fact," Naipaul deduces:

> It was more than a matter of an off day. The waiters, impeccable the day before, were casual, vacant. There were long delays, mistakes; some of the portions were absurdly small; the bill, when it came, was wrong. Someone was missing, perhaps the French or European manager. And with him, more than good service had gone: the whole restaurant idea had vanished. An elaborate organization had collapsed. The waiters—Ivorian . . . seem to have forgotten . . . why they were doing what they did. . . . They were not waiters now, in spite of their flowered tunics. Their faces and manners radiated various degrees of tribal authority. I saw them as men of weight in the village: witch doctors, herbalists, men who perhaps put on masks and did the sacred dances. The true life was there, in the mysteries of the village. The restaurant, with its false, arbitrary ritual, was the charade; I half began to see it so. (141)

It is quite clear that Naipaul sees the Ivorians (symbolic of Africans as a whole) as caught in the clutches of tribal traditions, rooted in a mystical, magical way of life belonging to the "old world," a world of "darkness," a world that is therefore "mysterious" to the sophisticated, "civilized" outsider who belongs to the "new world" (the world of "light"). Although Naipaul grants that this rootedness in mythical traditions of the past is what gives the Africans a sense of identity, of cultural "completeness" or "wholeness," ultimately it is this very sense of self-sufficiency and essential completeness that negates the possibility of true change in Africa.

Thus, it is not surprising that the president of the Ivory Coast—despite his desire to "modernize" his country by having fancy hotels, highways, and schools built, by mechanizing farming, by trying to "democratize" the country—remains, in Naipaul's opinion, the tribal chieftain that he in actuality is.

The crocodiles kept outside his palace in his native village of Yamoussoukro become a symbol of his power as tribal chief; and the "crocodile ritual"—that of sacrificing a chicken and feeding it to one of the crocodiles every afternoon—becomes a ritual meant to instill fear into the hearts of his enemies, not merely an intriguing tourist attraction. It becomes, in other words, a symbol of the primitive, magical "night world" to which the Africans in reality belong, and thus negates the world of "light" that the modern aspects of Yamoussoukro stand for:

> Down one side of the palace there is an artificial lake, and in this lake turtles and man-eating crocodiles have been introduced. These are totemic, emblematic creatures and they belong to the president. . . . No one knows precisely what they mean. But to all Africans they speak at once of danger and of the president's, *the chief's magically granted knowledge of his power* as something more than human, something emanating from the earth itself. (76; emphasis added)

Having established the totemic significance of the crocodiles, Naipaul then goes on to describe the ritual of feeding the crocodiles:

> The feeding ritual takes place in the afternoon, in bright light. There are the cars, the tourists in bright clothes, the cameras. But the crocodiles are sacred. A live offering—a chicken—has to be made to them; it is part of the ritual. *This element of sacrifice, this protracted display of power and cruelty*, is as unsettling as it is meant to be, and *it seems to bring night and forest close again to the dream of Yamoussoukro*. (78; emphasis added)

The "dream" of Yamoussoukro is of course the dream of bringing "light" and "civilization" to the bush, in the shape of modern highways, hotels, and, yes, even a presidential golf course. Yet, as Naipaul so astutely observes, the "night world" representing the "real" Africa is too close and too powerful to let the "dream" of Yamoussoukro become a reality. "Away from the stupendous modern frivolities of the golf course and the golf club and swimming pool of the Hotel President there is the presidential palace with its artificial lake . . . [where] the president's totemic crocodiles are fed with fresh meat every day" (77).

Naipaul concludes that it is futile to speculate or feel anxious about how Africa will cope with its entry into the "new world," since, in fact, Africa will always remain rooted in its mythic, mystical past, forever "complete" and unchangeable, forever in a state of historical petrification:

> To the man from outside . . . Africa can often seem to be in a state of becoming. . . . So it arouses hope, ambition, frustration, irritation. And even the success of the Ivory Coast induces a kind of anxiety. Will it last? Will the Africans be able to take over from the French and the Israelis and the others who have built it all for them and still effectively run it?
>
> And then, at a place like Yamoussoukro, where the anxiety becomes most acute, it also begins to feel unreal. *You get a glimpse of an African Africa, an Africa which—whatever the accidents of history . . . has always been in its own eyes complete, achieved, bursting with its own powers.* (78; emphasis added)

From this analysis of "The Crocodiles of Yamoussoukro," it should be clear that Naipaul is using myth here not as a strategy of liberation (as Rushdie does by debunking the genre itself), but rather, as countless Western Orientalists have before him, to contain Africa as other—the "dark continent" still caught in the grip of magical, sinister forces of the "night," so directly opposed to the rational, civilized world of "light" symbolized by the modern West.

He uses the same metaphor of darkness to label and contain India, his country of origin, as well. In his autobiographical nonfiction narrative about India, entitled *An Area of Darkness,* Naipaul writes:

> To me as a child the India that had produced so many of the persons and things around me was featureless, and I thought of the time when the transference was made as a period of darkness, darkness which also extended to the land, as darkness surrounds a hut at evening. . . . The light was the area of my experience, in time and place. And even now, though time has widened, though space has contracted and I have traveled lucidly over that area which was to me the area of darkness, something of darkness remains, in those

attitudes, those ways of thinking and seeing, which are no longer mine.[9]

The rest of this "nonfictional" tract reinforces the fiction of Orientalism: that India is indeed an "area of darkness" that will perpetually remain so because, like the Africa described in "The Crocodiles of Yamoussoukro," it is caught in the grip of age-old superstitions and traditional beliefs that prevent its inhabitants from undergoing fundamental change. Thus, the examples of an errand boy turned tycoon who still retains a cubbyhole for an office, of the entrepreneur clerk who continues sleeping on the pavement even after striking it rich, and of the Brahmin leather-goods manufacturers still anxious to protect their children against caste contamination are seen by Naipaul to be symbolic of a mythic Indian attitude that reveres the ancient traditions of caste and degree; so that even when people rise above their poverty-stricken backgrounds (as in the examples cited above), they nevertheless adhere to the rule of degree in their everyday pattern of living. "A knowledge of degree is in the bones" asserts Naipaul, "and no Indian is far from his origins" (*Area*, 59). Even Parsis, who seem to constitute one of the more "progressive" communities of India owing to a certain amount of westernization, are not really so, according to Naipaul. "But that little corner of merry England which they have created in Bombay is also Druidical. It worships fire; its ways are narrow and protective, and at the end lie Towers of Silence and the grim rites behind those walls whose main portals are marked with a symbol from the ancient world" (60).

If the deprecating language and imagery used here to describe India and its people appears strikingly similar to that employed in "The Crocodiles of Yamoussoukro," it is because, in fact, it is; and, as such, it reveals the depth of Naipaul's self-hatred, which drives him incessantly to demarcate the difference between who he is today (an inhabitant of the world of "light") and what his very distant past (with its link to India) was (a world of "darkness"). What he is today, he repeats obsessively throughout the book, is an Anglicized West Indian with a remote Indian ancestry—with the emphasis on "Anglicized." "London," he writes, "had become the center of my world, and I had worked hard to come to it" (45). As the westernized native par excellence, Naipaul succumbs to the syndrome of alienation so astutely described by Frantz Fanon: "At a given stage, [such

9. V. S. Naipaul, *An Area of Darkness* (1964; reprint, New York: Vintage Books, 1981), 32. All subsequent references to this work will be cited parenthetically in the text as Naipaul, *Area*.

a writer] feels that his race no longer understands him, or that he no longer understands it. Then, congratulating himself on grasping this fact, he enlarges the difference, the disharmony, the incomprehension, and finds in them the meaning of his real humanity."[10] In so doing, Naipaul creates a literature of self-hatred that duplicates Orientalist strategies of containment in which myth is used neither to debunk itself nor to glorify the past, but as a symbol of petrified societies enshrouded in perpetual darkness.

No account of Naipaul's self-hatred would be quite complete without a reference to his 1963 travel book *The Middle Passage: The Caribbean Revisited.* In September of 1960, Naipaul was given a scholarship by the government of Trinidad and Tobago to revisit his homeland and other countries of the Caribbean, out of which came this book. I would here like just to point out a few key passages where Naipaul's intense dislike of and revulsion toward his place(s) of origin and his people are felt most palpably. This antipathy starts to rear its ugly head from the moment that the sophisticated, Anglicized Naipaul steps foot on the train carrying scores of West Indians to the ship in Southampton that will carry them "home" for a return visit and bring back scores more of suchlike "immigrants" to Mother England. These people are described as at a remove from the worldly and westernized Naipaul: the women are dressed in gaudy pink satin petticoats, pink tights, and felt hats, sweaty-faced and visibly uncomfortable; the men, touting "Nat King Cole" hairstyles, are loud-mouthed and uncouth; and, of course, there are the interminable babies, typecast as "fat, bonneted . . . gift-wrapped in ribbons and frills,"[11] with rubber nipples sticking out of their mouths from which emanates a seemingly unstoppable flow of spittle.

The picture only gets uglier, because it loses the hints of irony lurking beneath the descriptions above, and even when Naipaul's criticism of postcolonial society "back home" has the ring of authenticity, it nevertheless estranges the reader because of the total absence of empathy. For instance, once back in Trinidad, the land of his birth, Naipaul feels free to make the most sweeping generalizations about what he considers to be despicable and faulty about the people and the place, without ever historicizing his statements. In the following passages, he sardonically critiques the Trinidadian drive to "modernity" without pausing for a

10. Frantz Fanon, *Black Skin, White Masks* (New York: Grove Press, 1967), 16. All subsequent references to this work will be cited parenthetically in the text as Fanon.

11. V. S. Naipaul, *The Middle Passage: The Caribbean Revisited* (New York: Macmillan, 1963), 11. All subsequent references to this work will be cited parenthetically in the text as Naipaul, *MP.*

moment to genuinely examine the historical reasons for and ramifications
of such a condition:

> To be modern is to ignore local products and to use those advertised
> in American magazines. The excellent coffee which is grown in
> Trinidad is used only by the very poor and a few middle-class
> English expatriates. Everyone else drinks Nescafe or Maxwell
> House . . . which is more expensive but is advertised in the
> magazines and therefore acceptable. The elegant and comfortable
> morris chairs, made from local wood by local craftsmen, are not
> modern and have disappeared except from the houses of the poor.
> (Naipaul, *MP*, 46)

From these general observations, Naipaul draws the following astounding,
ahistorical conclusion: "Modernity in Trinidad, then, turns out to be the
extreme susceptibility of *people who are unsure of themselves and, having
no taste or style of their own, are eager for instruction*" (46–47; emphasis
added).

Naipaul, on the other hand, sees himself (in contradistinction to the
poor, easily duped natives) as the man of style, taste, and class par
excellence. What he fails to acknowledge, however, is the fact that this
"style" of his is as imitative, if not more so, of the West than that of his
other compatriots. Thus, the irony of Naipaul's disparagement of the local
taste for Hollywood's "B" movies, instead of for the "higher-class" French,
Italian, or Swedish films that he prefers, is entirely lost on him. No small
wonder then, that having castigated Trinidadian society for lacking an
authentic culture of its own, for being "a colonial society, with no standards
of its own . . . [a society in which] minds are rigidly closed" (61), Naipaul
can be blind to the self-hatred he reveals in expressing his revulsion toward
anything that is "authentically" Trinidadian, including his physical presence in Trinidad itself.

> . . . on the quay . . . I began to feel all my old fear of Trinidad. I
> did not want to stay. . . . the city throbbed with steel bands. A
> good opening line for a novelist or a travel writer; but the steel band
> used to be regarded as a high manifestation of West Indian Culture,
> and it was a sound I detested. . . . The years I had spent abroad
> fell away and I could not be sure which was the reality in my life:
> the first eighteen years in Trinidad or the later years in England. I

had never wanted to stay in Trinidad. . . . and for many years afterwards in England, falling asleep in bedsitters with the electric fire on, I had been awakened by the nightmare that I was back in tropical Trinidad. (41)

For Naipaul, not only Trinidad and the West Indies but the Third World in general is a nightmare of history he seeks desperately to avoid by living in the world of light—the West. He is not interested in recovering the authentic voice of Third World societies, because it is their very authenticity (one aspect of which is symbolized by the steel drums of Trinidad) that serves to remind him of his own otherness in Western culture—a fact he so desperately wishes to efface. The more he wishes to ally himself to the West, the more he must distance himself from and disparage colonial and postcolonial societies.[12]

Naipaul's use of the genre of myth thus contributes to the kind of denigrating imagery of the Third World that Markandaya (see Chapter 3) speaks so stridently against and that all of the four writers under discussion try to counteract in some way through their writings. It should be clear then, that acceptance of the image of postcolonial peoples and cultures as other can lead, in the case of the native writer, only to a literature of self-hatred, as is evident in Naipaul's case. Such literature further perpetuates the Orientalist ideology of containment and can be refuted effectively only by those writers who choose, consciously or not, to transform such an ideology into one of liberation in their works.

12. In fairness to Naipaul, it should be acknowledged that some of his earlier fiction, such as *Miguel Street* (1959) and *A House for Mr. Biswas* (1961), both set in his native Trinidad, seems far less bitter and self-hating than the nonfiction work I have focused on. In his earlier work, empathy does seem within reach, and in his most recent nonfiction book on India, entitled *India: A Million Mutinies Now* (1990), Naipaul's approach seems mellower, his tone less strident than before. Could it be that there are, perhaps, two Naipauls? Gordon Rohler (quoted in Amritjit Singh's article "The Uses of Exile," *Commonwealth Literature* [Madras: Macmillan India, 1981]) recognizes that Naipaul is partially successful in achieving sympathy in some of his earlier fiction. Biswas, according to Rohler, is "fully presented as a person whose every quirk and idiosyncrasy we know, in a world whose every sight, sound and smell is recorded with fidelity and precision" (178). D. J. Enright, another critic quoted in Singh's article, says of Naipaul's latest novel, *A Bend in the River* (1979), that "Naipaul is not being merely satirical, or sour, or prickly. . . . There's an extra depth to Naipaul's grief here. . . . What he says originates in reality rather than . . . in his own private nervous sytem" (179). Nevertheless, Singh's own argument is that such instances of "empathy" are the exception, rather than the rule, in Naipaul's work, both fiction and nonfiction.

For a defense of Naipaul that rests its case on analyzing the idiom of his work, see chap. 7, "Naipaul's Arrival," in Sara Suleri, *The Rhetoric of English India* (Chicago: University of Chicago Press, 1992).

As we shall see, such an ideological transformation is not easy to achieve, and again runs the risk of creating an oversimplified dichotomy. Yet, it is a dichotomy inherent in the colonial mentality itself. Frantz Fanon points this out when he says, "White ontology . . . does not permit us to understand the being of the black man. For not only must the black man be black; he must be black in relation to the white man. And the converse of this is not true . . . because the black man has no ontological existence in the eyes of the white man" (110).

According to Fanon, colonization has created a Manichean world that posits an opposition between black and white values, so the colonized writer is forced to choose between the two. Abdul JanMohammed, in his ground-breaking study of the ideological structures in the novels of six African novelists (colonialist and native), effectively agrees with Fanon's thesis that the colonial world is a Manichean world:

> Fanon's definition of colonial society as a manichean organization is by no means exaggerated. In fact, the colonial mentality is dominated by a manichean allegory of white and black, good and evil, salvation and damnation, civilization and savagery, superiority and inferiority, intelligence and emotion, self and other, subject and object.[13]

Thus, if the writer chooses "white" values within the allegorical framework of Manicheanism, then clearly he will feel, at a given stage, that his race no longer understands him, or that he no longer understands it—as is true of Naipaul, for example. The only other option the writer has, it seems, is that of choosing a system of "black" values and constructing an alternative ideology; but this also, according to Fanon, is full of dangerous pitfalls because, more often than not, it results in historical petrification: "More rarely [the colonized writer] wants to 'belong' to his people. And it is with rage in his mouth and abandon in his heart that he buries himself in the vast black abyss. We shall see that this attitude, so heroically absolute, renounces the present and the future in the name of a mythical past" (16).

Given this issue of alternative or competing ideologies, generic form is

---

13. Abdul JanMohammed, *Manichean Aesthetics* (Amherst: University of Massachusetts Press, 1983), 4. All subsequent references to this work will be cited parenthetically in the text as JanMohammed.

the most important tool available for shaping ideological intentions. As Fredric Jameson explains: "Generic affiliations and deviations from them provide clues that lead us back to the concrete historical situation of the individual text itself, and allow us to read its structure as ideology, as a socially symbolic act, as a proto-political response to a historical dilemma."[14]

At this point, it would be appropriate to ask which genre best serves the purpose of a writer wishing to "belong" to his people. Northrop Frye's description of the romance genre in its mythic/magical mode supplies one important answer: "The Romance is nearest of all literary forms to the wish-fulfillment dream . . . the perennially child-like quality of romance is marked by its extraordinarily persistent nostalgia, its search for some kind of imaginative golden age in time or space."[15]

Certainly, a writer like Chinua Achebe uses romance in its mythic mode in *Things Fall Apart* to create a totality of an indigenous Igbo cultural past that is both mythical and mystical. He thus liberates his people from an imperialist ideology that had sought to contain them. At the same time, however, his mythification creates a society that is historically static, or petrified, because it is forever fixed in a mystical past.[16]

As an alternative to romance/myth, the writer may employ the generic form of realism to portray his or her society. "Critical realism," as defined by Georg Lukács, is a genre that is concerned with showing the tension in a society between man as an individual entity and man as social phenomenon and ultimately to resolve that tension by allowing its characters to achieve a balance between the two modes of existence, thus ensuring a harmonious survival of society.[17] Realism, then, becomes a tool for dealing with the present, for dealing with the current problems of man-in-society. It therefore helps the novelist avoid the pitfalls of petrification associated

14. Fredric Jameson, "Magical Narratives: Romance as Genre," *New Literary History* 7 no. 1, 157. All subsequent references to this work will be cited parenthetically in the text as Jameson, MN.

15. Northrop Frye, *Anatomy of Criticism: Four Essays* (1957; reprint, New York: Atheneum, 1970), 186.

16. I would like to point out that although I derive the term "historically petrified" from Abdul JanMohammed's discussions of African novels in *Manichean Aesthetics*, my interpretation of Achebe's use of form/genre in his novels is quite different from JanMohammed's. He does not feel as I do, that Achebe uses mythical strategies of liberation, resulting in "historical petrification." On the contrary, he sees Achebe's novels as "products of a conflict between the desire to retain traditional values . . . and the recognition, manifested in the adaptability of the society, that change and assimilation are absolutely necessary for survival" (JanMohammed, 183).

17. Georg Lukács, *Realism in Our Time: Literature and the Class Struggle* (New York: Harper and Row, 1964), 54–56.

with myth (due to its fixation on the past) while allowing the writer to portray his or her characters in all their realistic, sometimes painful, complexity, keeping them at the same time constantly rooted in the ongoing process of history.

It is this historicist understanding of humankind—arrived at by the realist school in the traditional Aristotelian dictum "Man is a social animal"—that reveals the differences in ideology between "great realist literature" and the work of the leading modernist writers, according to Lukács. "Achilles and Werther," writes Lukács,

> Oedipus and Tom Jones, Antigone and Anna Karenina: their individual existence—their *Sein an sich,* in the Hegelian terminology; their "ontological being," as more fashionable terminology has it—cannot be distinguished from their social and historical environment. Their human significance, their specific individuality cannot be separated from the context in which they were created.[18]

Lukács contrasts this sense of "rootedness" in history and society, which is the ideological hallmark of realism, with the concept of Man as an ahistorical being that arises out of modernism. "Man," for the leading European modernist writers (such as Kafka, Beckett, Joyce, Musil, etc.) "is by nature solitary, asocial, unable to enter into relationships with other human beings" (Lukács, *Meaning,* 20). Their solitariness is not a specific fate, as might occur in realist works, but rather a universal *condition humaine.* The problem, then, is ideological, or, to be more precise, poses an ideological choice between a form that presents a dialectic between abstract and concrete potentialities of human beings and one that negates the very distinction.

To explain more fully, let me quote from Lukács again: "The literature of realism, aiming at a truthful reflection of reality, must demonstrate both the concrete and abstract potentialities of human beings in extreme situations. . . . A character's concrete potentiality once revealed, his abstract potentialities will appear essentially inauthentic" (23). Thus, the case of Richard Dudgeon, in Shaw's *Devil's Disciple,* is one that shows how abstract potentiality can be converted into a concrete potentiality when Dudgeon sacrifices himself as Pastor Anderson, demonstrating the dialectic

---

18. Georg Lukács, *The Meaning of Contemporary Realism* (London: Merlin Press, 1963), 19. All subsequent references to this work will be cited parenthetically in the text as Lukács, *Meaning.*

between man as individual and man as social phenomenon. Lukács further elucidates the difference between "abstract potentiality" and "concrete potentiality":

> Abstract potentiality belongs wholly to the realm of subjectivity; whereas concrete potentiality is concerned with the dialectic between the individual's subjectivity and objective reality. The literary presentation of the latter thus implies a description of actual persons inhabiting a palpable, identifiable world. . . . But the ontology on which the image of man in modernist literature is based invalidates this principle. If the "human condition"—man as a solitary being, incapable of meaningful relationships—is identified with reality itself, the distinction between abstract and concrete potentiality becomes null and void. (24)

This distinction between realist literature on the one hand and modernist literature on the other, the latter leading to an attenuation of reality and a dissolution of personality, is an important one to bear in mind for discussion of the generic modes employed by the writers discussed in this volume. For often the modernist ideology tends to exhibit itself through an extreme of realism in which the individual fails to achieve a balance between self and society, or when surrealist fantasies displace realist tendencies. Sometimes, realist and modernist tendencies coexist in the same writer, as in the oeuvre of Salman Rushdie. Thus, the notion of ideology and its expression in literary form becomes very complicated indeed. Yet, it is essential to note that the choices made by European writers did have ideological underpinnings as well as consequences, and it seems safe to say that in the case of Third World postcolonial writers, the ideology of modernism would lead to an ahistoricism that could scarcely qualify as a "strategy of liberation."

In this sense, the modernist impulse is very much akin to the mythic one, in that it tends to negate the ongoing dialectic of history. In validating isolationism as a *condition humaine*, the modernist ideology points to its own political and moral nonviability in the postcolonial context, as well as to the nonviability of those aspects of realism and myth that, as alluded to earlier, are retrogressive in some way. For Lukács, the least retrogressive form of realism would be a blend of critical and socialist realism, eventually giving way to an entirely socialist realism:

> Both [forms of realism] work with the same material, but they apply
> themselves in different ways to be exploration of social reality. The
> deeper they probe, the closer will social reality approximate to the
> desired socialist society, and the closer will grow the ties between
> critical and socialist realism. In the process, the negative perspec-
> tive of critical realism will gradually be transformed into a positive,
> socialist perspective. (114)

The "negative perspective" for Lukács is the fact that critical realism as
a genre is intimately linked to portraying the contradictions of the individual in a capitalist society, so that a typical bildungsroman will end with
the hero either accepting his place within the status quo or resigning
himself to his society's wishes despite his contrary ideals. A socialist
realist novel, however, portraying a socialist society, departs from such a
pattern and, in doing so, proves its moral superiority to the genre of critical
realism:

> In socialist society, the situation is different. A *Bildungsroman,*
> set in a socialist society, only apparently conforms to this pattern
> [of the critical realist novel]; experience itself will convert bourgeois
> individualist into social being. The end is not resignation. On the
> contrary, the end begins with resignation and leads on to active
> participation in the life of the community. Nor does the hero end
> up in isolation, as in so many of the later novels of critical realism.
> (113)

In examining the realism practiced by some of the writers under discussion
in this book, it will become clear that with the exception of Markandaya,
whose vision most closely approximates that of a socialist realist, the others
are practitioners of a critical realist mode (as far as they employ this
generic strategy), which is, for reasons stated earlier, nevertheless the most
morally and politically viable strategy of liberation available to these
writers.

However, I would like to remind the reader that myth and realism have
been, and still are, used as strategies of containment rather than liberation
by countless Orientalists when applied to "other" cultures. (It seems
perfectly appropriate, in the light of my comments on Naipaul, to consider
him in such company.) It is therefore all the more intriguing and important

that these strategies be overturned in their ideological usage by postcolonial writers.

Ruth Prawer Jhabvala is a good example of a contemporary European writer (in contradistinction to the "native" Naipaul) who uses a combination of realism and myth as an ideological strategy for containing the other. In this respect, it is very important, as Rubin notes, to see Jhabvala as a Westerner writing about India, and not as an "Indian" writer, as she is so fondly dubbed by many of her Indian and Western critics alike. Rubin asserts: "I believe, however, that she should not be viewed as an Indian writer but that she actually belongs to the tradition of the Anglo-Indian writers . . . those novelists who for the most part regard India with the critical and often indignant eye of the superior (if lonely) outsider" (77). Viewed in this light, it is easier to understand the persistence of certain myths about India and Indians in Jhabvala's work—chief among them the myth of India as Destroyer—which is so central to the story and structure of *Three Continents*. Rubin's comments in this regard are illuminating:

> It is interesting to observe how powerful the old mythic patterns remain, as Jhabvala, in so many stories and most of the novels, continues to fabricate a basic structure in which individuals are somehow employed to dramatize the powerful and often destructive fascination of race, sex, and spirituality—an apparently indissoluble and threatening Indian trinity that seems still to dominate virtually all Anglo-Indian fiction. While many of Jhabvala's stories debunk the myth to some extent, they subtly reinforce many of its elements: India does destroy, Indian men, no matter how fatuous and without character, remain irresistible to European women. (73)

Her "realism" in her latest novel to date, *Three Continents* (1987), consists in strategically placing her central white (American) characters, the teenage twins Harriet and Michael, in the midst of a social setting that demands of them to make a choice: to be egoistic, self-centered materialists (like their divorced parents) or to "give of themselves" to some noble, "higher" cause. As an Orientalist, Jhabvala makes sure that the reader views the white protagonists as mythic upholders of light and reason and thus expects of them to follow the morally righteous path of critical realism. From the beginning, Jhabvala presents Harriet and Michael as lovers of truth and of noble ideals; this is borne out even in the way their bedrooms are (un)decorated: "His [Michael's] room was the same as mine. Both of us loved *bare* walls, *bare* floors, and no curtains, *to let in as much light as possible*" (emphasis added).[19]

Interestingly, both Harriet and Michael are described as extremely pale skinned, truly "white." The leaders of the "World Movement"—whom Michael and, later, Harriet come to view as representatives of a "cause" worth donating their personal wealth and energy and even love to—on the other hand, are all dark skinned, mysterious, and rather ostentatious (in direct contradiction to their supposed ideal of uniting East and West in a nonmaterialistic spirit of brotherly love). What Jhabvala then exhibits through this use of binary images to depict her European and Indian characters is the age-old mythic consciousness underlying the Orientalist view of self and other. The self here, though naive, is clearly noble and pure in its impulses, until it comes into contact with the crass evil of the fake Indian spiritualists; the other continues to be portrayed as murky, mysterious, and ultimately evil. Hence, the Rawul, the ostensible leader of the movement, is an Indian prince of a dubious, derelict state, whose greatest pleasure seems to be good food—hence his portly figure (nothing ascetic here!). The "rani," his "queenly" consort in America and England, is half-Indian, half-European, and loves to dress lavishly but is filthy underneath (Indian filth beneath a European cover-up?), and is neither the Rawul's wife nor a queen (her real name is Renee)—dubioser and dubioser! Finally, there is Crishi, the "heir apparent," adopted son of the Rawul and rani—again of Indian origin, but of an Assamese mother, hence the slanted eyes, to complete his devilish character.

Crishi is associated in the novel with the mysterious, magnetic ocean; he is a man who loves to lie on the beach on a black rock—a force of darkness, threatening the light of reason. During one of the swims he takes with Harriet, she remarks:

> The farther out I swam in the ocean—and Crishi was making us swim much farther than we wanted to—the more helpless I felt, not so much against the waves as against everything beneath them, all the mysterious unknown dark goings-on there like some vast cosmic unconscious threatening to overwhelm the light of day or reason. But for Crishi, the ocean seemed to be his favorite element. (Jhabvala, 109)

19. Ruth Prawer Jhabvala, *Three Continents* (New York: William Morrow, 1987), 16. All subsequent references to this work will be cited parenthetically in the text as Jhabvala.

This passage essentially sums up the book. Crishi, along with the Rawul and the rani (or Renee), come to exert a mysterious power over Michael and Harriet, who become deeply involved with them. Michael is attracted to the trio for idealistic reasons, and Harriet, because she falls in love with, then marries, Crishi. The conclusion is appropriately horrific: after making over almost their entire wealth to the Indians, Michael realizes his error in judgment—but it is too late. Harriet has by this point lost all power of reason—she is totally, madly, obsessively in love with Crishi. Even though she suspects him of having orchestrated Michael's timely disappearance and death, she, at the end, is shown to be willingly signing over the entire family inheritance (of which, due to Michael's death, she is now sole heir) to Crishi. It seems safe to assert, then, that the book is ultimately about the cosmic struggle between good and evil. What is disturbing is that through the generic strategies of myth and realism, good comes to be represented by scions of a once-noble white family, whereas evil is perennially associated with the characters belonging to the darker races of the ancient, mysterious East. From Conrad's *Heart of Darkness* to Jhabvala's *Three Continents*, the stereotypes of Orientalism have remained the same, and surely one of the tasks the writers under discussion must tackle is the task of liberating themselves and their cultures from the effects of such stereotyping.

Then there is still the case of the writer who neither wishes to "belong" wholeheartedly to his or her culture nor wishes entirely to reject it. What kind of generic strategy would serve the more complex and ambiguous motives/needs of this third group of writers? This is a question that will be raised and addressed largely in the chapter on Rushdie, whose work resists classification along binary lines.

The focus of this book, then, will be an examination of the generic strategy, or combination of strategies, each of the four Indian authors under consideration—Narayan, Desai, Markandaya, and Rushdie—uses to refute the ideology of containment with one of liberation, and how far each is successful in his or her endeavors. Before turning to a discussion of each author, however, it will be useful to elaborate a little more here on the critical definitions of the genres of myth and realism that will be used in the following chapters.

The definitions of the terms "myth" and "mythic mentality," as employed in this study, arise largely out of Ernst Cassirer's descriptions of modern myths in his essay "The Myth of the State" and, as such, blur the distinction between myth as a literary device and myth as an ideological tool in service of the social state. As Cassirer points out, the mythic mentality has been associated by ethnologists, sociologists, anthropologists and psychologists with the "primitive mind." It is therefore associated with a stage of human culture that is "gone forever." According to the well-known theory of Lucien Levy-Bruhl, "there is a deep gulf, an insurmountable barrier between the primitive mind and our own mind. They do not belong to the same genus; they are incomparable and incompatible." He goes on to state, "Primitives see with eyes like ours, but they do not perceive with the same minds. . . . The profound difference which exists between the primitive mentality and our own is shown even in the ordinary perception of the simplest things. Primitive perception is fundamentally mystic . . . ours has ceased to be so."[20]

However, the question Cassirer poses of such a theory of myth, and one that is very relevant to this study, is, "If myth is a typical outcome of the primitive, that is to say the prelogical and mystical mind, how can we account for its sudden reappearance under the conditions of our own highly sophisticated culture?"[21] Of course, Cassirer's reference to a highly sophisticated culture is to the post-Enlightenment, postindustrial culture of the West; and I am dealing with the uses of myth and mythic mentality in a literature produced by a people belonging to a less industrialized culture (which is therefore "sophisticated" in an ancient, rather than a modern, sense). Nevertheless, the writers under discussion are all heavily influenced by the West (not least evidenced in their use of the English language itself), and therefore their work falls within the parameters of Cassirer's debate.

To continue with Cassirer's line of inquiry, he points out that many thinkers have described myth as a kind of "atavism." However, this does not adequately answer the question of myth's power in modern culture, since an atavism is an exception, not the rule. As Cassirer notes, "An atavism of a whole nation would be a very paradoxical and almost inexplicable thing." He refers here to the atavism practiced by the nation of Germany under the rule of Hitler and national socialism. Political myths of the modern world, then, may belong, in Cassirer's opinion, to the same family as the primitive myths of prehistoric cultures, "but do not resemble

20. Lucien Levy-Bruhl, *How Natives Think* (1926; reprint, New York: Arno Press, 1979), 44.

21. Ernst Cassirer, *Symbol, Myth, and Culture* (New Haven: Yale University Press, 1979), 244. All subsequent references to this work will be cited parenthetically in the text as Cassirer.

their brothers" (Cassirer, 245). Indeed, these new myths "appear in broad daylight, they do not fear the light of the sun and cannot be expelled or exorcised; they stand their ground firmly and stoutly" (245). All this leads to the conclusion that myth is not just a "mere relic"—the remains of a dead past, as thinkers of the school of Levy-Bruhl would have us believe. "It is not an outgrowth of primitive mentality; it still has its place in the most advanced stages of human culture. To banish myth, to eradicate its root and branch, would mean an impoverishment. What would become of poetry and art if we would no longer be able to understand the language of myth?" (Cassirer, 245).

Thus, at the same time that myth connotes a reversal to the past, to a state of stasis, there is something enriching about the use of myth, especially in literature. Myth can become an energizing force by firing our imaginations, and as such become the bedrock of ideology. (This concept of "energizing myth" has also been put forward by Martin Green in his brilliant analysis of the myths of empire: *Dreams of Adventure, Deeds of Empire.*) For Cassirer, however, the ideological uses to which myth has been put in modern European society have been evil: witness the Holocaust. Elaborating on the age-old conflict between logos and mythos, Cassirer writes:

> In politics, we are never living on a firm and stable ground. In quiet and peaceful times, in periods of relative stability and security it is easy to maintain a rational order of things. But we are always standing on a volcanic soil and must be prepared for sudden convulsions and eruptions. In the critical moments of man's political and social life, myth regains its old strength. It was always lurking in the background, waiting for its hour and its opportunity. This hour comes if the other binding forces of our social life, for one reason or another, lose their influence; if they can no longer counterbalance the demonic power of myth. (246–47)

The passage quoted above poses an interesting problem in the value ascribed to the mythic mode in the present study; for the writers under discussion, the generic tug-of-war is surely between mythos and logos, myth and realism. In accordance with Cassirer's theory, myth seems to exert its strength as an ideological tool during the crisis created by colonialism and the political and social turmoil that has ensued. Recourse to a mythic mentality and a mythic literary mode affords the kind of respite

Frye has already hinted at—the recovery of some "lost Eden." In this sense, the mythic impulse is certainly regressive and antirationalist. But can it also be demonic as Cassirer claims? In exploring the tensions between myth and realism in the works of these four South Asian writers, this is a facet of myth that also will need to be explored.

Generally speaking, myths are traditional stories relating to religious beliefs, opposed to rational cause/effect explanations. The mythical attitude, therefore, usually signifies a retreat, an escape from the pressures of daily commercial life. Myth is also associated with the magical, the miraculous—again, neither quality being associated with the happenings of everyday social life. Because the mythic mode thus usually implies a retreat, an escape from the pressures and responsibilities of everyday existence, it often symbolizes a rather self-centered, isolationist stance. It sometimes signifies an irresponsible, even fatalistic attitude toward life and toward others. Yet there is something wonderful and energizing about it; it gives one traditions and old beliefs to cling to in the face of an unpleasant reality. Myth often becomes synonymous with tradition, since a retreat to the past is usually a retreat to traditional values eroded by modern society. In this context, myth sometimes comes to symbolize values of community, such as the communal values of the pastoral or village mode of life. Cassirer's definitions of the different ways of thinking implicit in a mythical versus a realistic approach might be usefully quoted here.

> It seems only natural to us that the world should present itself to our introspection and observation as a pattern of definite forms. . . . If we see it as a whole, this whole nevertheless consists of clearly distinguishable units . . . which preserve their identity that sets them apart from the identity of all the others [realism]. But for the mythmaking consciousness these separate elements are not thus separately given . . . but gradually derived from the whole. (13)

This differentiation between myth's tendency toward "wholeness" and the others' toward "individuation" is useful in defining the generic attributes of myth and realism, although, as already stated, such lines of difference do occasionally get blurred.

Often, the traditions of myth are rooted in spiritual and mystical beliefs; thus, although the mythic mode may not always provide for the material well-being of the community, it does provide for the spiritual and emotional needs of people. At other times, however, the mythic mode transforms itself into a mode of fantasy and romance and, instead of satisfying "spiritual" needs, ends up fulfilling a "baser" need for the fantastic, the exotic, and the grandiose in life, an attitude totally opposed to facing "humble" reality.

Realism, in the Lukácsian tradition, concerns itself with portraying everyday "real" life and problems of people: survival, making ends meet, or how to achieve the desired balance between individual desire and communal responsibility. It thus sets up as its ideal the achieving of a wholeness, or unity, of existence. Often, however, it falls short of its ideal and ends up celebrating or urging the choice of one extreme or the other. It addresses itself primarily to the material issues of life and society, without much concern for the spiritual and emotional needs of people. It is usually associated with Western values, for example, rationalism (though not reason, and that is an important distinction), and especially those of commercial enterprise, which, in turn, are the predominant values of modern urban life. It is also associated with the concept of industrial and mechanical progress.

These definitions of myth and realism suggest that several key terms or concepts may be associated with either mode, depending upon which subgenre the mode reflects in different works or even in the same work at different points. For instance, myth is often synonymous with tradition, or the past, which, though more often than not "glorious," suggests a quality of stasis and petrification. Myth is also associated with a pastoral way of life that may sometimes be sheer fantasy (in that it exists no longer) or may be symbolic of a romantic vision. The mythic response to life usually also endorses faith, religion, and may even lead to mysticism and deep spirituality—all associated with a "higher" level of human consciousness and therefore desirable ends. Yet, the egolessness evoked by intense spiritualism can lead to isolation, which in turn can result rather perversely in a kind of ego-aggrandizement. Conversely, when the mythic response occurs within a pastoral setting, it often bespeaks a communal harmony and stands for a vision that transcends the purely individual frame of mind for a more collective one.

Realism, on the other hand, is a mode of much less moral ambiguity than myth. It clearly is the voice of the present and the future, and of modernity. It represents all that is synonymous with Western-style "progress": rationalism, materialism, industrialism, technological innovation. As opposed to the stasis of myth, realism is associated with flux, change, and achievement. Carried to an extreme, the realist individual's will to succeed can lead to extreme egocentrism; yet, the ideal goal espoused by realism is one of achieving an equilibrium between individual needs and communal responsibility.

The choice between these two generic strategies seems relatively clear, then, within the postcolonial writer's context: progressive realism, rather than outdated myth. However, just as my description of myth's concepts indicates ambiguities in its interpretation, so too is the postcolonial writer's situation fraught with ambiguities, such as that raised by the question "How appropriate or desirable is Western-style progress in non-Western societies?" It is this thought that the curious reader should bear in mind as she or he continues to read: given that these modes are, after all, Western formal strategies, how will our Indian writers, choosing to write in the master's tongue and using the master's forms, steer between the Scylla and Charybdis of myth and realism? Further, what generic alternatives are available to writers like Rushdie and, lately, Anita Desai, whose ideological motives resist binary classification?

As a person of South Asian background, I have chosen to concentrate on the works of Indian writers writing in English—two male and two female— in trying to understand the effects of colonialism and neocolonialism on contemporary life. The four writers discussed in this book happen to belong to roughly that period in Indian history when India, having been granted independence by Britain, was (and still is) struggling to overcome its colonial legacy. (Of the four, Narayan is the only writer whose work spans both pre- and postindependent India.) Issues of neocolonialism are undoubtedly of great relevance to the literature and culture of most regions in the world today. Thus, although I have focused on Indian writers writing in English, my analysis is based on definitions of genre and ideology and their function in a postcolonial context that would apply to the works of writers from most geographical areas that were once colonies of the British or other European powers.

# R. K. Narayan

## The Realm of Mythic Realism

The works of R. K. Narayan, who combines Indian myth with critical realism in his "serious" comedies, reveal their ideological implications quite clearly. As William Walsh, in his book *R. K. Narayan: A Critical Appreciation*, points out:

> The reader will have felt the effects of the principle which orders the pattern and affects the structure of Narayan's fiction, namely that of balance. This is a principle of the greatest significance in novels which are comedies of sadness, works in which the material and attitudes appropriate to different genres flow in and out of one another.[1]

In other words, there is a balancing of various genres in Narayan's novels, a harmonious coexistence symbolizing a unity, a wholeness, toward

---

1. William Walsh, *R. K. Narayan: A Critical Appreciation* (Chicago: University of Chicago Press, 1982), 60, emphasis added. All subsequent references to this work will be cited parenthetically in the text as Walsh, *Narayan*.

which Narayan's protagonists are constantly progressing and which they must achieve if they are to mature fully. The wholeness—which, as I will show later, becomes a hollowness for Salman Rushdie (the most modern of the four novelists to be considered)—is possible in the Malgudi of Narayan's novels because it is a world rooted in Indian myth and tradition, a town that is still pastoral in its innocence of the political reality of modern, twentieth-century India. "It is clear that Malgudi, although a small region, is a place of ancient myth and history, which Narayan does not choose to reexamine."[2] Here, what matters most is not how the natives deal with the aftermath of political fragmentation, but whether they will achieve an authentic and sincere identity as Indians in an "authentic" Indian setting (Malgudi).[3]

The issue of authenticity is tied closely to that of sincerity, which can be achieved only through the growth of self- and social-awareness; and most of Narayan's protagonists are able to achieve some measure of both. The goal of Western realism (as seen in Jane Austen's novels, for example) is for the individual to achieve a state of balance between individual autonomy and social responsibility (neither extreme being viewed as good) and this is usually achieved through becoming honest, or sincere, about oneself and one's motives, which, in turn, leads to sincerity and responsibility toward others. Although such authenticity of character and maturity are achieved primarily in the Western realist mode in Narayan's work, the part played by Indian mythical and mystical tradition in achieving these desired ends cannot be underestimated. Narayan, it seems, cannot get away from mythification, because it is through the use of Indian myth that some measure of an authentic Indian past can be recreated. However, it should be clear at the outset that the petrifying effects of myth are not always offset by the balancing effects of realism. Not all of Narayan's protagonists choose to respond to the call of social or familial duty, or to

2. Keith Garebian, "The Spirit of Place in R. K. Narayan," *World Literature Written in English* 14 (November 1975): 292. All subsequent references to this work will be cited parenthetically in the text as Garebian, "Spirit."

3. This concept of the "sincere" and "authentic" self would have found an echo in Rousseau's thought, as explained at length in Lionel Trilling's work, *Sincerity and Authenticity*, (Cambridge: Harvard University Press, 1971). Trilling himself goes on to make a distinction between these two terms, indicating his preference for "authenticity" over "sincerity." The concept of "sincerity" implies a discrepancy between the "inner" (or "sincere" self) and the "outer" (societally defined) self, whereas the "authentic" self simply is, unmindful of societal constructs. In Narayan's worldview, the "sincere" and the "authentic" must come together to form the "whole" individual. All further references to this work will be cited parenthetically in the text as Trilling.

the demands and pressures of "real" life. Some (like Krishna in *The English Teacher* and Jagan in *The Vendor of Sweets*) choose to retreat from the pressures of social living into a world of mysticism and myth. In other words, they choose against maturity and sincerity in the realist mode, although they may achieve authenticity and wisdom within the mode of myth. Thus, it is important to remember that there are contradictions to be found in Narayan's work, symbolic of the inherently confusing situation in which the Indo-English (or, for that matter, any postcolonial) writer finds him or herself. Yet, by and large, the pattern of Narayan's novels is one that, according to one critic, "gives us the account of an evolving conscious-ness beginning in isolation and confusion and ending in wholeness,"[4] and, as another critic points out, such a wholeness is often indicative of "a spiritual maturity that does not deny the demands of life."[5] In other words, the demands of the mythic and the realist modes often coalesce, and in responding to those demands the protagonist often achieves a balance of both.

Thus, the *Bachelor of Arts* (1937) deals with the protagonist Chandran's passage from rebellious adolescence to a fairly acquiescent adulthood; from being an egocentric individualist with modern (that is, westernized) notions of love and marriage, to becoming a fairly well-adjusted and authentic member of his social community, with some sense of duty to family and adherence to age-old customs and mythic beliefs.

From the moment of Chandran's introduction, the reader is made aware of his desire to avoid commitments to others. Natesan, secretary of the college union, asks Chandran:

> "You remember your old promise?"
> "No," said Chandran promptly, to be on the safe side.[6]

The thought of assuming any kind of social responsibility frightens Chan-dran, because he sees in it a threat to his individual selfhood, having formed as yet no concept of balance. Thus, at college, when he is forced to assume extracurricular responsibility by being appointed secretary of

4. Charles R. Larson, "A Note on R. K. Narayan," *Books Abroad* 50 (1976): 352.

5. K. Venkatachari, "R. K. Narayan's Novels: Acceptance of Life," *Indian Literature* 13 (March 1970): 74. All subsequent references to this work will be cited parenthetically in the text as Venkatachari.

6. R. K. Narayan, *The Bachelor of Arts* (1937; reprint, Chicago: University of Chicago Press, 1984), 13. All subsequent references to this work will be cited parenthetically in the text as Narayan, *Bachelor*.

the historical association, he feels that he is "on the verge of losing his personality" (Narayan, *Bachelor*, 54).

On one of his solitary river ramblings after passing his B.A. examinations, he espies a young girl, Malathi, and becomes infatuated with her. Despite his desire to be bold and "indifferent to the public's observation and criticism" (108), Chandran is unable to approach the girl and introduce himself, although with the help of an old college friend, Mohan, he is at least able to find out her family's name and caste. Having done this, he blurts out to his parents his desire to marry the girl. The first reaction of Chandran's mother is a hysterical no, since the girl is too old to be eligible (she is all of sixteen years!). However, when Chandran remains unhappy, his parents come around to the extent that they are willing to consider the match if, according to custom, the proposal comes from the other side. Chandran's rebellious, if predictable, response to this is the somewhat ludicrously phrased statement "To the dust-pot with your silly customs." Voicing of such modern sentiments has very little effect on Chandran's mother, who replies that she "at any rate belonged to a generation which was in no way worse than the present one for all its observances; and as long as she lived she would insist on respecting the old customs" (118).

The rest of the book describes the process by which Chandran is brought around to a more traditional way of thinking. When his prospects for marriage with Malathi are thwarted by a mismatching of their horoscopes, and Chandran learns she is to be married elsewhere, he has a minor breakdown of sorts. When he recovers, he asks his parents to send him off to Madras for a change. His father gives him some money and wires to Chandran's uncle in Madras to fetch Chandran from the train station and look after him; this is Chandran's chance to escape from an "oppressive" family system that had sought to confine him to outdated customs. He can now, at last, have a taste of the "freedom" he has so long yearned for. Chandran's first stop in Madras is a hotel where he puts up for a few days. Here he meets a disreputable character by the name of Kailas, who takes him around town. When the latter offers Chandran a drink, he refuses, on the grounds that he had "made a vow never to touch alcohol in my life before my mother." Thus, without knowing it, Chandran is very much a product of certain customs from which he cannot disassociate himself, and that this adherence to traditional symbols is good is confirmed by the pathos of Kailas's response:

> He [Kailas] remained solemn for a moment and said, "Then don't. Mother is a sacred object. It is a commodity whose value we don't

realize as long as it is with us. One must lose it to know what a
precious possession it is. If I had my mother I should have studied
in a college and become a respectable person." (161–62)

However, the truth of such a sentiment is, as yet, lost on Chandran, who
still wishes to remain far from Malgudi because of its associations with
"astrologers, horoscopes, and unsympathetic Mother" (166). He still has to
learn the value of home and of social custom, and interestingly enough, it
is his dabbling with the tradition of Indian mysticism that brings him the
necessary awareness.

Chandran now dons the garb of a sanyasi, "one who has renounced the
world and was untouched by its joys and sorrows" (174). His renunciation
"was a revenge on society, circumstances, and perhaps, too, on destiny"
(176). Chandran's renunciation, then, is symbolic of the supremist act of
self-centered individualism, meant to inflict hurt on family and friends. It
is not an act born of a desire to achieve a selflessness However, in spite of
himself, Chandran does achieve a measure of selflessness and self-knowl-
edge when he realizes he can no longer take advantage of the Kropal
villagers' simple faith in him as a saintly figure:

> They had all brought gifts for him, milk and fruits and food. The
> sight of the gifts sent a spear through his heart. He felt a cad, a
> fraud, and a confidence trickster. . . . He had deserted his parents,
> who had spent on him all their love, care and savings. He told
> himself he had surely done this to spite his parents, who probably
> had died of anxiety by now. This was all his return for their love
> and all they had done for him. (180)

And so Chandran decides it is time to stop this charade and go home.
Naturally his parents are delighted to see him, having been worried sick
about his welfare. This theme of the reversal of cause and effect, of
someone becoming sincere through being insincere, is a paradox that
delights Narayan and is central to his ironic vision of life. This same
pattern is repeated in many of his other books, most prominently in *The
Guide* (which I shall discuss later), in which the protagonist Raju begins
by playing a role but ends up assuming it for real. Although such a reversal
rarely implies self-transformation, it does lead to self-discovery, as is
obvious in Chandran's case. What is interesting to note is that such a
reversal leading to self-discovery and a measure of authenticity and

sincerity occurs often in a state of mystical withdrawal. George Woodcock, in an article on Narayan, sheds some light on the implications of such a withdrawal:

> Can a modern Indian reject westernization, with its political and ultimately moral implications? The only way to attempt it, Narayan suggests, is by withdrawal into one of two Indian worlds that remained relatively untouched by the intrusion of the raj. . . . These are the interlocking worlds of villages, still living largely by traditional techniques as well as beliefs, and of the wandering holy men. . . . In Narayan's novels such withdrawal rarely provides a way to self-transformation but it does often lead to self-discovery.[7]

Although the outcome of such a withdrawal is often an awakening in the protagonist of a sense of sincerity to himself, leading to sincerity and responsible behavior toward others (which is the ultimate goal of realism), such an attitude in Narayan's work generally results from a symbolic immersion in the rituals of Hindu mysticism and mythic beliefs.

Upon his return, Chandran is a changed man. He settles down to a life of "quiet and sobriety" and decides to take up the responsibility of earning his living, instead of toying with the idea of going to England. To secure the chief agency of a Malgudi newspaper, Chandran journeys for the second time to Madras to obtain the help of his uncle. This time around, however, Chandran journeys willingly into the world of social custom, obligations, and favors, unlike his first journey, which had symbolized a retreat from the very society he now embraces.

He secures a job with a local newspaper and, through it, achieves a sense of connectedness with the world around him. His transformation from being a radical individualist to becoming a more balanced conventional social being is completed with his acquiescence to an "arranged" marriage. The marriage is arranged according to custom, with Chandran making, for the most part, a very happy bridegroom. Thus, a happy balance between man as rebel and man as self-determiner has been achieved in the critical realist mode. But this happens only with the help of social customs, Indian mythical beliefs in such things as horoscopes, and the Indian tradition of ascetic mysticism.

7. George Woodcock, "Two Great Commonwealth Novelists: R. K. Narayan and V. S. Naipaul," *Sewanee Review* 87 (Winter/Spring 1979): 17.

*The Dark Room*, Narayan's third published novel (1938), is a bit of an anomaly among the rest of his oeuvre. This is the only time Narayan chooses to write directly about the plight of (middle-class) Indian women within the traditions of marriage, and though he views their pitiful condition with sympathy, he is unable to envision a better alternative for them. In this novel, then, neither realism nor myth seems to offer any hopeful solution to the age-old problems faced by the majority of women even in modern postcolonial India.

Savitri, the protagonist of the novel and wife of Ramani, is a typical, self-effacing Hindu wife who has put up with the petty tyrannies of her husband for the fifteen-odd years of their married life. As she herself admits "How impotent she was, she thought; she had not the slightest power to do anything at home, and that after fifteen years of married life."[8]

Indeed, Savitri is at the extreme of man as social phenomenon, for she is constantly attending to the needs of her husband, her children, her friends, without once being able to articulate her own needs and desires, let alone fulfill them. No wonder, then, that when her husband drags her (without any consideration for her wishes in the matter) to the movies, Savitri ends up so totally engrossed in the mythic world represented on the screen that she has no desire to leave this fantasy world and return to the mundane world of reality:

> The picture carried Savitri with it, and when in the end Kuchela stood in his pooja [prayer] room and lighted camphor and incense before the image of God, Savitri brought her palms together and prayed. The switching on of the lights, the scurry of feet, and a blue-coated husband yawning, had the air of a vulgar anticlimax. . . . She loathed the drab prospect of changing her Saree, dining and sleeping. (Narayan, *Dark Room*, 30)

When Ramani starts an affair with one of his employees, Savitri finds that she can no longer tolerate this indignity on top of everything else, and so she finally lets out her pent-up hurt and anger and asks Ramani to give up "the other woman," telling him that otherwise she, his wife, will no longer live with him.

Ramani merely scoffs at her "threat" and tells her she is quite free to

8. R. K. Narayan, *The Dark Room* (1938; reprint, Chicago: University of Chicago Press, 1981), 30. All subsequent references to this work will be cited parenthetically in the text as Narayan, *Dark Room*.

leave, since he will not be browbeaten by a woman into giving up anything he desires. When Savitri says she will also take the children with her, Ramani, with the full force of patriarchy behind him, refuses to let her do so, saying, "They are *my* children" (113; emphasis added). And Savitri once again realizes the powerlessness of her situation as an economically dependent woman: "Yes, you are right. They are yours, absolutely. You paid the midwife and the nurse. You pay for their clothes and teachers. You are right. Didn't I say that a woman owns nothing?" (113). And so Savitri leaves, even though she has no money and nowhere to go. When she tries to commit suicide by drowning, she is saved from such an end by a locksmith cum burglar, who later helps her get a job, at her own request, as a cleaner and helper at the village temple; it seems that the mythic mode will finally come to her rescue and that within it she will be able to obtain the peace she couldn't within the realist mode: "What more fitting life, she thought, could one choose than serving a god in his Shrine? She would dedicate her life to the service of God, numb her senses and memory, forget the world, and spend the rest of her years thus and die" (170).

However, the promise of peace within the detached mythic mode turns out to be illusory. Not only is the priest of the temple unsympathetic and unhelpful, but Savitri herself is unable to reconcile herself to the loss of her children. Although she chides herself for her "foolish yearning for children, this dragging attachment" (170), she nevertheless cannot bring herself to forget them and, soon enough, decides to return to them.

The novel ends with her rather ignominious return to her children and husband. Nothing changes, her husband continues to treat her as before, and once again Savitri acquiesces to the system. At the very end, as Savitri is lying in the hall half-asleep one afternoon, she hears the locksmith's cry "Locks repaired!" from the street. Though she initially becomes excited at the thought of seeing Mari again and maybe offering him some money or food as thanks, she recalls the cook before he goes out to fetch him: "As Ranga [the cook] was about to step out she changed her mind: 'Let him go, don't call him.' She thought: Why should I call him here? What Have I?" (210). And on such a depressing note, the novel ends. Neither realism nor myth, nor any combination thereof (nor any other genres, for that matter), provides appropriate fictive strategies for resolving the problems of the majority of middle-class Hindu housewives in the Narayan world. (Since I see genre not only as an artistic mode but also as symbolizing a particular attitude toward life, I think it quite appropriate to demand that a generic mode be a vehicle not only of conveying or describing life's problems but also of providing some means of solving them.)

According to one critic, the ending can be construed as a triumph of the mythic tradition that upholds womanly selflessness and sacrifice (even though he is himself critical of such a tradition):

> *The Dark Room* . . . operates within a social setting in which the Dharma Shastra [mythic tradition or religious code] gives woman a position of perpetual dependence, while custom extols her qualities of endurance, suffering and sacrifice. In *The Dark Room*, the heroine rebels against her tyrannous husband, but returns to suffer indignities for the sake of her children. *Here, her selflessness and sacrifice could well be construed as a vindication of her key role in saving the family from disintegration.* Does not such an idea, however true to a tradition, in effect relegate woman to a position of permanent subservience and subordination under the glorifying guise of an upholder of family integrity and honor?[9] (emphasis added)

The ending hardly glorifies Savitri's return. On the contrary, the reader is made to feel pity for this woman who had no other alternative but to return. Thus, neither the mythic nor the realistic mode has been seen to be capable of providing any satisfactory solutions to Savitri's plight.

Myth, in its pastoral romantic mode, operates in a much more positive way in *The English Teacher* (1945), where it helps wean the protagonist, Krishna, away from his emotionally dry, highly self-oriented life as an English teacher at the local missionary college to a more emotionally and spiritually fulfilled state as husband and father and, later, teacher of an authentic indigenous school.

The reader learns, through Krishna himself, that he guides the students through the mazes of Elizabethan English not "out of love for them or for Shakespeare, but only out of love for myself."[10] Nor does Krishna have any

9. Satyanarain Singh, "A Note on the World-View of R. K. Narayan" *Indian Literature* 24 (January–February 1981): 106. All subsequent references to this work will be cited parenthetically in the text as S. Singh.

10. R. K. Narayan, *The English Teacher* (1945; reprint, Chicago: University of Chicago Press, 1980), 12. All subsequent references to this work will be cited parenthetically in the text as Narayan, *Teacher*.

respect for his colleagues. He thinks of Rangappa as a "dry philosopher," a "hopeless man," a person whose problems are "not my business" (Narayan, *Teacher*, 9).

In the midst of this isolationism come two letters—one from his father, the other from his wife, Susila—announcing the impending arrival of the latter, their nine-month-old daughter, and Krishna's mother from the village. Of course, what this means is the end of Krishna's rather solitary existence in the college hotel, and although one part of him looks forward to the arrival of his wife, mother, and child, the other part is naturally quite apprehensive.

Just as Susila reintroduces Krishna to the pastoral traditions of his past, so the presence of his mother invokes other age-old Indian customs and traditions. For example, when Susila arrives, the mother, who had arrived earlier, performs all of the customary rites, such as circling a pan of vermilion solution before the young mother and child, before she lets them enter the house. The presence of the old continues even after she returns to her own village, because she sends as her surrogate an aged friend to cook and nurse for the young couple. It is in this historical context, then, with time past, time present, and time future, embodied in the three generations in a world threaded with religion, custom, and immemorial habit, that Narayan shows the growth and realization of Krishna's love for his wife and child. Through Krishna's growing devotion to his daughter and wife, he rejoins the world of genuine response and human reality, that is, goes from being an isolated individual in danger of drying up within formal relationships, to a man connected to a social unit. With Susila's arrival, then, the English teacher's life achieves some semblance of serenity and harmony.

When she dies, therefore, the teacher is inconsolable in his grief. No longer a traditional believer, he does not know where to turn for comfort or hope, until one day a boy delivers him a note from his father stating that the latter has been in touch with Susila's spirit. Skeptical at first, the English teacher comes to believe strongly in the authenticity of this "spirit medium," and it is with the help of his séances (which are always conducted in a pastoral setting, Nallapa's grove) that he begins to come to grips with his loss. In developing this second theme of spirituality, Narayan daringly attempts one of the most extraordinary feats in realistic fiction. He persuades the reader to accept Krishna's efforts to bring his wife back from the dead. It is the cheerful ordinariness of the spirit medium that gives the mystical experience some footing in common life and thus helps make it believable. Here again the realistic blends with the mythical/ mystical modes, a generic coexistence that reveals Narayan's desire for the wholeness of realism and his simultaneous awareness that such a unity and balance can be achieved only with the help of something un- or suprareal, such as, in this case, a belief in mysticism and myth.

The initiation into a rapidly disappearing pastoral tradition that had begun with his marriage to Susila is thus continued with her death and finally completed by his friendship with the headmaster of the children's school. The school is described unequivocally as a pastoral haven: "The floor was uneven and cool and the whole place smelt of Mother Earth. It was a pleasing smell, and seemed to take us back to some primeval simplicity, intimately bound up with earth and mud and dust" (134).

The exposure to this man's educational philosophy, based on a return to native pastoral traditions, serves as the catalyst that completes the English teacher's growing alienation from his former "real" life and leads to his resignation. He realizes that what he had thought of as "real" education (that is, English education) was "the dead mutton of literary analysis and theories and histories." His epiphany is complete when he realizes that "this education had reduced us to a nation of morons; we were strangers to our own culture and camp followers of another culture, feeding on leavings and garbage" (178).

With this realization comes the decision to pursue his social obligation to instruct the poor children of his town in their native heritage, something that would have infinitely more meaning than teaching Shakespeare to bored college students merely to satisfy the selfish motive of earning a hundred rupees. However, judging from Krishna's resignation speech, it is quite clear that his authenticity, his growth from self as individual to self as social phenomenon, is achieved to some extent on the basis of a withdrawal from reality. Krishna's desire to enter the world of the child may have its socially noble motives, but it symbolizes, nevertheless, a rejection of the "adult" world of realism and responsibility in favor of the child's world of fantasy and romance, once again revealing Narayan's ironic stance toward realism. Krishna says, "I'm seeking a great inner peace. I find I can't attain it unless I withdraw from the adult world and adult work into the world of children. And there . . . is a vast storehouse of peace and harmony" (183).

Thus, Narayan's desire for his characters to achieve the wholeness of realism, to be people who have achieved the perfect balance between individualism and social responsibility in a society that sets store by its myths and traditions, is realized only when realism is counterbalanced by myth, when some kind of a retreat into a mythical (pastoral, romantic) past is still possible.

Once again, myth blends with realism to create a fictional genre that affects neither the complete historical petrification associated with myth, nor the Rushdian kind of cynicism about realism being an impossible gesture. In Narayan's world, it seems that often both an indigenous authenticity (born of sincerity) and a unified sensibility are realizable ideals for the protagonists.

In *Mr. Sampath: The Printer of Malgudi* (1969), the central value and goal once again is the achievement of balance, and the struggle the protagonist, Srinivas, must go through is the struggle to achieve such a balance in his life. At the outset he is a young man ready to go to any lengths to start his newspaper, the *Banner*. He leaves his wife and child behind in his ancestral village, thus neglecting a primary social duty, to come to Malgudi and try his luck. After meeting up with Mr. Sampath, a printer who promises to publish his paper, Srinivas's career as editor is launched, and he becomes completely engrossed in his professional life, to the exclusion of all else. Before long, however, wife and son arrive on the scene and accuse him of familial neglect:

> [Srinivas] cast a look at his wife: she wore a very inferior discolored cotton saree, patched here and there. "Am I guilty of the charges of neglect?" he asked himself. "Family duties come before any other duty. Is it an absolute law? What if I don't accept the position?"[11]

This, of course, is one of the main issues Srinivas must resolve in order to achieve full maturity. The realization dawns on him almost immediately that "family preoccupation is no better than occupying oneself solely with one's body and keeping it in a flourishing condition" (Narayan, *Mr. Sampath*, 34). In other words, no kind of preoccupation with any one thing is good; rather, moderation leading to balance is the key to a harmonious and "whole" existence, where each issue receives its due consideration, and no more.

11. R. K. Narayan, *Mr. Sampath: The Printer of Malgudi* (1949; reprint, Chicago: University of Chicago Press, 1981), 33. All subsequent references to this work will be cited parenthetically in the text as Narayan, *Mr. Sampath*.

Ironically, it is through interacting with and observing closely the behavior of "unbalanced" people like Sampath, printer turned movie producer, and Ravi, accountant/artist, that Srinivas begins to acquire, albeit very slowly, the technique of existence necessary for a "harmonious" or balanced life. The source of this balance, the reader realizes early on, will be mythical, since Srinivas's apprehension of this principle of life has mythological overtones:

> As an example: Here was the printer [Mr. Sampath] telling Ravi imaginary stories about his ability to find the other's sweetheart. Ravi's head was in the clouds on account of these stories; and here was the artist helping the printer also to keep his head in the same cloud-land with promises of sketching his child: these two seemed to balance each other so nicely that Srinivas felt astounded at the arrangement made by the gods. (63)

Here, once again, is the Narayan paradox: balance born of imbalance, sincerity out of insincerity, holiness out of unholiness.

This little anecdote reveals not only that balance is achieved with the help of supernatural deities but also that Sampath and Ravi are characters at two extreme poles of behavior. The former will do or say anything to "help" another, even to the extent of fabricating stories; whereas the latter is one who is so obsessed with his own peculiar fantasies that he can't be bothered with anything or anyone else. Thus, the one represents the extreme of man as social phenomenon, whereas the other is the epitome of man as individual entity. Sampath helps others, but at the expense of neglecting his own family, whereas Ravi helps his family by bringing in money but is otherwise completely alienated from them, especially after the arrival of Shanti. What Srinivas must do is strive for some kind of middle ground between these two extremes.

He does so, as already hinted, with the intervention of the gods, quite literally. After a short stint as editor of the *Banner* Srinivas is informed by his printer, Sampath, of a workers' strike, which renders their mission of printing newspapers an impossibility. However, Mr. Sampath, ever resourceful and helpful, tells Srinivas not to worry, since he has another project at hand—the making of a movie—for which he could use Srinivas's services. The latter, after some initial misgivings, goes to work on the script. Before long, Srinivas has succumbed completely to the magical charms of the mythical theme of Shiva's burning of the love god—according to which Shiva, in order to prevent himself from falling too extremely into the throes of lustful passion, burns up the "God of Love," Kama, with his powerful third eye—thus burning away all of love's "grossness" until "only its essence remains" (103).

The connection between myth and daily life is here made quite explicit, and once again the myth points out the desirability of balance. However, at this stage Srinivas goes overboard in his involvement with the mythical story to the extent of neglecting his "real" duty by his family. So, at this point, myth has not yet helped him achieve a balance: "His mind had become a veritable stage for divine beings to move and act and he had little interest in anything else" (102).

Soon, though, the sordidness of "real" happenings around him finally makes Srinivas wake up to the reality of things. He realizes that he not only must help his friends Ravi and Sampath to the best of his ability but also must say no to their demands after a point if he is to retain some vestiges of sanity and achieve some equilibrium in life. "He felt he had been involved in a chaos of human relationships and activities. He kept saying to himself, 'I am searching for something, trying to make a meaning out of things' " (196).

Of course, what he has been searching for, and what has thus far eluded him, is the principle of balance. He has either been too self-involved or gotten over-involved with the affairs of others, such as Ravi and Sampath. Although now, with the help of the inspector, he is able to find another printer to restart his old newspaper, Srinivas is still too much caught up with helping Ravi and his family through the period of Ravi's insanity. Once again, it is with the help of mythical forces that Srinivas is able to place reality in proper perspective and acquire a balanced view of things. When an exorcist is hired by Ravi's mother to drive out the "mad demon" besetting her darling son, Srinivas, watching the ceremony cynically at first, is later led to recreate the mythical past of his Indian heritage in his mind's eye. He imagines the present Market Road as an avenue of wild trees, on which appears Srinivas Rama, the hero of Ramayana. By scratching a nine on the sand with his arrow, Rama magically creates the river Saraya. Then Srinivas pictures the coming of the Buddha, and in the next millennium the great Shankara, who built his temple on the river bank where "the extremes meet . . . [where] the cobra, which is the natural enemy of the frog, gives it succor." This is the place, Srinivas realizes, that always had "its rebirth and growth," a place where extremes ultimately balanced each other out, "Ravi with his madness, his well-wishers with their panaceas and their apparatus of cure" (207).

As the historical pictures fade out of Srinivas's mind, he asks himself, " 'Who am I to bother about Ravi's madness or sanity? What madness to think I am his keeper?' This notion seemed to him so ridiculous that he let out a laugh" (208). With the help of myth, Srinivas has achieved a balance, if not in the realist mode, then certainly in a metaphysical one. As Keith Garebian remarks, "Life, as Srinivas discovers in *The Printer of Malgudi* (1949), is largely a hysterical distraction whose madness must be dispelled in order that the individual might attain clarity of direction, meaning in life, and a metaphysical balance" (Garebian, "Spirit," 297).

Yet, the balance achieved is not purely of a metaphysical nature. Srinivas does not shelve all responsibility to others; rather, he realizes that his duty is both to himself and to others, which is why he is so eager to start work on the *Banner* again, a symbol both of self-interest and of service to society. Srinivas's desire not to get too "involved" with the affairs of others by the end of the novel symbolizes the new state of balance and harmony that Srinivas has attained. He still retains the humanity and sense of responsibility to ask Sampath to dine with him but now also has the wisdom not to tie himself up in knots over something that is, ultimately, not his concern, such as Sampath's affair with Shanti. Once again, a wholeness is achieved and harmony reigns, though not without help from a mythical past and, in some instances, by dispensing with realism.

Narayan's next novel, *The Financial Expert* (1952), is once again a blend of exact realism with poetic myth, although here the connection with Indian myth is made much more tactfully and obliquely than in *Mr. Sampath*. It should be borne in mind here, however, that the move toward myth (at least in this book) is neither good nor bad in a moral sense; it is only when viewed in a long-term "cultural" sense that it can be considered "good."

Margayya, the central character, is the moneylender who makes money in "realistic" circumstances, squatting under the banyan tree across from the cooperative bank, advancing "a little loan" ("for interest") to the villagers:

So that the little loan might wedge out another loan from the Co-operative Bank, which in its turn was passed on to someone in need for a higher interest. Margayya kept himself as the center of all the complex transaction, and made all the parties concerned pay him for his services.[12]

However, when he is demeaningly ordered by the secretary of the bank to remove himself from the premises, Margayya, after his initial rage has subsided, realizes that he is treated with such contempt because "he had no money." Later, when his wife asks him by what right the secretary can threaten him, Margayya replies, "He has every right because he has more money, authority, dress, looks—above all, more money. It's money which gives people all this. Money alone is important in this world" (Narayan, *Expert*, 21).

Thus, Margayya's desire for money is deeply rooted in social motives. However, when Margayya seriously sets out to discover the right way to become wealthy, it is toward the mythical powers that he turns for help. Seeing a temple priest walk down his street, Margayya is immediately struck by the idea that "he was a wise man, well-versed in ancient studies, and he might be able to give advice" (29). He goes to the priest and confesses his desire to make money, to which the priest replies, "That means you should propitiate Goddess Lakshmi, the Goddess of Wealth. When she throws a glance and it falls on someone, he becomes rich, he becomes prosperous, he is treated by the world as an eminent man" (50).

Margayya agrees to do whatever is necessary to "propitiate" the goddess, but before he embarks on this course, the priest warns him of the rivalry between goddess Lakshmi and goddess Saraswathi, the deity of knowledge and enlightenment. He tells Margayya that if the one favors a person, the other usually withdraws her blessing, to which Margayya, intoxicated by the vision of wealth, replies arrogantly, "A man whom the Goddess of Wealth favors need not worry much. He can buy all the knowledge he requires. He can afford to buy all the gifts that Goddess Saraswathi holds in her palms" (51).

Clearly, such arrogance is folly, partly because it hints at imbalance. Needless to say, the truth of the mythic parables is borne out as Margayya's life unfolds along realistic lines. He does indeed achieve a great deal of wealth, through means that are sordidly "real"—for example, with the publishing of a sex manual, euphemistically entitled "Domestic Harmony." At the same time, what the priest had foretold comes true: Balu, Margayya's

12. R. K. Narayan, *The Financial Expert* (1952; reprint, Chicago: University of Chicago Press, 1981), 8. All subsequent references to this work will be cited parenthetically in the text as Narayan, *Expert*.

son, for whom the latter has the noblest academic ambitions, turns out to be a complete dud. Margayya indeed tries to "buy" knowledge for his son by hiring the most expensive tutors, but to no avail—what the ancient myths uphold must come to pass.

The pursuit of wealth, to the exclusion of all else, results in an imbalance in Margayya's life, for he has begun to neglect his family duties. What is important, then, is that Margayya attain some kind of balance and harmony in his life; ultimately his financial insolvency provides him with such an opportunity: "Margayya, the financial expert, learns from his tortuous waywardness that his proper destiny consists of a return to his modest roadside business as a financial expert of sorts and a resubmergence in domestic community" (Garebian, "Spirit," 295).

Moderation in everything seems once again to be the key to achieving a balanced, or harmonious, existence. However, the balance and authenticity or sincerity are, by and large, found here not in the growth or development of the characters (for Margayya, despite some redemption, remains to the end the small, ignoble character fixated on money, as he was in the beginning) but rather in the theme and plot themselves. The friction between the gods is the permanent reality of which the events in Malgudi and in Margayya's life are the merest reflection; thus, myth and realism balance each other out.

In *Waiting for the Mahatma* (1955), Gandhi is portrayed as both a man—a real, worn, ordinary person—and a god. It is politics in the mythical/magical shape and proportion of Gandhi's Quit India movement that provides the context for the protagonist Sriram's development.

But though this development proceeds against the mythical backdrop of the Gandhian movement, it does so in a classical, realist mode. Sriram goes from being a solitary adolescent living with his old grandmother to becoming a Gandhian disciple out of very individualistic motives (he falls in love with Bharati, another disciple, and wishes to be near her). His stint as a Gandhian "freedom fighter" alienates him from his grandmother, the only family he has. It is only when he is informed of her impending demise that he rushes home and realizes how socially irresponsible and selfish he has been in running away from home. Luckily, his granny revives on the funeral pyre (a truly comical scene), but unluckily, Sriram, being a "wanted" revolutionary, is hauled off to prison by the police.

In the company of fellow prisoners (jailed for various nonpolitical offenses), Sriram realizes the extent to which he has led a self-centered, isolated existence: Their's "was a fresh outlook that had not occurred to Sriram in his self-centered political existence. He had a feeling that he was running up against a new species of human being, speaking like monsters, but yet displaying sudden human qualities."[13]

He is now assailed with memories of "all the good things that his granny had made for him" (Narayan, *Waiting*, 193), and is filled with remorse at his callous behavior toward her. Slowly, but surely, "his admiration for the old prisoners became genuine; his sympathies were really widening" (206).

By the time Sriram is released from jail, he has achieved some balance between being an isolated individualist and one who is responsive and sensitive to the needs and views of others. Now all that remains is that he meet and convince his beloved Bharati to display the same sense of balance by agreeing to marry him, for all along she has been at the other extreme of man as social phenomenon. When Sriram does meet up with Bharati again and begs her to marry him after all that she has put him through (he had, after all, become a Gandhian merely out of love for her), her response is that she will do so only if "Gandhiji" (the "ji" being a suffix connoting respect) will sanction it. In other words, "the approval of the gods," here symbolized by Gandhi, is essential if humans are to coexist harmoniously in a realm of social realism. Fortunately for Sriram, Gandhi's blessing is granted—and not a minute too soon, for almost immediately thereafter, he is tragically assassinated.

According to Walsh, the final impression left on the reader by this novel is

> the authority and conviction with which what seems to be a straightforward realist narrative, can include, without jar or friction, the spiritual [and mythic], the tragic, the comic, in a whole in which the parts are consistent with one another, in which fable, theme, history and documentary fit together with the naturalness of life. (Walsh, *Narayan*, 94)

Yet this novel doesn't work quite as well, either dramatically or aesthetically, as most of Narayan's other novels, primarily because Gandhi takes the place here of the mythical gods of the other books. Gandhi, as a symbol of the gods, poses an aesthetic difficulty for Narayan, since in reality he

---

13. R. K. Narayan, *Waiting for the Mahatma* (1955; reprint, Chicago: University of Chicago Press, 1981), 193. All subsequent references to this work will be cited parenthetically in the text as Narayan, *Waiting*.

was a mortal who stood for certain moral imperatives that the mythical deities, by and large, did not. Thus, he cannot be "played with" in any sense, which in turn leaves the novel neither comic nor totally serious, one in which the tensions between the real and the mythic are never satisfactorily resolved.

In the books discussed so far, the path of the protagonist's progress has usually been from a state of isolated individualism to a state of involvement with others and with issues that transcend the self.

In *The Guide* (published in 1958, and considered by many critics Narayan's best novel to date), however, the protagonist, "Railway Raju" (so called because he serves as guide to tourists who get off at the train station in Malgudi), must reverse this direction to some extent if he is to achieve the true ideals of balance and sincerity. Raju must strike a balance between extreme modes of behavior in order to become a "sincere" man, deserving the confidence of himself and others. This dialectic between himself as individual and himself as social phenomenon establishes him firmly within the Lukacsian mode of critical realism that insists that man, despite his individual autonomy, is an ineluctably social animal.

At first, however, Raju is too much the social animal and has very little sense of himself as an autonomous being with individual integrity. He is Railway Raju, who exists, it seems, only in the public/social role of guide to tourists.

> I came to be called Railway Raju. Perfect strangers having heard of my name began to ask for me when their train arrived at Malgudi station. It is written on the brow of some that they shall not be left alone. I am one such, I think.[14]

But of course he brings this lack of space for his individual, solitary self on himself, and much of this action of "pleasing others" consists in being false. As he himself admits, there are times when his responses to questions of tourists are "an utter piece of falsehood." In going overboard to be of service to others, he loses all sense of personal integrity, as for example, in his relation to Marco, the archaeologist. Despite the latter's bullying and demeaning treatment, Raju continues to play guide for him, even though he admits:

14. R. K. Narayan, *The Guide* (1958; reprint, New York: Penguin Books, 1980), 47. All subsequent references to this work will be cited parenthetically in the text as Narayan, *Guide*.

I felt annoyed with him [Marco] at this stage. What did he take me
for? This fellow, telling me that he wanted the car at this hour or at
that hour—did he think I was a tout? It made me very angry, but
*the fact was I was a tout, having no better business than hanging
around* between Gaffur and a snake-charmer and a tourist and
*doing all kinds of things.* (Narayan, *Guide*, 59; emphasis added)

It is no wonder, then, that becoming a projection of what Rosie, Marco's
wife, needs, he becomes her lover. He takes on the role of sympathetic
admirer of Rosie's dancing talents, thus becoming someone she is desperately in need of, since her husband views this side of her with great
disdain. When her cold, archaeological husband discards her because of
her affair with Raju, the latter takes on the role of Rosie's financial
manager and helps put her back on the stage where she belongs.

However, in his zeal to be helpful to Rosie, he ends up ultimately being
unhelpful to her and neglectful of his duties to others in his family,
especially his mother, and, above all, neglectful of his duty to himself to
be a morally sincere person.

Despite, or perhaps because of, his extreme accommodation to others,
Raju's "sincerity" consists in being false (see, for example, Trilling, 69–
70). He is false to Rosie (who now takes on the stage name Nalini) because
he loses his appreciation of her art and her commitment to it; rather, he
becomes obsessed with the material benefit accruing from her performances
and overbooks her to such an extent that when he talks to her of taking a
vacation and "enjoying ourselves," she can only reply viciously, "I don't
think it's going to be possible until I fall sick or break my thigh bone. Do
you know the bulls yoked to an oil-crusher—they keep going round and
round and round in a circle, without a beginning or an end?" (Narayan,
*Guide*, 179).

Thus, Raju is unable to have a "real," harmonious relationship with the
one person for whom he has given up any claims to a private individual
existence (since, as Nalini's manager, he lives the most public of lives). By
being too eager to play the "required" role, Raju ends up by being false,
not only to Rosie, but ultimately to himself. And from being too much the
person involved with others (in this case with Rosie), he swings to the other
extreme and becomes an egocentric individual concerned with making
money and aggrandizing himself in the name of Rosie and her art. In fact,
as he later admits, he becomes so conceited as to think himself responsible
for all her fame and success, though he ought to have known better:

I became known because I went about with her, not the other way
around. She became known because she had the genius in her and
the public had to take notice of it. I am able to speak soberly about
it now—only now. *At that time I was puffed up with the thought of
how I had made her.* (161; emphasis added)

And he also begins to think of her as his "property" (167). Clearly, Raju
has lost himself in a sea of self-deception, and something must be done if
the impediments of insincerity resulting from extreme modes of behavior
are to be removed from the path of his self-actualization and maturity. Until
he becomes someone that he himself wishes to be and, in being that, is
neither wholly egocentric nor utterly subservient to others' wills, he cannot
be said to have achieved a balanced maturity or an authentically sincere
identity.

It is now that myth and mysticism intervene in the realm of critical
realism as a force to help Raju attain the goals of the latter genre. Having
forged Rosie's (alias Nalini's) signature on some documents sent to her by
her former husband, Marco, Raju is about to be sent to jail for forgery,
although he does not yet know it. The fact that this jail sentence will
change Raju's life irrevocably, nay, remove the impediments to his true,
"sincere" self and social growth, is underscored by the mythic song and
dance performed by Rosie on the night that he is arrested: "She entered,
carrying a brass lamp, with a song in praise of Ganesha, the elephant-
faced God, the remover of impediments" (187). Then she goes on to
perform the snake dance, which, Raju notes, is "unusual." This dance is
one that elevates the serpent by bringing it out of its "underground reptile
class" and transforming it "into a creature of grace and divinity and an
ornament of the gods" (188). In parallel fashion, Raju is elevated through
his experiences in the jail, and later, with the villagers, is elevated from a
low-life (like the snake) to a "holy man," from a "confidence man" to a
man deserving of others' confidence.

In the final and crucial phase of the novel the reader sees "how the outer
fit becomes an inner one, how the manner turns into the identity" (Walsh,
*Narayan*, 126). For while in prison, Raju discovers the mythic life of
pastoral pursuits, and this puts him in touch with the earth and with a side
of his nature (a very individual, solitary side) that he had never known
existed:

I worked incessantly on a vegetable patch in the backyard of the
superintendent's home. I dug the earth and drew water from the

well and tended it carefully. . . . I loved every piece of this work.
. . . Oh, it seemed to be so good to be alive and feeling all this—
the smell of freshly turned earth filled me with the greatest delight.
If this was prison life, why didn't more people take to it? . . . I'd
have been happy to stay in this prison permanently. (Narayan,
*Guide*, 202–3)

Of course, Raju cannot remain in prison permanently, nor can he remain
totally cut off from his fellow beings, or the goals of realism would remain
unfulfilled. When he is released, he seeks shelter in a deserted temple
and there is perceived as some kind of "guru," or holy man, by the village
community. Once again, Raju finds himself taking on, albeit reluctantly, a
role assigned to him by others and, in so doing, becomes (as before) a
projection of what people need.

There is, however, a marked difference in the situation this time around.
Now, at last, Raju's own will matches his receptivity to others' suggestions.
His decision to play the role required of him by others, by society, becomes
now a matter of individual choice. Thus, "the inner pattern and outer
events flow together" (Walsh, *Narayan*, 172). When the village people force
him to fast as an appeal to the gods for an end to a drought, Raju's initial
resistance gives way to a supportive resolve:

"If, by avoiding food I should help the trees bloom, and the grass
grow; why not do it thoroughly?" For the first time in his life, he
was making an earnest effort; for the first time he was learning the
thrill of full application, outside money and love. (Narayan, *Guide*,
212)

For the first time, toward the end of his life, Raju does succeed in
achieving a measure of self-awareness and authenticity. He finally achieves
wholeness by striking a balance between individuality and social
responsibility.

At the end of the novel, then, Raju is both an individual alienated from
the crowd and yet also a character who is constituted, not simply influenced, by the expectations of others. When he stands at the very end up to
his knees in water, he is utterly isolated from the crowd; yet it is his
collaboration, in some sense, with their expectations that produces their
sense of a "miracle." The suggestion, at the conclusion, that rain may be
on its way is again symbolic of divine/mythic intervention in the realist

mode. Raju's transformation is in fact achieved through mythic and mystical means—the godlike heroism of a "holy man" that seems to have the approval of the "gods of life" (Walsh, *Narayan*, 133). Thus, the goal of realism—achievement of balance, sincerity, and maturity by the protagonist—is achieved within the mode of the Indian mythic and mystical tradition: the idea of the holy man achieving a miracle for his people.[15]

If, in the novels discussed thus far, the reader senses an implicit approval of the values of the past (symbolized by the ancient Indian mythological and mystical traditions), in Narayan's next three novels this approval becomes an explicit theme.

In *The Man-Eater of Malgudi* (1961), Vasu, the taxidermist-hunter, with his "black halo" of hair, comes to symbolize not only the present, as opposed to the past, but also a darker influence opposed to light and grace. In sharp contrast to him, Nataraj and his friends represent a style of life and habit of sensibility that has been sanctioned by the experience of generations. They are products of history and mythic tradition, whereas Vasu is one in whom the individualistic will is unqualified by the past.

Thus, Nataraj and his friends exist in a world that is very real, but whose realism is very much dependent on acknowledging the presence of myth. In fact, several critics, including M. K. Naik and Meenakshi Mukherjee, have pointed out how closely the novel recreates the old Hindu myth of Bhasmasura in modern form, and that it is perhaps the only novel by R. K. Narayan that has a definite, sustained, mythical structure.[16]

Nataraj, then, is portrayed in the critical realist mode, supplying his son with adequate toys, books, and sweets, and his wife with silk saris, running a fairly successful business as printer; yet all this is possible because he hung up "a framed picture of the goddess Laxmi poised on her lotus . . . and through her grace [he] did not do too badly."[17] His friend, the poet, is one "who was writing the life of God Krishna in monosyllabic verse" (Narayan, *Man-Eater*, 7). When Nataraj wakes up in the mornings, the first thing he does is to recite "a prayer to the Sun to illumine my mind" (9).

15. For a different interpretation of the conclusion of *The Guide*, see O. P. Mathur, "*The Guide:* A Study in Cultural Ambivalence," *Literary Endeavour* 3 (January–June 1982): 70–79.

16. Shyam M. Asnani, "The Use of Myth in R. K. Narayan's Novels," *Literary Endeavour* 3 (January–June 1982): 27. All subsequent references to this work will be cited parenthetically in the text as Asnani, "Myth."

17. R. K. Narayan, *The Man-Eater of Malgudi* (1961; reprint, Harmondsworth, Middlesex: Penguin Books, 1983), 7. All subsequent references to this work will be cited parenthetically in the text as Narayan, *Man-Eater*.

He then goes to his office and spends a pleasant day doing his work and chatting with his various friends, especially the poet and Sen, a would-be journalist, who constantly drop by. This harmonious existence is shattered, however, with the arrival of Vasu, who not only forces the mild-mannered Nataraj into printing cards for him free of charge but also takes over the attic of Nataraj's office to live in and to stuff animals in.

That Vasu is indeed the voice of a present which has no respect for the myths and traditions of the past becomes evident during a visit Nataraj pays him in the attic. Horrified at seeing all the birds and animals Vasu has killed and stuffed, but in particular the sacred eagle, Nataraj exclaims:

> "Don't you see it is a garuda?"
> "What if it is?"
> "Don't you realize that it's sacred? That it's the messenger of God Vishnu?"
> "I want to try and make Vishnu use his feet now and then." (50)

Vasu's irreverence does not stop there. He goes on to inform Nataraj that he believes he is serving the religious Hindu community in his own way by providing them with stuffed eagles that they can worship in the comfort of their own homes. Nataraj can't help but shiver at the thought of how Vasu's mind works. He realizes that "nothing seemed to touch him. No creature was safe if it had the misfortune to catch his eye" (51).

Vasu's nihilistic and menacing air, his bullying of everyone around him, becomes, in the Indian context, then, "a force not negotiable on human terms" (Walsh, *Narayan*, 137). When Vasu's behavior becomes intolerable, and the foul smell of dead animals stinks up Nataraj's entire press, Sastri, Nataraj's printer, appraises Vasu as "a 'rakshasa' or a demoniac creature who possessed enormous strength, strange powers and genius, but recognized no sort of restraints of man or God" (Narayan, *Man-Eater*, 72). However, according to mythical belief, such a creature contains within itself a seed of destruction, in order that the balance of the universe remain intact: "Every rakshasa gets swollen with his ego. He thinks he is invincible, beyond every law. But sooner or later, something or other will destroy him" (72). And Sastri expatiates on the lives of various demons in the puranas to prove how each one was destroyed by a flaw in his own armor.

What is interesting, of course, is that as the story unfolds along traditional realist lines—with the reader following the day-to-day life and problems of Nataraj and his somewhat futile efforts to maintain some

individual integrity in the face of Vasu's belligerency—the myth of the
rakshasa actually resolves itself in the way foretold in the puranas (religious
stories), thus helping Nataraj and others regain the lost balance. Vasu
mocks the religious efforts of Nataraj and the other Malgudi residents to
celebrate the publication of the poet's book on Krishna and decides to
shoot the elephant that will be heading the carnival procession. Muthu, the
elephant-keeper, warns Vasu that the "elephant belongs to no one but the
Goddess on the hill road. If anyone tries to harm it . . ." (141). But Vasu,
in characteristic fashion, cuts in irreverently, "Why don't you mind your
tea-shop and keep off the flies, and leave these issues for others? Don't try
to speak for any elephant" (141). Needless to say, Vasu gets his just reward.
Sitting at his window, waiting to shoot the elephant, unprotected by his
mosquito net, he is plagued by mosquitoes and, in trying to kill them, kills
himself. Sastri, picturing the scene in his mind, describes it thus for
Nataraj's benefit:

> Rangi [the prostitute Vasu slept with] . . . saw him [Vasu] flourish
> his arms like a madman, fighting them off as they buzzed about his
> ears to suck his blood. Next minute she heard a sharp noise like a
> thunderclap. The man had evidently trapped a couple of mosquitoes
> which had settled on his forehead by bringing the flat of his palm
> with all his might on top of them. . . . It was also the end of Vasu.
> . . . That fist was meant to batter thick panels of teak and iron.
> (173)

When Nataraj, in a moment of softheartedness, tries to point out Vasu's
virtue in never hitting anyone with that mighty hand, Sastri's puckish
response, faithful to the mythic fable, is, "Because he had to conserve all
that might for his own destruction. Every demon carries within him,
unknown to himself, a tiny seed of self-destruction, and goes up in thin air
at the most unexpected moment. Otherwise what is to happen to humanity?" (173–74).

Sastri's remarks at the end offer a modest word of hope about the
possibility of human survival and also indicate the quality of the quietly
complex tone of Narayan's fiction, a tone that suggests that balance and
unity can be achieved only by setting realism in a mythological context, by
living in a social present that is well grounded in the mythical traditions of
an authentic past.

In his next novel, *The Vendor of Sweets* (1967), Narayan seems a little less sure of the possibility for simultaneous coexistence of the two modes of realism and myth, present and past.

From the opening incident, it seems that Jagan, the sweet-vendor, exists successfully not only in a realistic present (running a sweetshop for personal profit) but also in a realm that symbolizes continuity with the past. For sitting under a framed picture of the goddess Lakshmi, Jagan says to his listener, "Conquer taste, and you will have conquered the self." When the listener asks, "Why conquer the self?" Jagan replies, "I do not know, but all our sages advise us to do."[18] This is a small excerpt from experience, issuing not only from a single lifetime but from generations; it is itself an emblem and instance of continuity, of connection with the past.

However, this happy coexistence does not last long, for with his son Mali's return from America with a Chinese American "wife," all the peace and harmony and traditional notions of Jagan are shattered—Mali, full of modern notions about setting up a business of novel-writing machines, tries to force his father into financing his scheme. Jagan, ever the traditionalist, just cannot see the sense of it, and thus commences a long period of prevarication on Jagan's part and what amounts to belligerent bullying on Mali's part. Mali's attitude wears Jagan down as the presence of his own son's foreign casteless "wife" disrupts his notions of propriety. Just when it appears that the domestic crisis has reached unmanageable proportions, the arrival of the "image-maker" at his shop provides Jagan with succor from pastoral, mythical sources. The man takes Jagan to Nallapa's grove (always a symbol of a mythical retreat in Narayan's fiction) and there shows him the statues of gods and goddesses carved by his master.

> Watching him in this setting, it was difficult for Jagan, as he mutely followed him, to believe that he was in the twentieth century. Sweetmeat vending, money and his son's problems seemed remote and unrelated to him. The edge of reality itself was beginning to blur. (Narayan, *Vendor*, 84)

As the man continues to talk about the intricacies of image-carving and recites stories about the mythic powers of the gods, Jagan realizes how narrow his whole existence has been until this point and wonders if he

18. R. K. Narayan, *The Vendor of Sweets* (1967; reprint, Harmondsworth, Middlesex: Penguin Books, 1983), 19. All subsequent references to this work will be cited parenthetically in the text as Narayan, *Vendor*.

might be on the verge of a spiritual rebirth. And indeed, after being shocked even further by the revelation that Mali and the American woman are not really man and wife, Jagan decides to give up all efforts to try and keep pace with realism and social responsibility in an increasingly modern setting. He decides, in fact, to retreat to the mythically pastoral setting of Nallapa's grove, symbol of a traditional past, where, as he explains to his cousin, "I will seek a new interest—different from the set of repetitions performed for sixty years. . . . *I am going to watch a goddess come out of a stone*" (140; emphasis added).

Jagan's renunciation of the world is a renunciation, on Narayan's part, of the critical realist mode, a largely Western mode. As Garebian points out:

> Mali, in the *Sweet-Vendor* is so victimized by the luxuriousness and unorthodoxy of the West that he cannot reconcile himself to his native place and consequently suffers a malign fate. Jagan, his father, on the other hand, accepts his ashrama, and while it is true that he extricates himself from the cares of Malgudian society, it is also true that he embarks upon his duty within the bounds of Malgudi's forest shrine and Hindu canons. (Garebian, "Spirit," 296)

In other words, by renouncing the goals of realism, Jagan succeeds in achieving the authentic existence and sincere identity available to him through Indian mysticism. Thus, there is an authorial awareness here that a balance may not always be achievable through a felicitous mixing of different genres or modes of behavior; in fact, here, harmony and peace of mind are achieved only through a one-sidedness, a rejection of "unity," and this is a resolution already hinted at as early as *The English Teacher*.

*The Painter of Signs* (published in 1977, ten years after his last novel) also sets out to point to the desirability of balance, but ends up proving its impossibility.

Raman is a modern-day rationalist who wishes to establish an Age of Reason. That his is an extremist philosophy totally at odds with the traditional beliefs in myth and ritual cherished by the older generation is quite apparent from the following exchange between him and his old aunt. She describes a particular ritual performed by her father:

Occasionally, he also brought in a cow, which as you know, when gifted to a brahmin, helps a dead man's soul to ford a difficult river in the next world.

"How?" questioned the rationalist.

"Don't ask me all that," Aunt said. "That's what our shastras say, and we don't have to question it." . . . Raman felt irritated at her beliefs. How could the Age of Reason be established if people were like this! Impossible.[19]

Indeed, it is impossible to establish such an Age of Reason when Raman is himself shaky in his convictions about the value of rationalism.

When Raman comes into contact with Daisy, the supremely rational individualist bent on the modern social mission of forcing birth control on the population, he realizes the value of "balance." He starts to feel a bond with her that cannot be explained in rational terms, but rather calls for spiritual, mystical terms. He tells her, "I feel as if we had known each other several Janmas," to which he receives her coldly rational response, "It is imagination, really" (Narayan, *Painter*, 73).

Later in their relationship, Raman finds himself wishing that Daisy were just a little more conventional and begs her to marry him, in order to make their relationship legitimate in the eyes of the very society he has mocked so long. She agrees at first, and it seems that a balance can be struck between the old ways and the modern, between tradition and reason, between the mythic and the real.

However, at the last minute, Daisy backs out of her commitment to Raman, explaining that "married life is not for me. I have thought it over. It frightens me. I am not cut out for the life you imagine. *I can't live except alone*" (139; emphasis added). Thus, in this case, the effort to achieve a "marriage" between extreme individualism and real connectedness to another person (as opposed to a less concrete commitment to a social ideal) fails. Myth, once again, has been unable to exercise its influence in the critical realist mode, and the result is an unhappy disunity and disharmony.

The reason for this failure perhaps could be that Raman, despite a few attempts at unifying the old with the new and certainly trying to achieve a "whole" relationship with Daisy, is nonetheless too much the modern

19. R. K. Narayan, *The Painter of Signs* (1977; reprint, Harmondsworth, Middlesex: Penguin Books, 1982), 19. All subsequent references to this work will be cited parenthetically in the text as Narayan, *Painter*.

rationalist, fundamentally cut off from his ancient, authentic roots. Daisy, of course, is no believer in ancient myth or custom either. "In fact," says Walsh, "Daisy is a peculiarly modern young woman for whom the cult of independent individuality is the supreme value in life" (*Narayan*, 161). Maybe Narayan is hinting that without connections to an authentic past and traditions, one can never achieve a balanced or "whole" life. In other words, realism must be tempered by myth in order to achieve the unity that is its goal. If the "real" world has no use for myth and tradition, then perhaps one is better off like Jagan, retreating to a haven where at least peace of mind, if not unity, is still possible. Such a haven, constituted by Narayan's religious sense of myth, forms part of his grip on reality.

In turning to the characters and situations of ancient epics and myths, then, Narayan, "is not only faithful to his national tradition, but also evinces that his questionings and solutions are firmly rooted in his own cultural ethics" (Asnani, "Myth," 21).

His latest novel, *Talkative Man* (1987), provides further proof that Narayan does not view with optimism the thrust toward modernity in Indian life. The brunt of Narayan's ironic disapproval falls on the shoulders of Rann, the westernized Indian, whose philandering presence in good old Malgudi leads to (among other disturbances) a scandalous affair involving a "fresh young virgin." She is saved from a "fate worse than death" only because of the saviorlike behavior of the narrator of the novel, TM (short for "talkative man"). TM is a "native" of Malgudi, a resident of the famous Kabir Street, whose family has lived there generation after generation. That the role of the traditionalist, of the preserver of old values, be assigned to a man of his background and temperament should come as no surprise. In fact, in the earlier passages of the book, TM's relationship with the intruder, Rann, resembles that between an earlier hero/villain pair, Nataraj and Vasu of *The Man-Eater of Malgudi*. Not only does Rann, a stranger, demand that TM help him find a place to live while he's in Malgudi, but when no place suits his fancy, he succeeds in manipulating TM into letting him move into his house on Kabir street.

In this most "modern" of his novels, Narayan tackles head-on one of the most vexing issues in contemporary Indian urban life: the changing roles and aspirations of women, which obviously come into collision with age-old ways of defining male-female relationships. The rather slim plot of this short novel in fact explores the breakdown of conventional decorous behavior between man and woman (specifically between Rann and his innumerable mistresses and wives) that occurs, so Narayan seems to be suggesting, when traditional values and beliefs are diluted by the forces of modernity. Whereas Daisy of *The Painter of Signs* was willing to sacrifice conventional norms of Indian society and was even willing to forgo intimacy with a man in favor of a single-minded devotion to career, Rann's former wife, Sarasa, and current girlfriend, Girija, both refuse to make such a choice. These "modern" women want both a traditional home and a career, and a man who is both lover and respectable husband. This desire to have the best of both worlds is a notion Narayan wishes to discredit, for neither woman is successful in achieving her aim. Rann, the archmodernist, refuses to submit to the traditional expectations people, especially women, have of him. He is the quintessential rootless man, forever on the run.

Although TM is meant to serve as a foil to Rann, and does indeed perform the role of helper/savior to the two women in question, he too is enamored sufficiently with the spirit of modernity to fail adequately to respond to the challenge facing him. Thus, although he is successful in getting Girija out of Rann's clutches, he is unable to offer much consolation at the end of the novel to the powerful but hysterical "Commandant Sarasa," Rann's "wife." Having tracked Rann down once with the help of a news item TM had published, and having subsequently dragged him "home," Sarasa is unable to hold on to her errant husband for long. The ever slippery Rann, a modern man on the lookout for new adventures and scientific discoveries, absconds yet again, this time to Europe—surely a more appropriate "home" for him. Sarasa returns to Malgudi to inform TM of this latest development, hoping, perhaps, that TM might have received some news from Rann. As her closing statement indicates, she holds TM responsible for revealing Rann's whereabouts (the article on Rann) and for causing her, however inadvertently, the pain of a doomed reconciliation. Although her logic appears somewhat warped, it is true that TM, in his fascination for the modern Rann and all that he represents (scientific "progress," change, mystery, etc.), is indeed the one who sets in motion the rather ill-fated sequence of events that form the plot of the novel. These result not only in the unhappiness of the two leading ladies of the story but also in a disastrous lecture by Rann that in turn leads to mass pandemonium and general riot in one of Malgudi's lecture halls. And so, by the end of this unceremonious novel, one can lend some credence to Sarasa's accusations against TM, as well as empathize with TM's sense of impotence in the face of events and attitudes that are rapidly eroding the old, stable world of traditional Malgudi:

At this point she broke down, and began to sob uncontrollably. Between her fits of sobbing she managed to say, "I should have been far happier if I had never met you or noticed your news item about the Timbuctoo man. . . ."

It was distressing to see a mighty personality, generally self-possessed, crumbling down. My eyes were wet too. Presently finding it embarrassing to continue in my presence, she abruptly got up, rushed back to the waiting room, and bolted the door.[20]

And on that inconclusive, rather pessimistic note, Narayan's latest novel ends. By virtue of its pessimistically "real" ending, *Talkative Man* stands as a bit of an anomaly in the rest of Narayan's oeuvre, although *The Painter of Signs* can be said to presage it somewhat, and even, perhaps, *The Dark Room*. It might be more appropriate to say that this latest novel marks a more pronounced awareness in Narayan that realism is the way of the future and that myth and tradition are merely relics of a fast-disappearing cultural past.

Nevertheless, ideologically speaking, Narayan stands in sharpest contrast to Rushdie. The latter can see no possibility for a "whole" identity in a culturally and politically fragmented world, and conveys this belief through fiction in which all genres cancel each other out, and where even Myth debunks itself. In Narayan's fiction, on the other hand, not only do different genres and modes, myth and realism, comedy and tragedy, hold their own, but, for the most part, they interfuse with, rather than defuse, each other; and myth, far from debunking itself, often reigns supreme. This creates the possibility of a whole existence for the fiction as well as the characters. But, of course, this wholeness is made possible only if present reality is diluted or made more palatable by the comforting presence of an enduring indigenous past, and as my discussion of Narayan's last few novels has shown, even for Narayan this is not always possible. However, as Harsharan Ahluwalia sees it, Narayan, for the most part, "has got along prosperously with one little spot called Malgudi to the almost complete exclusion of any concern with socio-political forces at work in the country."[21] In other words, Narayan, in most of his oeuvre, chooses to deal with the present only on his terms—and these include ignoring whatever is unpleasant in the past and current sociopolitical history of India.

20. R. K. Narayan, *Talkative Man* (New York: Viking, 1987), 119.
21. Harsharan S. Ahluwalia, "Narayan's Sense of Audience," *Ariel* 15 (January 1984): 64.

# 2

## Anita Desai

## The Morality of Realism Versus the Aestheticism of Myth

In this chapter, the call of realism is, by and large, the call of community, of communication with others, and requires the individual to connect with, and thus take some responsibility toward, others. It thus forms the moral bedrock, or content, of Anita Desai's novels. It is conveyed in her work largely through the medium of her prose style, which often borders on the poetic and richly lyrical, rather than the down-to-earth, crystal clear, ironic prose employed by Narayan.

Myth, on the other hand, here stands for isolation and retreat from society and its values, and characters who operate within this mode are, or wish to be, quite cut off from the rest of humanity. There is a certain glamor and attraction in this mode because it allows its characters to operate in a realm of imagination and fantasy not available to those who must live their lives in a more mundane, down-to-earth, socially responsible fashion. It is such a pull between the aesthetic attractiveness of myth and the moral weight of realism that gives Anita Desai's fiction its tension and interest.

Anita Desai, like R. K. Narayan, is struggling to find a voice that can (in an "authentic" way) bridge the gap between a glorious (pre-British, precolonial) Indian past and a much diminished, more sordid, postcolonial present. Whereas Narayan had struggled with the question of how his characters were to achieve sincerity and balance in a "native" (that is, authentic) Indian setting and had come up with the response of diluting realism through myth, Desai's response to the colonial dilemma does not, I think, have the total optimism that underlies Narayan's formal choices, for ultimately she is in favor of diluting myth with realism, rather than vice versa. Although one critic seems to think that "so long as her moral vision remains subservient to the poetic and metaphysical urges of her imagination, there cannot be much hope for her development,"[1] I feel that, on the contrary, Desai ultimately subordinates her poetic and mythic imagination to her moral vision. In other words, she is morally much more in favor of a "realistic" approach to life. By this is meant an approach that faces up to life and leads one to shoulder one's burdens, do one's duties to others responsibly. It means facing up to the fact that a "glorious past" is nothing but a myth and not something which, like "Paradise Lost," can be regained. In fact, the very idea of achieving some kind of mythic retreat or escape from the burdens of reality, no matter how attractive, is rejected at the end of her novels. Such a response, for Desai, is unacceptable because it is ultimately a rejection of life in all its variety and leads only to insanity for those who choose it. At the same time, however, Desai is aesthetically very much a practitioner of the mythic mode. Her lyricism, her poetic imagery, places her formally more within the mythic rather than the realist mode. And some of the more interesting characters in her fiction are those conceived within the mythic mode, which lends them a certain grandeur and appeal that the more mundane characters of realism lack. Yet morally she is on the side of the critical and social realists, although she herself does not seem to think she is composing any kind of social criticism in her earlier works; she does, however, acknowledge a change of style in her later fiction, indicative of a broader interest in social and political reality.[2]

1. Darshan Singh Maini, "The Achievement of Anita Desai," in *Indo-English Literature*, ed. K. K. Sharma (Ghaziabad: Vimal Prakashan, 1977), 228. All subsequent references to this work will be cited parenthetically in the text as Maini.

2. In an interview with Florence Libert, which she gave in Cambridge, England, in 1989 (published in *World Literature Written in English* 30, no. 1 [1990]: 47–55), Desai states that "various people have said that they've noted a change in my writing with *In Custody* and going on to *Baumgartner's Bombay*." She goes on to confirm the validity of such observations by admitting that she has moved away from her previous interest in "interior monologue really, the interior self" to larger issues that can be expressed only through the use of dialogue. Although later in the interview she eschews the novelist's conscious

Needless to say, I find this strain of critical realism overshadowing the mythic pull of her poetic prose and her interest in the "solitary individual" even in her earlier works.

It might be useful, for the purpose of illustrating the mythic quality of her prose style, to quote an excerpt here from Desai's earliest novel, *Cry, the Peacock*. In the following passage, the young heroine, Maya, in her choice of language and imagery, stands revealed as a romanticist; her desire to see the extraordinary in the ordinary, the beautiful in the humdrum, and, above all, the solitary nature of her musings place her within a mythic mode, which, as later discussion of the novel will show, is the kind of aesthetic pull she has to fight against to fulfill her realist desires for communion with others.

Says Maya of her husband, the "cold rationalist" (who turns out, in the novel, to be bound to the male myths of the Bhagavad Gita):

> Looking down at his thin face, gray and drawn upon the white pillow, it seemed to me that I was climbing a mountain from the top of which could be seen the entire world, unfolded like a map, with sun-silkened trees and milk-mild rivers and jeweled townships . . . which he, because he did not care for walks, or views . . . remained behind in the dusty, enclosed cup of the small plain down below. . . . Oh unprivileged to miss the curved arc of a bird's wing as it forces itself against the weight of air into the clear sky . . . the persistent, sweet odor of a ripe pineapple . . . moonlight, its quality and coolness, playing upon papaya leaves, its silver glint cutting sharp, black silhouettes . . . and then the papaya tree itself . . . I contemplated that, smiling with pleasure at the thought of bridal flowers that flow out of the core of the female papaya tree and twine about her slim trunk, and the firm, wax-petalled blossoms that leap directly out of the solid trunk of the male.[3]

The last several lines of the passage indicate the crucial battle in Desai's fiction, here emblematized by the struggle in Maya between form and content, myth and realism. The lyrical imagery employed herein indicates a poetic and withdrawn sensibility at odds with the prosaic reality of the

---

role as social critic, she nevertheless admits that "if you are uncompromisingly telling the truth about yourself, about your characters and about society, then you become willy-nilly a social critic."

3. Anita Desai, *Cry, the Peacock* (1963; reprint, New Delhi: Orient Paperbacks, 1983), 17. All subsequent references to this work will be cited parenthetically in the text as Desai, *Cry*.

world, symbolized partially by the husband. On the other hand, Maya *is* drawn to the concept of connectedness, of true communion with an other (which is an intrinsic concept and goal of realism), as evidenced, ironically, in the poetic, mythic metaphor of the mating of the papaya trees.

The question of genre is also closely tied to the "woman question" in many of her books. Many of her female protagonists tend to choose the mythic over the realist mode primarily because they are women and, as such, have too much responsibility and very little liberty within the realist mode of Indian life. In making such a choice for her female protagonists, Desai is much like the British and American nineteenth-century women novelists, such as the Brontë sisters and Sarah Orne Jewett, who also chose to cast their heroines in the modes of myth and romance for, I think, similar reasons as Desai. Of course, there were exceptions, such as Jane Austen and George Eliot, whose women were conceived within the realist genre. It is therefore interesting to note that Desai herself prefers the writing of Emily Brontë over that of Jane Austen:

> "I was nine years old when I first read *Wuthering Heights* and although obviously I could not have understood half of it, it struck me with the force of a gale and I still vibrate to it. . . . On the other hand, when I first read Austen I was left cold. . . . There is something about her that is totally alien to my own writing and which strikes no sympathetic chord in me. Is it that she is so entirely social or entirely the opposite of solitary?"[4]

The solitary stance of myth is very attractive to Desai. Yet, when her characters choose to respond in such a way, especially the women, their response is somehow not seen as ultimately viable by Desai, because, finally, we do have to take on responsibility for life if we are to remain within history; and, as she shows in *Cry, the Peacock*, the Indian mythic mode does not really provide women with a strategy for liberation from male (and colonialist) hegemonies. In fact, the Indian mythic image of woman most prevalent in the literature of the time was that of the Patrivrata tradition: the Sita, Sati, Savitri image of the silently suffering, sacrificial wife, mother, and daughter. A Western critic, Dorothy Spencer (quoted in Shirwadker), recognizes this phenomenon and comments:

4. Atma Ram, "An Interview with Anita Desai," *World Literature Written in English* 16 (April 1977): 95–103. Quoted by Peter Alcock in "Rope, Serpent, Fire: Recent Fiction of Anita Desai," *Journal of Indian Writing in English* 9 (January 1981): 15.

It seems clear that in woman as wife we are dealing with a literary tradition. Sita, Savitri, Shakuntala. . . . At any rate, they exemplify the ideal and thus express society's values . . . that "a husband is a woman's god—how Sita submitted to Rama; she followed him into the wilderness and afterwards when he banished her, she turned and went without one word, though she was innocent."[5]

Thus, Desai rebels against myth at the same time that she is cognizant of and attracted to some of its benefits.

Maya, the heroine of *Cry, the Peacock* (1963), is rebellious from the outset—one who questions tradition in every form through her senses and emotions. Her husband, Gautama, is the very opposite; although he professes to mock mythic traditions through the power of logic and intellect, he ironically uses his logic to support the most traditional views of Hindu philosophy: resignation and acceptance of whatever life brings, by virtue of the philosophy of nonattachment and the fatalism of reincarnation.

When Maya mourns the death of her beloved dog, Gautama launches a tirade against all forms of tradition, including the one that insists on giving a "fitting" burial or cremation to a dearly departed one: "Now what is there in the ancient rites of cremation that is worth remembering?" When Maya defends the tradition of burial as something people do because it "matters to them," Gautama, irritated, replies, "Why should it matter? It doesn't—not only because their lives are trivial and expendable in any case, but also because our religion trains us not to believe in these empty rites. The Gita does not preach involvement in tradition. It preaches—recommends, rather—detachment on every count" (Desai, *Cry,* 17).

Although Gautama vehemently rejects all "traditions," by adhering so closely to the doctrine of the Bhagavad Gita, he is in fact allying himself with all that is traditional and mythic in Hindu thought and philosophy.

It is just such a traditional (and male) philosophy of detachment from life that Maya rebels against; the rebellion, slow and muted at first, ends ultimately in Maya's cathartic killing of her husband.

From the beginning, the contrast between Maya's and Gautama's value systems is established, and the fact that Maya is the narrator makes it clear where the writer's own sympathies lie. Thus, when all Gautama says to the bereaved Maya to console her for the death of her dog is, "You need a cup of tea," Maya's whole being cries out:

---

5. Meena Shirwadker, *Image of Woman in the Indo-Anglian Novel* (New Delhi: Sterling Publishers, 1979), 49. All subsequent references to this work will be cited parenthetically in the text as Shirwadker.

"Yes," I cried, "yes, it is his hardness—no, no, not hardness, but the distance he coldly keeps from me. His coldness, his coldness, and incessant talk of cups of tea and philosophy in order not to hear me talk, and talking, reveal myself. It is that—my loneliness in this house." (9)

The tradition based on the mythic content of the Bhagavad Gita, of which Gautama is the pallbearer, stands for a kind of isolation, a rejection of the critical realist mode of existence (which demands that man act within society). Such isolation is anathema to a deeply sensuous person such as Maya because, being sensuous, she believes in unity between body and mind, self and society. As she herself admits, she yearns for "the peace that comes from companion life alone, from brother flesh. *Contact, relationship, communion . . .*" (18; emphasis added).

Highly strung and sensitive to her own loneliness in her husband's house as she is, Maya remembers, one moonlit night, a fatal prophecy of her youth: a "horoscope Wallah" had prophesied that four years after her marriage, either she or her husband would die. The memory of this prophecy unsettles Maya terribly (especially as her marriage to Gautama has just completed its fourth year), and in her agitation she wishes she could return to visit her father, the idol of her youth, for help and comfort. And so she mentions her desire to Gautama: "I wish I could see father again. It always helps" (53). But his puzzled response is, "Helps what? Whom?" Hearing this response, Maya reflects:

Without realizing what he had done, Gautama had laid his finger and forced mine upon the fatal vulnerability of what I had believed in like a fond fool. My father, with his quiet words, would have done nothing to allay my fears or dispel my conviction, but merely underlined their power by asking me, however sadly, to "accept for it must be so." In his words, "It must be so." If he saw disaster he saw it as being inevitable, and if he saw rebellion, he saw it as being hopeless. (54)

Her father, then, becomes merely another facet of her husband. For Gautama's philosophy of nonattachment is intimately linked to the traditional philosophy of resignation and fatalistic acceptance inherent in the Hindu doctrine of reincarnation (which Maya's father so strongly believes in). Anticipating Maya's rejection of the "logic" of reincarnation, Gautama says to her:

> You will say—"what, are we bound to this cycle then, tethered to it? But that is fatalism?" Ah, but see the logic of it—the perfect logic of it: one incarnation acting upon the other, the action performed in one incarnation bearing fruit in the next, as surely as autumn must follow summer, as surely as the rising tide must ebb. (122)

Maya's horrified response to such a coldly mechanical and unjust view of life is:

> To think—to think that we are to pay, in this life for what we *may* have done in a past one, to think that we may have to pay horribly, oh horribly, for something terrible, something terrible that we *might* have done—it is terrible! (124)

It is quite obvious, then, that Maya, who is perceived by Gautama as the traditionalist, is in fact the very opposite. Horrified by the male "logic" that goes hand in hand with the most sacred yet terrifying of Hindu myths and traditions, Maya wishes to throw off the double yoke. For if she accepts the view of life preached to her by her husband and father, she must resign herself to her fate and thus must die, as the soothsayer had foretold, in order, perhaps, to atone for sins committed in some previous life (as well as to preserve her husband's life). Enmeshed in such a nightmare, Maya cries out in anguish, "Father! Brother! Husband! Who is my savior? I am in need of one" (98). Of course, the reader realizes that Maya cannot look for salvation to any of her male "helpers."

Slowly the moon, symbol of the female imagination, starts to dominate Maya's life, and although it is seen as ominous by Maya at several points, it nevertheless symbolizes the rebellion and anger raging within her and in the end turns out to be her savior. Thus, when Maya needs to remember the "language . . . of hieroglyphs [which she had] once known" (27), in order to understand the childhood prophecy, the moon supplies her the answer:

> In the end, it was not the stars which told me, but the moon, when it rose out of the churn of my frenzy, vast and ghost-white, written

> ever with dim, tortuous signs in ash-grey . . . it was not the gentle
> moon of love-ballads and fairy revels . . . but a demoniac creature
> . . . a phantom gone berserk trying to leap the threshold of my
> mind. (27)

And the moon presides over her ultimate sliding into insanity, or, as the perceptive reader can't help but think, her final "liberation." When, on a moonlit night, Maya pushes her husband over the edge of the roof, she has, in fact, achieved victory over fate, over all the traditional myths of acceptance and resignation that the men in her life had tried to force on her. She has done this, however, not by acting within the realist mode, but by empowering herself through the symbols of female mythology (for example, the moon). Thus her "deliverance" is only partial, for she has escaped the yoke of the masculine mythic mode only to yield herself to the female mythic mode.

The price she has to pay for such a partial liberation is extremely heavy—the price of sanity. Yet, the reader can't help but feel that this was a better alternative than remaining forever a prisoner to the male myths of Hindu tradition, petrified in a state of isolation and acceptance as Gautama and her father had been.

Seen from a postcolonial perspective, Maya stands for change, even if it is nihilistic, whereas Gautama and her father symbolize the continuance of patriarchal, neocolonialist traditions.

Although, at the end, Maya has lost her sanity (which means, of course, that her response is not ultimately endorsed by Desai), the novel does not end on a totally pessimistic note, for Gautama's mother and sister, cool and detached as they have been trained to be by their men in the earlier parts of the book, now come to the aid of Maya. Maya's desire and vision to achieve "communion . . . with others" finally comes true, and it is among women. Here Desai shows the desirability of the critical realist mode in which people take responsibility for each other, as opposed to the mythic mode that is essentially isolationist and unhistorical. Thus, when Maya's cries are heard at the end, both her mother-in-law and sister-in-law go to her aid:

> The old lady [Gautama's mother] was up on her feet first. "Someone
> must go to her," she said, and her quick voice was so low and
> reassured that the tenseness in the younger woman relaxed imme-
> diately. "She is frightened," said the mother, and hurried out of

the room. Nila heard her climbing the stairs, pounding them in urgency. She rose too and went after her to the door. (218)

The central issue in Desai's next novel (1965), *Voices in the City*, is that of communication. The three major characters of the book, Nirode and his two sisters, Amla and Monisha, are caught up in the by now familiar dialectic: whether to create an isolated, mythic world to live in, remote from the pains and unpleasant realities of the past and present, or to accept the burdens of history and, with that, one's responsibilities to others, to society, and thus to give one's life some meaning, through communication and responsiveness to others. Nirode, who is the central character of the first section of the book, is the one most obsessed with his own past and, in his desire to escape it, finds that he must create another myth to live by, a myth that will isolate him from the need to communicate with, and thus care for, others. Yet, ironically, the role he creates for himself, that of being an idealistic, bohemian young writer and editor of "meaningful" journals, is one that has its basis in communication.

Thus, Nirode thinks he can escape the past, because the past is dead, over with; yet, he keeps reliving it at almost every step, and his present mode of life is based in an obsessive desire to reject it. At the start, then, Nirode is envious of his younger brother's success in his studies, in being able to "escape" India and go off to study in England—something Nirode wishes he could have done. Yet, after waving goodbye to his brother, and after a bout of self-pity, Nirode convinces himself that he does not want what his brother has—the "light of success"—because, he says to himself, "This light was crass, it stung his eyes, and what he wanted was shadows, silence, stillness."[6] What he is doing here is repressing the very real desires of his childhood past, to be like his brother, to be a success, rather than a "shadow," a failure. Later, gazing out over a graveyard from the window of a friend's apartment, Nirode, in thinking about India's British past, commits the same act of repression by insisting that everything about British colonialism is dead, finished, a thing of the past:

> At the window, Nirode . . . counted grave stones in the night. The founders of the British empire lay buried in the sleazy Bengal ooze where they had first founded their colonial power. . . . Young

6. Anita Desai, *Voices in the City* (1965; reprint, New Delhi: Orient Paperbacks, 1982), 8. All subsequent references to this work will be cited parenthetically in the text as Desai, *Voices*.

> English roses seized once by glorious ambition and then, finally,
> by dysentery—and so a career of balls and crinolines and harsh
> voyages *ended* (emphasis added) (Desai, *Voices*, 17)

Of course, what Nirode in his cynicism wishes to deny is the fact that
the past is never quite "ended," that on the contrary, it always encroaches
on the present and shapes our identities in subtle ways. Thus, as far as
British influence is concerned, Nirode later admits (albeit unknowingly),
"They [his family] had outgrown it [Bengali] and brothers, sisters and
mother now conversed and corresponded almost exclusively in English"
(35).

What Desai seems to be saying in this novel is that pleasant or
unpleasant, happy or unhappy, our past and our memories of it have to be
confronted realistically: ultimately we have to reconcile ourselves to our
past and accept it. If not, like Nirode, we will be forever adrift on a sea of
cynicism and negativism, unable to get on with our lives in any fruitful
way.

The past Nirode has to confront and accept is his childhood, particularly
his memory of his mother's infidelity to her husband (true or otherwise the
reader is never told). Unless he can accept his mother for what she is, his
dreams of his childhood will remain nightmarish:

> Into Nirode's sleep the bright birds of the past came serenely
> winging and the wide gestures of their wings ushered into his sleep
> the gemmed loveliness of a holiday home of his childhood. . . .
> [Then] anger and impotence tore at the light sheet of his sleep, tore
> holes into it and admitted a new, harsh and uncolored light upon
> the dream scene. Something about all this prettiness and brightness
> turned macabre and horrifying, and he soon saw why; . . . between
> him and his mother's brilliant territory was erected a barbed wire
> fence, all glittering and vicious. To his astonishment, he found at
> his side, also on the wrong side of this cruel division, his father,
> lying slovenly, asleep, the buttons of his silk coat undone. He
> looked at his mother to ask her to explain this unsightly apparition
> of the dead man, but . . . something distracted her, footsteps, a
> voice, and she turned to greet, with a ravishing smile, her neighbor,
> that retired major, or brigadier who, with his bestial jaws and hairy
> hands, repelled Nirode . . . his mother sat on the veranda, smiling
> a slow, sensuous smile. Hideous to see in his mother, hideous to

see in the heroine. . . . He turned over, *away from her*, and in his sleep groaned. (26; emphasis added)

This "turning away" becomes Nirode's modus operandi with the rest of the world as well. Having been hurt, betrayed once, Nirode thinks all relationships, all attempts at communication are hopeless, doomed to destruction: "Marriage, bodies, touch and torture. He shuddered and, walking swiftly, was almost afraid of the dark of Calcutta, its warmth that *clung to one. . . .* All that was Jit and Sarla's, he decided, and indeed *all that had to do with marriage was destructive, negative, decadent*" (35; emphasis added). Thus, Nirode feels of himself "that he was a man for whom aloneness alone was the sole natural condition, aloneness alone the treasure worth treasuring." Having created this myth of the "lone ranger" for himself, Nirode is able to say to a friend, when asked why he doesn't start a newspaper (instead of a magazine), that "the newspaper carries the writer further and further into the impersonal, it only follows the You. The You is everything in news. There is never an I. It is the I that interests me now" (24).

Yet Nirode is torn by the desire, the need to communicate, as his questions to the professor attest: "Unless one has decided upon one's chosen audience, one's readers, what sort of material can one feed them? What does one collect for them? How put it across? How communicate?" (23).

But because of his cynicism, his retreat into a state of solitude and self-centeredness in the face of unpleasant memories of the past, Nirode's ventures into the world of communication are doomed to self-defeat. Thus, when asked by a "friend," David, about the state of his magazine, Nirode replies:

> "Ah, the magazine," Nirode spat in disgust. "What has the magazine to do with my journey? It has only to do with my days—it occupies me, it gratifies my friends. It feeds me meals and drinks at their expense. . . . But at night what answer, or reassurance does the bloody thing give me then? How can it? It is only a collection of little pieces . . . written by little men. . . . I want it to fail—quickly. Then I want to see if I have the spirit to start moving again, towards my next failure." (39)

In the face of such cynicism (which creates a totalizing mood in Nirode, a mood that is "mythic" in its total rejection of the redemptive power of communication and of connection with others), David can only reply, "That is more than defeatism—Nirode, it is absolute negation" (40). And indeed Nirode's entire life-style is a negation of life because it is a negation of love, of the power to redeem one's failures by communicating with and caring for others.

Living in this isolated mode, cut off from his mother (to whose letters he never replies) and his sisters, Nirode one day receives a letter from Monisha that tells him she and her husband's family are in Calcutta and that she wishes to see him. Thus begins the second section of the book, narrated in first person by Monisha, who envies Nirode his nonattachment and wishes her life too could become like his:

> Look at me, my equipment, my appurtenances. My black wardrobe, my family, my duties of serving fresh chapaties to the uncles as they eat, of listening to my mother-in-law as she tells me the remarkably many ways of cooking fish, of being Jiban's wife. If all this were to blow away, what would be left would be very small. Yet, it would be lighter to bear. Nirode is lighter now. (112)

However, Monisha's desire to escape social responsibility does not stem from a neurotic desire to escape the past, as Nirode's does. Rather, it is an understandable, even justifiable response of an intelligent woman whose creativity and freedom are completely curtailed within the bounds of a traditional marriage. However, Desai still does not wish to favor a response that rejects social responsibility. Being primarily a writer who believes in the philosophy of the critical realist mode, she chooses once again to reject the myths of the Bhagavad Gita, even though her style of writing about the siblings is a mythic one.

Thus, even Monisha, fervent reader of the Bhagavad Gita, who believes in the words of the mythic Keshava—that "he who is free from all attachment . . . his wisdom is well established" (128)—even she realizes that the element she and Nirode lack is love, and that this lack is tantamount to a lack of conscience. Having been introduced to David, Nirode's friend, Monisha discovers in him

> that vital element that is missing from Nirode and myself—the element of love. . . . In place of this love that suffuses the white face of this mystic waif [David], we possess a darker, fiercer element, fear. *I see now that both Nirode and I shy from love, fear*

*it as attachment.* If only love existed that is not binding, that is free
of rules, obligations, complicity and all stirrings of mind or con-
sciences, then—but there is no such love. (135; emphasis added)

No, there is no love without obligation, duty to others, and in avoiding this
responsibility to others, one is avoiding one's conscience, as Monisha
admits, "Mine has withered and died away" (136). The third sibling, Amla,
is superficially different from Nirode and Monisha, in that she arrives in
Calcutta full of energy and hopes to make it big in the communicative
world of advertising. At least initially, she seems neither burdened by an
oppressive past nor desirous of a retreat into solitude; to the contrary, she
mingles in society and goes to several parties in order to establish a
clientele for herself. However, all the communicative hustle and bustle
soon comes to an end. Amla suddenly realizes the emptiness of her life:
"Then the rot set in—overnight, without warning. Amla was melancholy.
. . . The thread of communication was broken, she saw how friable it had
been" (179).

Jit, a "friend" of Nirode's, meeting Amla in this mood for the first time,
realizes how similar she is, after all, to her other siblings: "I don't
understand it—this terrible destructiveness in all of you. You destroy—you
destroy yourselves, and you destroy that part of others that gets so fatally
involved in you. There is this—this dreadful attractiveness in your dark
ways of thinking and feeling through life towards death" (175). And indeed,
unable to love, to communicate, the siblings are living a kind of death,
which in itself is a rather mythic idea, similar to the one Thomas Mann
employs in describing the rather unnatural relationships of the siblings in
"Blood of the Walsungs."

Nirode, seeing his sister Amla in this mood, decides "it is time I took
you to meet a friend of mine" (185), an artist named Dharma, who like
Nirode has retreated from life and for years has painted no human figures,
but only insects and plants. On meeting Amla, however, Dharma shocks
Nirode by expressing a desire to paint Amla's portrait, to which request
she agrees. Thereafter ensue a series of meetings between Amla and the
artist, which bring about a curious transformation both in Amla and in the
nature of Dharma's work. Amla, for the first time in her life, begins to feel
the power of love and does not shy away from it, even though she can't
express it: "Amla's love, knowing no possibility of manifestation, became
one uncontrollable desire to communicate" (193).

This urge to communicate impresses itself upon the consciousness of the reclusive Dharma and transforms his hitherto grotesque, surrealistic vision of the world to one that is whole, unified. The contrast between Dharma and Nirode at this point becomes quite clear. As one critic points out, "If Nirode's escape can be termed from nowhere into nowhere, Dharma's is an escape into involvement."[7]

From painting Amla in isolated portions, Dharma ends by painting a complete, a whole, portrait of her. Amla dared not at first calm and console herself with the heady thought that she was

> the cause of this great change. . . . But when the fetishes, the symbols and the dream images began to slowly disappear from his paintings, and more and more of Amla began to appear whole and alive and meaningful in herself, then apprehension made her very heart darken and tumble. Over the weeks she had watched the incorporate horror of his earlier surrealisms filter softly out of his whorled paints . . . and a *new, refreshing realism* push its way through as though from the rubble of a post-war ruin—at first tentative, then shocking in its rawness and finally marvelous by the very virtue of its existence. (Desai, *Voices*, 212; emphasis added)

The wholeness of realism, achieved by Dharma toward the end of his career, is finally also achieved by Nirode and Amla, although only after, and because of, Monisha's suicide.

Shocked and brought together by their sister's death, Nirode and Amla both sense the message that Monisha was trying to convey to them by taking her own life—the importance of feeling, of love, of caring and reaching out to others—for she herself had been unable to reach out or become involved with those around her, and the loneliness had ultimately made it impossible for her to go on living. (Of course, her uncommunicativeness was not entirely her fault, but was due in large part to a cold, unresponsive husband, who could not be bothered to take note of her sensitive nature.) Amla realizes

> that Monisha's death had pointed the way for her and would never allow her to lose herself. She knew that she would go through life with her feet primly shod, *involving herself with her drawings and*

7. Ramesh K. Srivastava, "Voices of Artists in the City," *Journal of Indian Writing in English* 9 (January 1981): 51.

*safe people like Bose,* precisely because Monisha had given her a glimpse of what lay on the other side of this stark, uncompromising margin. (248; emphasis added)

And though this may sound like a somewhat timid response to life, it is nevertheless a more sane, balanced, and communicative response than that of Monisha's. Even more revolutionary is the change in Nirode. Sitting with his sister and aunt, watching over Monisha's body till morning, he seems unable to remain still or silent:

> . . . *he was filled with an immense care of the world that made him reach out,* again and again, to touch Amla's cold hand when he saw it shake, or embrace the old woman . . . when he saw her weep. He pressed them to him with hunger and joy, as if he rejoiced in this sensation of touching other flesh, others' pains . . . which till now had been agonizingly neglected. There was so much he wanted to tell them—to reassure them that no outrage had been committed, that *Monisha had died from an excess of caring, in a fire of cure and conscience and that they too must accept with a like intensity, the vigilance of heart and conscience,* . . . allowing no deed of indifference or incomprehension to drift by but to seize each moment, each person, each fragment of the world. (248; emphasis added)

Thus, for Desai, the only way to cope with life is through involvement with and caring for others (the goals of realism), not by withdrawal and isolation, which are the ideals of the heroes of Indian myth. It is only by eschewing his mythic goals of solitude and isolation and by embracing instead the realistic ideals of communication and involvement that Nirode finally achieves a wholeness, a unity of body and spirit, an understanding of life's grand design:

> He felt himself elevated to an unimaginably high vantage point from where he could see the *whole* fantastic design of life and death . . . this lucidity made him transparent, allowing night and sorrow to merge with his own ecstasy, till everything became *one, became unified,* and understandable . . . he had listened to silence, till out of silence . . . music had sprung. (249; emphasis added)

It is only fitting that Nirode, having achieved some measure of "understanding," should, at the end of the book, be able to look forward to a reconciliation with his mother, with the past. Ultimately, so Desai's message seems to be, we must accept the burdens of our past and continue to live within the pale of history, in as socially responsible a way as possible, because the only alternative to this is annihilation.

In her next two novels, *Where Shall We Go This Summer* (1975) and *Fire on the Mountain* (1977), Anita Desai continues to explore the theme of mythic escapism versus social responsibility (reality) and in so doing examines which of the genres, myth/romance or critical realism, is morally appropriate as a novelistic strategy within the Indian context.

In *Where Shall We Go This Summer,* Manori, the island of myth and magic, Sita's childhood home, competes for her attention with Bombay, the metropolis of the present, Sita's home after marriage and thus symbolic of the adult world and its responsibilities.

When Sita, the central character, mother of four children and living in her husband's home in contemporary Bombay, discovers she is pregnant for the fifth time, she has a kind of breakdown. Having grown up in the sheltered, peaceful atmosphere of Manori—the island that her father, a well-known preindependence politician, had received as a gift from an admirer and where he had carried out his magical pastoral experiments—Sita has never reconciled herself to the violence and the frenetic quality of life in postindependence Bombay. It is also clear that as a wife and mother, her life in the realist mode is hopelessly circumscribed and that she has very little influence either on her husband or children. Thus, when she discovers she is about to bring another human being into the world, something snaps within her, and she informs her shocked husband, Raman, that she will not have the baby. Horrified, he asks her if she means to abort it, to which her hysterical response is, "I want to keep it—I don't want it to be born,"[8] and she thinks she can somehow prevent the birth by going back to the mythical Manori, where stranger miracles are known to have happened. This, of course, is another example of mythic fiction and of its aesthetic appeal for Desai. As Darshan Singh Maini points out, "The mad idea of containing the baby in the womb for keeps is surely one of the classic cases of regression and retreat from reality" (Maini, 228).

8. Anita Desai, *Where Shall We Go This Summer?* (1975; reprint, New Delhi: Orient Paperbacks, 1982), 35. All subsequent references to this work will be cited parenthetically in the text as Desai, *Where.*

In other words, Sita wants to keep the unborn baby forever safe from the cruelty and violence of the "real" world (which, as she sees it, is a world of the masculine values of competitiveness and aggression). As she tells her husband, the spirit of violence has infected everybody living in the present, including (and this is what horrifies her most) her own children. She thinks to herself:

> Everyone fights. They are all violent . . . like the waves incessantly, tiresomely crashing into each other, her sons hurled their bodies at each other as if they were made for attack and combat. . . . No one offended her so much by violence as Menaka [her daughter] in her carelessness. She watched disbelievingly as Menaka, telling her about a party she had been to, idly reached out her fingers and crumbled a sheaf of new buds on the small potted plant. . . . [Menaka] had done it unconsciously, had not meant to destroy anything at all. Destruction came so naturally; that was the horror. (Desai, *Where*, 44–45)

It is to prevent her fifth baby from being born into a world where "destruction comes so easily" that Sita retreats to Manori, dragging her daughter Menaka and one son, Karan, with her. At this point, the writer's (and the reader's) sympathy is clearly with her and with the mythic mode she represents, with its "feminine" values of passivity and nurturance.

Awaiting her arrival at the island with great anticipation are Moses, caretaker of her father's house, his wife Miriam, and a host of villagers who still remember the mythic stature of her father when he had been alive and the virtual ruler of Manori. Thus, as the villagers sit around reminiscing, the entire atmosphere takes on a mythological coloring: "Moses . . . sat amongst jars of pink biscuits and cream horns and calendars with *lush mythological themes* and drank sweet tea out of a thick glass" (7; emphasis added). Trying to recall the time when the father was alive, Moses coaxes the other villagers into recalling the myths as well:

> "Who has forgotten the father?" Moses harangued them, but in a sing-song tone, ritualistic, almost dreamy.
> "Not us, not us," neighed the goats [that is, the other villagers], wagging about the table. . . . "He rid my house of snakes and scorpions and no one was bitten again," [says one]. . . . "He made my wife bear who had been barren for twelve years, and she bore

sons," sang another. . . . "Who has forgotten the well?" Moses roared to rouse them again. "The only well in Manori that gives sweet water?" "Ah, the well, the well, we remember, we know." "He dug it," cried Moses. (11–12)

And, of course, it is to rekindle the old myths, to achieve another miracle, that Sita returns to the island:

She was on the island, in order to achieve the miracle of not giving birth. Wasn't this Manori, the island of miracles? Her father had made it an island of magic once, worked miracles of a kind. His legend was still here in this house, and he might work another miracle, posthumously. She had come on a pilgrimage, to beg for the miracle of keeping her baby unborn. (31)

But almost as soon as she arrives, with Menaka and Karan unhappily in tow, Sita begins to sense that the magic is no longer there. The old house is in shambles, no food is available, and she has arrived "at the old house on the once magic island [only] to find the past all burnt to white ashes" (37). Slowly, as she begins to relive the past, Sita realizes that in fact the past was not all she had made it out to be. The "pastoral haven" her father had supposedly created on the island was a myth in the most literal sense of the word. And thinking back to the first time she had ever glimpsed the island (when her father, brother, stepsister, and she had first arrived there), Sita realizes that even then she had sensed that there is no perfect, magical retreat, a place where one can escape the realities of life: "She saw the island as a piece of magic, a magic mirror—it was so bright, so brilliant to her eyes after the tensions and shadows of her childhood. *It took her some time to notice that this magic, too, cast shadows*" (63; emphasis added).

Once she has conceded to herself the illusory nature of the mythical paradise created by her father, Sita begins to remember how most of the "miracles" attributed to her father seemed to her, even as a child, less than what they were supposed to be. Thus, she recalls her disappointment at the "miracle" of the well-digging:

The well was dug—no more a miracle, perhaps, than the wells in any village, but somehow it seemed one. The very presence of the father, watching and directing his "chelas" all in white, all still pure and clear as glass after their prayers and devotions made it seem one. . . . The first bucketful was drawn out and father ladled out the water to each of those who had helped with the digging.

"Sweet!" they cried, ecstatic. . . . "Sweet!"

Sita also came forward and her father, after hesitating for a second, smiled and filled her cupped hand from the ladle. She drank and pulled a face, understanding in an instant his hesitation, for the water was not sweet. . . . Only later, down on the beach with her brother, she confessed to its awful taste—and felt contrite, all night, for her betrayal, her failure to find the well water sweet. (68–69)

Sita's father, in his mythical role, thus comes to represent not only his daughter's past but, as innumerable details suggest, the Father of the Nation himself. He is referred to as the "Second Gandhi"; he lives among the poor and acquires a life-style dangerously similar to the original's. In casting such a character in the mold of Gandhi himself, Desai is unquestionably asking the reader to challenge the mythification of national heroes, of history itself. As Charmazel Dudt observes, "The author has succeeded in enlarging the function of the traditional psychological novel to include not merely an individual's struggle with his past, but also a nation's conflict with its history."[9]

Finally, Sita too realizes that she must challenge and reject the lure of a mythic past, in order to reenter the present and the future. There are no easy solutions to life's problems, she realizes, and running away from life and responsibility will certainly not solve anything, even though it may seem like an attractive alternative. Thus, when Raman comes to take the daughter and son back to Bombay in time for school and to persuade Sita to get to a hospital, Sita realizes the worth of his mode of life—the critical realist mode of life (which is balance and moderation):

He never hesitated—everything was so clear to him, and simple: life must be continued, and all its business—Menaka's admission to medical college gained, wife led to hospital, now child safely brought forth, the children reared, the factory seen to, a salary earned, a salary spent. There was courage, she admitted to herself

9. Charmazel Dudt, "Past and Present: A Journey to Confrontation," *Journal of Indian Writing in English* 9 (January 1981): 91.

in shame, in getting on with such matters from which she herself squirmed away, dodged and ran. It took courage. That was why the children turned to him, sensing him to be the superior in courage, in leadership. (Desai, *Where*, 139)

With this realization comes Sita's decision to return to Bombay with her husband and children, to the world of social responsibility. Although she feels that in her initial refusal to give birth to the child she had "had the imagination to offer it an alternative—a life unlived, a life bewitched" (139), such an alternative implies petrification, a refusal to enter history, and therefore, ultimately, death. Thus, Sita cannot retreat to a preindependence, even precolonial India, of which Manori is a symbol: in Manori there are no reminders or remnants of the political and religious strife that tore India during and after independence. Since "articles about the perfidy of Pakistan, the virtuousness of our own India" (55), are one of the factors that make Sita feel that in giving birth "to the child now so safely contained" within her, she would be "releasing it in a violent, pain-wracked blood-bath" (56), Sita sees the act of separation at childbirth as a reflection of the violent division of Pakistan and India. In avoiding childbirth, then, she thinks she can somehow avoid the pain of history (and the pain of being a woman), but of course, as Desai points out, such an alternative is contrary to the laws of nature and is therefore, finally, undesirable. In making Sita ultimately reject the comfort of myth, Desai has once again shown her moral disapproval of any stance that refuses to shoulder the burdens of history (however violent it may have been) and one's responsibilities to one's fellow beings. Critical realism both as a genre and a moral attitude toward life is upheld over the genre of myth, which romanticizes some kind of retreat from everyday life and history.

In *Fire on the Mountain*, the reader is again presented with a female protagonist who, like Sita, wishes to retreat from the responsibilities of adult life into a realm of solitude, where she can indulge the myths and fantasies of her childhood. Unlike Sita, however, Nanda Kaul has fulfilled her duties as wife and mother for most of her life, and she chooses to "escape" only after the death of her husband and after all her children and even grandchildren are grown and married. Having thus spent most of her grown life looking after the needs of others, Nanda Kaul is entitled, one feels, to some privacy and solitude toward the end of her life. And, indeed, Desai does view Nanda's desires with some sympathy, and as in her other books, she is to some extent attracted to a life of withdrawal, of escape from the onward process of history and responsibility, especially when it promises to relieve women of their onerous duties within a patriarchal culture. Yet here, as in her other books, critical realism as a genre and an attitude toward life wins out over myth. Balance (the ideal upheld by realism) is ultimately the most important thing in life, and it is when a sense of balance is lost that things go wrong. Thus, it is not that the desire to be left alone itself is wrong; it is only when Nanda Kaul lets this desire completely annihilate her sense of responsibility to others that things go wrong.

Hence, when her daughter writes to Nanda that the latter's great-granddaughter, Raka, is being sent to her for the summer holidays, Nanda Kaul is very annoyed: "It annoyed her intensely that she should once again be drawn into a position where it was necessary for her to take an interest in another's activities and be responsible for their effect and outcome."[10] Having finally succeeded in escaping familial and social responsibilities by purchasing for her new home a solitary house, Carignano, on a remote hill station, Nanda is obviously unhappy at having the yoke of responsibility thrust around her neck once again. Although understandable, it is nevertheless a callous reaction, since Raka, child of an unhappy marriage and broken home, has been very ill and now needs some loving care in order to recuperate, both physically and emotionally. However, Nanda Kaul is unable to look beyond her own selfish needs at this point and so is pleased when she discovers Raka to be a quiet child, with a penchant for isolation. Instead of being concerned at this rather abnormal trait in a child, Nanda is pleased, since she can now leave the girl to her own devices and not have to bother with her. Rather perversely, Nanda Kaul admires Raka for rejecting her [Nanda] and for being such an isolated, self-contained little person. She wonders at Raka's

> total rejection, so natural, instinctive and effortless when compared with her own planned and willful rejection of the child. . . . Nanda Kaul saw that she [Raka] was the finished, perfected model of what Nanda Kaul herself was merely a brave, flawed experiment. . . .
>
> Nanda Kaul felt a small admiration for her rise and stir. (Desai, *Fire*, 47–48)

10. Anita Desai, *Fire on the Mountain* (1977; reprint, New York: Penguin Books, 1981), 46. All subsequent references to this work will be cited parenthetically in the text as Desai, *Fire*.

Insensitive to the real reason behind Raka's attitude of withdrawal from the world of people—which, as the reader learns in chapter 11, is the terrible relationship between her parents—Nanda Kaul continues to leave her alone. When, during a storm, Nanda finds herself in enforced companionship with the child, her desire to communicate with Raka, instead of making her act (as one would expect) within the critical realist mode, leads her further into the mythicized realm of her childhood past. Thus, she starts to tell Raka stories about her own father's trip to Tibet, a land of myth and magic where, like a mythic hero, he undertook daring feats: "He was away in Tibet—oh for years and years. He went every step of the way on horseback, or on foot. The Mustagh Pass, the Baltoro glacier, the Aghill Pass . . . a terribly hard, dangerous route . . ." (83). And he witnessed strange, fantastic sights: "He went to Lhasa, saw the Potala. . . . there he ran into the strangest people of all, Lamas and sorcerers . . . [who] could do magic: they could make idols speak, turn day into night" (84–85).

Yet, even as she is relating these stories to Raka, as well as other stories about her wonderful, mythical childhood in Kashmir, Nanda Kaul realizes that one cannot really return to the past (especially when it only exists as myth). For, when Raka asks her, "Why did you come here . . . instead of going back to Kashmir?" Nanda Kaul eventually replies, "One does not go back. . . . No, one does not go back" (93).

But, if one cannot go back, one must go forward; one must live in and assume responsibility for present reality. One cannot with impunity reject the duties that real life thrusts upon one, no matter how onerous the burden. In order to drive this point home, Desai shows us the tragedy that results when we say no to life's responsibilities and withdraw into a mythical past. At the end of the book, Ila Das, an old childhood friend of Nanda Kaul's, telephones and Nanda is forced to invite her to tea. Through the course of their conversation, the reader realizes that Ila Das has always looked to Nanda Kaul for support and guidance. Being from a less privileged background than Nanda's, Ila has frequently relied on any help her friend could give her, such as getting her a decent job or a decent place to live.

It becomes clear from her conversation with Nanda on this particular afternoon that Ila is once more in need of help and caring from her old friend. When Nanda asks her, "Are you managing, Ila? Can you make ends meet?" Ila is forced to admit, "Not since Rima's [her dependent sister's] troubles grew so bad. . . . I've been sending a tiny sum for her board and lodging—the barest minimum, but oh . . . the barest minimum was all I had" (126).

From the rest of Ila's conversation, it becomes increasingly evident that not only is she in dire financial straits (though she tries to make light of it), she is also being threatened by several men in the village where she lives and works as a social worker, because of her progressive beliefs. At this point, Nanda Kaul realizes that the only decent thing to do would be to offer Ila Das a room in her house, which could considerably ease her burdens. But she cannot bring herself to do so:

> Dumbly, Nanda Kaul shook her head. She held the arm of her chair very tightly in an effort to speak, to say "Come and stay with me, Ila," and then clutched it tighter still to keep herself from saying what would ruin her existence here at Carignano. She simply shook her head. (*Fire*, 127)

Nanda Kaul's refusal, in this climactic instance, to end her mythic isolation and take on responsibility for her friend results in a horrifying death by rape for Ila. Forced to return to the village where, as a "modern" social worker, Ila Das has roused the ire of many men by trying to stop them from marrying their daughters off at a very young age, Ila Das is attacked, raped, and murdered by one of them.

Clearly, Desai here demonstrates how tragedy can result when we say no to life's responsibilities, when we retreat into a mythic realm of isolation (resulting from the mystical aspect of myth, rather than its pastoral and communal aspect) that prevents us from connecting with and caring for others.

As if to drive her point home even more strongly, Desai ends the book with a symbolic act of annihilation. Raka, Nanda's isolated great-granddaughter, as if to wreak vengeance on the "cold," withdrawn world around her, sets fire to the mountainside. This ultimate act of social irresponsibility that Desai ends the book with once again points out the grave consequences that will result if we choose to reject the critical realist mode in favor of the mythic, which does not take responsibility for changing a past, present, or future reality based on class, gender, religious oppression, and inequality.

> The message is only obvious that one must learn "to connect" in order to make one's life meaningful, which both Nanda and Raka have failed to do. It is this imbalance in the lives of these female

protagonists in the novel, which is its real strength, throwing its
real insight into the missing essential link, in absence of which life
becomes but a long tale of woe and suffering.[11]

*Clear Light of Day* (1980) also deals with the issue of realism versus myth,
but here, although the central character, Bim, conceived in the realist
mode, gets the reader's (and the writer's) sympathy, the reader is made
aware (as she herself is) that she has lived in too extreme a fashion, has
become too much of the socially responsible one—in other words, she has
failed to achieve the balance between self and social responsibility that is
the ideal of realism. What is truly ironic is that despite her realism, Bim
is the only one of her family (not counting Baba, the retarded brother) who
lives in a state of petrification, the past that for her hasn't changed, because
realism, in this instance, has meant taking responsibility for the past,
rather than for the present and the future.

Thus, when Bim asks her younger sister, who is home on a visit
reminiscing about old times, whether she would really like to return to
those days and whether she knows anyone who "would—secretly, sincerely,
in his innermost self—*really* prefer to return to childhood?," Tara, bewil-
dered at first, asks Bim in return, "Prefer to what?" To which Bim replies,
"Oh, to going on—to growing up—leaving, going away—into the world."
And Tara's answer, clear now, is, "But you didn't, Bim."[12] What she means
is that Bim did not "go on"; rather, she chose to stay behind and to
shoulder the responsibility for her brothers, sister, and Aunt Mira after the
parents passed away. Although an admirable thing to do, this realist stance
has left Bim embittered in her old age and without any of the romantic
ideals and myths that she shared with her brother Raja.

Ironically, Raja, who had as a youngster lived in a world of romance and
prepartition mythic ideals of Hindu-Muslim unity, who had retreated from
his responsibilities to his immediate family in order to go off and become a
"poet and a hero," has ended up, in fact, marrying a Muslim girl, raising
a family, and fulfilling his responsibilities to them in postpartition India.
The younger sister, Tara, has also gone on to make a life for herself, has
married and raised two daughters.

It is Bim, the most responsible of the siblings, the one who sacrificed

11. Shyam M. Asnani, "The Theme of Loneliness and Withdrawal in Anita Desai's *Fire on the
Mountain*," *Journal of Indian Writing in English* 9 (January 1981): 90.

12. Anita Desai, *Clear Light of Day* (Harmondsworth, Middlesex: Penguin Books, 1980), 4. All
subsequent references to this work will be cited parenthetically in the text as Desai, *Clear*.

her own desires to look after them all, who, ironically, is the one left alone at the end. Thus, in this novel, Desai seems to be modifying the moral meaning of her message a little (not surprising in view of her strong attraction to the form of myth): any genre of fiction or mode of existence can be a trap if it prevents us from "going on—growing up—leaving—going away into the world—something wider, freer—brighter" (Desai, *Clear*, 4). If, by existing solely within a critical realist mode, Bim is nevertheless caught in a web of the past, unable to live fully and happily in the present, unable to forgive and forget past mistakes (as she is unable to forgive Raja for his "desertion"), then perhaps she should reject such a mode (or at least modify it). And if a romantic sensibility, a sense of a mythical, heroic past, can aid one, as it does Raja, in creating a unified present despite all obstacles (of which his marriage to a Muslim is a symbol), then a mythic, romantic mode has its moral value too and should not be altogether discarded.

What Desai offers in this Chekovian novel, then, is a mixing of different genres that will allow a wholeness of character and of life to emerge, which are otherwise too fragmented, too one-sided. Toward the end of the novel, Bim realizes that her approach has indeed been too extreme, that her love for her family has been fragmented, made "unwhole" by her absorption in her "duty" to them. At the end, what she wishes for more than anything is to recover that "wholeness" (which, within the realistic mode, has somehow evaded her):

> Although it was shadowy and dark, Bim could see as well as by the clear light of day that she felt only love and yearning for them all, and if there were hurts, these gashes and wounds in her side that bled, then it was only because her love was imperfect . . . and because it had flaws. *All these would have to be mended,* these rents and tears, *she would have to mend and make her net whole* so that it would suffice her in her passage through the ocean. (165; emphasis added)

And the only way to "make her net whole," Bim realizes, is to forgive and forget her grudges against the past ("somehow she must forgive Raja that unforgivable letter") and move on with the present, into the future. But, of course, this unity is not to be achieved by repressing the past; rather, in keeping with the Chekovian tone of the novel, she must accept the past, make her peace with it, and in so doing also accept and understand her own tendencies to mythicize the past. Only through such tolerance can she ever hope to dominate the past, instead of letting it dominate her. Thus, at the end, when Bim hears verses being sung that remind her of her brother's (and her own) childhood romantic aspirations, she no longer rejects the memory. Instead, when the guru sings, "Your world is the world of fish and fowl, my world is the cry of the dawn," "Bim's hand flew up to brush aside the gray hair at her face, and she leant excitedly towards Baba. 'Iqbal's' she whispered. 'Raja's favorite' " (182).

It is this acceptance of the past and all its myths that leads to a wholeness for Bim, for finally myth and realism, past and present, have been interfused. Thus, Bim's final epiphany could not be more appropriate:

> Bim was suddenly overcome with the memory of reading, in Raja's well-thumbed copy of Eliot's Four-Quartet's, the line:
> "Time the destroyer is time the preserver."
> Its meaning seemed to fall out of the dark sky and settle upon her like a cloak or like a great pair of feathered wings. She huddled in its comfort, its solace. . . . With her inner eye she saw how her own house and its particular history linked and contained her as well as her own family with all their separate histories and experiences—not binding them within some dead and airless cell but giving them the soil in which to send down their roots, and food to make them grow and spread. . . . That soil contained all time, past and future, in it. . . . It was where her deepest self lived and the deepest selves of her sister and brothers and all those who shared that time with her. (182)

There can be no going forward without also going backward, no separation of realism from myth.

If Bim has tried to escape the past and its mythic quality by immersing herself in the critical realist mode, then Deven—the protagonist of Anita Desai's novel *In Custody* (1984)—in the same position, wishes to do the opposite. As A. G. Mojtabai points out in her review of the novel, "Deven's life is hopelessly compromised. Long ago, he set aside his ambition to write poetry in order to support a wife."[13] Not only has Deven set aside his

---

13. A. G. Mojtabai, "The Poet in All His Squalor," *New York Times Book Review*, 3 March 1985, 7. All subsequent references to this work will be cited parenthetically in the text as Mojtabai.

ambition to write poetry, but in order to earn a living to support his wife and son, he has also had to put aside his love of Urdu literature and instead find a job as lecturer in Hindi literature, a field in which he has little interest and no discernible talent.

Thus, Deven, trapped in the critical realist mode, fulfilling his responsibility to his family, caught up in "the sordid necessities of everyday life" (Mojtabai), is thrilled when given the opportunity to escape into the world of poetry and myth. This happens when he is asked by his editor friend Murad to interview Nur Shahjehanabadi, a great, aging Urdu poet. Yet, at first he resists this opportunity: "So firm is Deven's sense of failure and entrapment that, when the door opens and he is given a nudge toward it, he stalls, unable to grasp it" (Mojtabai). Not for long, though, because the temptation to escape from the onerous duties and the ordinariness of the realist mode, into the "transcendent, wondrously illuminated realm" of poet and poetry, is irresistible. What is more, Nur is the very poet whose poetry Deven's father had loved to recite and who, therefore, symbolizes for Deven a mythicized past: "He [Deven] went on reciting that great poem of Nur's that his father had loved to recite and that he still read, ceremoniously, *whenever he felt sad or nostalgic and thought of his father and his early childhood and all that he had lost.*"[14]

And so, when Deven, hesitatingly and with great trepidation, enters Nur's house and is actually summoned by the poet into his presence, he feels, as he begins to climb the stairs up to the poet's bedroom, as though he is truly about to leave behind his dross, drab life and ascend to a wonderful, mythic world:

> It was to him as if God had leaned over a cloud and called for him to come up, and angels might have been drawing him up these ancient splintered stairs to meet the deity. . . . This, surely, was the summons he had been waiting for all these empty years. . . . He had never conceived of a summons expressed in a voice so leonine . . . a voice that could grasp him, as it were, by the roots of his hair and haul him up from the level on which he existed— mean, disordered and hopeless—into another, higher sphere. *Another realm it would surely be if his god dwelt there*, the domain of poetry, beauty and illumination. (Desai, *In Custody*, 39–40; emphasis added)

14. Anita Desai, *In Custody* (New York: Harper and Row, 1984), 44; emphasis added. All subsequent references to this work will be cited parenthetically in the text as Desai, *In Custody*.

Deven mounts the stairs then, a literal ascent (since Nur lives in the topmost room of the house), and feeling as though with every step he is "sloughing off and casting away the meanness and dross" of his present existence, he fails to notice the broken bike, the dripping tap, and the dusty stairs themselves. However, once he enters the poet's room, Deven can scarcely fail to notice the "real" disorder, the shabbiness and filth that surrounds his idol, his mythic hero. According to Mojtabai, "It is a scene of squalor on a grand scale, for the poet lives surrounded by squabbling wives and drunken, loudmouthed toadies."

Although Deven's first impulse is to separate Nur from the sordid reality around him by "seeing Nur in this setting, but not of it," even he cannot ignore the evidence of Nur's humiliating, painful disease, born of squalor and inactivity—piles.

Deven, who, in coming to Nur, had hoped to trade in realism for myth, life for art, asks himself, "In taking Nur's art into his hands, did he have to gather up the stained, soiled, discolored and odorous rags of his life as well?" (Desai, *In Custody*, 158). Having looked to Nur to provide an escape from the burdens of realism, Deven naturally is disturbed to find that his task of recording Nur's poetry involves assuming responsibility for the poet's very real, sordid problems.

Deven, therefore, has little stomach for the task; his repeated impulse is to run. Nur senses his difficulty and later, during one of their recording sessions (held in, of all places, a brothel), finally looks Deven in the face and says, to his unease, "Has this dilemma come to you too then? This sifting and selecting from the debris of our lives? It can't be done my friend, it can't be done, I learnt that long ago—" (167). Having said that, Nur breaks into a verse that Deven has never heard before, a poem "that silences them all with wonder." This, of course, just goes to prove Nur's point that the real (that is, the ordinary, the sordid, the realm of social responsibility for the present) can never be separated from the mythic (the supraordinary, the romantic, the realm of escapism into the past here symbolized by his poetry).

And, finally, this is what Deven realizes too. Having turned his back for the last time (or so he'd thought) on Nur's incessant demands for money and help, Deven realizes the folly of such a response. He had forged an alliance not only with a mythicized poet but with a real man who had real needs. Such an alliance demanded responsible behavior from Deven and was an alliance he would not be able to break, should not break, even after the poet's death:

Where was the end? Was there one? He had a vision of Nur's bier, white, heaped with flowers. . . . He saw the women in the family weeping and wailing around it. . . . He saw the shroud, the grave open. When Nur was laid in it, would this connection break, this relation end? No, never—the bills would come to him, he would have to pay for the funeral, support the widows, raise his son. . . . *He had accepted the gift of Nur's poetry and that meant he was custodian of Nur's very soul and spirit. It was a great distinction. He could not deny or abandon that under any pressure.* (204; emphasis added)

In other words, the call of realism, of the present, cannot be, must not be, ignored in favor of a retreat from responsibility of the present, into a mythicized past. Neither must the past and all that is valuable in it be rejected—as Nur's poetry (and Urdu literature in general) are in danger of being forgotten, wiped out, in postindependence, postcolonial India. But of course the past can only be preserved if one takes responsibility for it, if, in other words, myth is given its rightful place within the critical realist mode.

Anita Desai's next novel, *Bye-Bye Blackbird* (1985), is a bit of an anomaly in the context of the rest of her oeuvre, in terms of both the setting and subject matter. It takes place in the England of the sixties, rather than in her native India, and deals overtly, for the first time in her work, with the theme of cultural conflict and cultural imperialism born of the colonial encounter between India and Britain. Yet, of course, the difference is superficial; for, as in her previous work, here too the underlying concern is coming to grips with a reality as unencumbered by mythic deification as possible, so that the ghosts of the past can be laid to rest and Indians and Britons, the colonized and the colonizers, can take up the task of living responsibly in the present.

Thus, in this novel, which centers around the lives of Indian immigrants in London, the three central characters, Adit Sen, his English wife Sarah, and Adit's friend Dev, newly arrived from India, must settle their scores with the past of empire before they can become fully functional within the critical realist mode with its imperative of balance.

From the beginning, it is evident that both Dev and Adit are out of balance in their respective reactions to the facts of empire; indeed, they have both chosen to inhabit the realm of myth, though from opposite ends of the spectrum. Dev inhabits the myth of the wronged native par excellence, in that he wishes initially to reject and refute all things British (even though he is subconsciously attracted to them) and to play the righteous role of an Indian who will return to his native India to impart the wealth of knowledge accumulated as a student in England-turning the tables on the colonizers, as it were. Adit, on the other hand, has mythified the glories of life in Britain to the extent that he has completely identified himself with it, at the expense of his Indian past. The following exchange between the two friends captures the essence of their respective "blindspots," or mythically static positions:

> Suddenly, Dev exploded. . . . "I wouldn't live in a country where I was insulted and unwanted," he said grandly.
> "No? Why have you come then?" Still, Adit's voice showed no hostility, only laziness.
> "To study. . . . I will go back to India, an England-returned teacher. . . ."
> "Oh noble, noble man. When you go back . . . they will award you the Padma Bhushan. . . . How fine you will look with it shining on the front of your dirty purple pullover."
> Dev threw grass at him. . . . "Laugh. Go on. That's all you people do—you lazy immigrants. God. You should go mad, when even schoolboys can call you names. . . . Adit, aren't you coming back at all? Do you mean to stay on?"[15]

To this tirade, Adit replies in the manner of an adoptive Englishman:

> "Yes," Adit said, "I do. I love it here. . . . I'm happy here. I like going into the local for a pint on my way home to Sarah. I like wearing good tweed on a foggy November day. I like the Covent Garden opera house. . . . I like steamed pudding with treacle. I like—I like thatched cottages and British history and reading the letters in the Times. . . . I like the pubs. I like the freedom a man has here: Economic freedom! Social freedom!" (Desai, *Blackbird*, 18)

15. Anita Desai, *Bye-Bye Blackbird* (New Delhi: Orient Paperbacks, 1985), 17. All subsequent references to this work will be cited parenthetically in the text as Desai, *Blackbird*.

Clearly, neither Dev nor Adit is a good model of a critical realist. The former is too extreme in his criticism of Indian immigrants and overly idealistic about the value of his projected role as an England-returned teacher in India. The latter is almost a caricature of the Indian who is "more British than the British"—one who cannot or will not face up to the multiple ironies of his life in England, or deal with the obvious racism that exists there. Both protagonists have mythified certain aspects of their lives: Dev, aspects of his past in India; Adit, his present life in England at the expense of his Indian heritage.

It takes a weekend in the country, at Sarah's parents' home, to break the spell for both Dev and Adit. In the process, Sarah's life also changes drastically. Dev's experience of the calm, orderly countryside somehow breaks down his extreme antipathy to things British, so that he ends up working and living in London and quite enjoying this new life, much in the way his friend Adit has. Adit, on the other hand, undergoes a crisis of identity and comes to feel that he has been living an inauthentic life in England; he therefore resolves to return to India, with his pregnant English wife in tow. Quite an about-face! Yet, what is implied by this dialectical movement is the necessity of arriving at some middle ground, some way of bridging what appear to be mutually irreconcilable positions. The fact that Dev and Adit seem to switch positions points to the difficulty of achieving the ideal of balance in a situation that is the result of such a fundamental imbalance as the colonial encounter.

In this regard, it is interesting to note that it is Sarah, Adit's long-suffering English wife, who represents, through her stoic acceptance of the life she has chosen by marrying an Indian man, if not an ideal, nevertheless a more critically responsible position on this difficult issue. Throughout the novel, she plays the morally responsible role of a genuinely caring wife to Adit, even though she seems aloof and even estranged from her own parents. Nevertheless, on trying occasions like the weekend when Adit and a party of his friends visit with her parents, she tries to maintain the peace between people who have little or no understanding of each other, and even less mutual tolerance. In the end, she agrees to accompany her husband back to India even though she does have her private moments of doubt about this major step she is taking. Yet, it is her overall spirit of openness to entering a different culture, acquiring a different self—which she sees as an adventure mixed with some regret—that marks her as a realist rather than a creature imprisoned by colonialist myths as Dev and Adit are:

> . . . stoically ignoring the weather. . . . Often she said to herself:
> This is one of the last walks I shall have. Soon I shall leave it all.
> She felt a small contraction of unwillingness followed by a large,
> warm expansion of heart that the adventurers of old must have felt
> when they cut loose from the shore and set sail for what was then a
> fabulous land. (208)

Sarah's "expansion of heart" is not based in fantasy or myth, like that of
the "adventurers of old," but stems rather from a genuine belief in human
connectedness and human complexity across differences of race and
culture. Thus, in reply to her mother's stereotyping of Indians, Sarah's
speech, though spoken in a doubtful and exploring tone, shows the largesse
of her spirit and establishes her well within the critical realist mode of
balance and fairness to all:

> "Do you call 'em—intro—intro—"
> "Introverts?"
> "Yes, yes. People say they are moody and self-conscious. But my
> dear, your—your husband and his friends, they are the very
> opposite, aren't they?"
> "Extroverts? Adit certainly is, and so are some of his friends,
> but not all. Dev, the one who is to stay on with you, he is moody
> enough to make up for all the others—at times. Then he can be
> very out-going too, in spurts. Rather like us, Mummy, and your
> friends—everyone a bit different from the other but not too much."
> (139)

It would seem then, that Desai's generic strategy for avoiding ideological
containment from both sides of the coin remains the same, despite the
difference of matter and theme: the balanced and reasonable approach of
critical realism that encourages one to retain faith in human complexity,
as opposed to the static stereotyping that results from fixation on ignoble
aspects of myth.

Anita Desai's latest novel, *Baumgartner's Bombay*, also feels like a
departure from the rest of her oeuvre in terms of style and content, though
again not, I think, in terms of message. The critic Judie Newman also
takes cognizance of the change: "In *Baumgartner's Bombay* . . . Desai
departs from her previous practice, in order to interrogate the relation of

discourse to history, the language of the interior to that of the outer world."[16] Desai relies here much more on dialogue than in any of her earlier books, and her main characters are Germans in India, not Indians. Hugo Baumgartner is a German Jew who comes all the way to India to escape the Nazis. In this novel, Desai seems concerned with a larger, though related, issue than that of being an authentic postcolonial writer of Indian culture. Here she confronts head-on the issue of being a "foreigner" in a world composed of nation-states created through centuries of war and destruction. It is in this novel that the tug-of-war between mythos and logos, myth and realism, is greatest. It seems that Desai's reactions to myth as a symbolic force in life and literature are highly ambivalent here— much more so than in any of her previous books. The power of myth, embodied largely (though not exclusively) in the figure of the protagonist's mother, is still clearly attractive. Yet, it is also, ultimately, a "demonic" force in the way Ernst Cassirer has described, an aspect expressed most forcefully through the character of Kurt, the young German who murders Hugo.

The mythic impulse to see grandeur in the past, of any culture, is, through Hugo Baumgartner's life experiences, decried as a kind of romantic blindness leading to conflict and hatred between individuals and nations, even though its converse, a kind of unabated realism (in art and in life), ends in a diminished and nihilistic "reality" too. Baumgartner, the protagonist of the novel, is an elderly German Jew settled in comfortable squalor in Bombay. He is a perpetual outsider who, through the course of the novel, recalls the perilous, sometimes happy years of his younger life, including a childhood in Berlin lived under the constant threat of the advent of Nazism.

It is through his recollections of his childhood days, as well as of his younger days in India (especially his relationship with Lotte, a German cabaret singer, and his removal to a wartime detainment camp), that one gets a sense of Desai's disdain for mythic structures of belief and behavior (although, as stated earlier, extreme realism/rationalism fares not too well either). For instance, Hugo's mother, described as a romantic, a lover of poetry and music and one who constantly harks back to memories of a "golden" past when faced with a threatening and unpleasant present, is held in some disdain by her son. Just as life begins to get frightening for

---

16. Judie Newman, "History and Letters: Anita Desai's *Baumgartner's Bombay,*" *World Literature Written in English* 30, no. 1 (1990): 37. All subsequent references to this work will be cited parenthetically in the text as Newman.

Jews in Germany, and thus also for Hugo's parents (his father was sent away to Dachau and returned a "broken man"), Hugo and his mother take a trip to the country to visit Frau Baumgartner's childhood friend, Adele Friedman, and her family. At the Friedmanns, seeing his mother relive her past, listening to her voice "lift and fly with lightheartedness and relief," Hugo is both attracted and repelled by the mythic mentality personified by his mother and by the mythic, pastoral surroundings in which he finds himself. As Frau Friedmann's son, Albert, takes him out in a boat, telling him of the deer that come to drink at the lake, it seems to Hugo that he is "stumbling through the illustrations of a book of fairy stories, the forest where Hansel and Gretel followed a trail of bread-crumbs, or in which Sleeping Beauty lay hidden by a wall of thorns—beautiful, hushed and vaguely sinister."[17]

Myth, then, becomes synonymous with both the beautiful and the sinister. When Hugo returns to the garden where he had left his mother and her friend reminiscing of poetry and music, he finds "the garden overtaken by a chilly shadow" and the ladies gone indoors. Inside, they are discussing the works of Rabindernath Tagore, a famous Bengali poet and mystic, winner of the 1913 Nobel Prize for literature. As he watches his mother immersed in this world of poetry and myth, Hugo feels, finally, a desperation overtaking him:

> He could not allow his mother to continue with her pretense that she had returned to her youth, that her adulthood could be ignored. Seeing her so childishly irresponsible and irresponsibly blithe, he was driven to an adult decision. Turning around, he saw them listening admiringly to Albert reading a poem about the deer by the lake . . . and blurted out "Mama, komm, we must go back to Papa now." In the tram, lifting her face out of a fold of her cape, she accused him in mortified tones, "How could you, Hugo, in the middle of such a beautiful poem?" (Desai, *Bombay*, 48–49)

Hugo has gone from wondering why his mother does not do this sort of thing more often if it pleases her so, to desiring more adult behavior, more "realistic" behavior from her. It seems that Desai, too, makes a parallel shift from logos to mythos in this section, since, when the duo get back to

17. Anita Desai, *Baumgartner's Bombay* (New York: Knopf, 1989), 47. All subsequent references to this work will be cited parenthetically in the text as Desai, *Bombay*.

their apartment in Berlin, they find that Herr Baumgartner has gassed himself to death. Had Hugo's mother remained within the realm of realism, had she fulfilled her adult duties, this might not have come to pass, and Hugo's life might not have undergone such a dramatic displacement as it did following his father's death. Such a conclusion, however, would require more than an individual resolution of the conflict between the mythic and the realistic impulses. The parallel argument that Desai seems to be making is that for the horror of the holocaust and the displacement of German Jewry (not just Hugo) to have been averted, an entire nation needed to have resisted the power of myth. Cassirer's comments on Judaism and modern political myths can be usefully quoted here:

> We fail . . . to understand the true character and the full signifi-
> cance of myth if, according to its Greek name, we see in it a mere
> "narrative"—a recollection or recital of the memorable deeds of
> heroes or gods. This epic aspect is not the only one and not the
> decisive one. Myth has always a dramatic character. It conceives
> the world as a great drama—as a struggle between divine and
> demonic forces, between light and darkness, between the good and
> the evil. There is always a positive and a negative pole in mythical
> thought and imagination. . . . In the mythical pandemonium we
> always find maleficent spirits that are opposed to the beneficent
> spirits. There is always a secret or open revolt of Satan against God.
> In the German pandemonium, this role was assigned to the Jew.
> What we find here is much more than what is usually described by
> the name "anti-Semitism." . . . Anti-Semitism could have led to
> social discrimination, to all forms of oppression . . . but it cannot
> account for the specific methods of the German anti-Jewish propa-
> ganda. What was proclaimed here was a mortal combat—a life-
> and-death struggle which could only end with the complete exter-
> mination of the Jews. (Cassirer, 238–39)

It seems that in *Baumgartner's Bombay*, the force of myth, linked here with the impulse toward communal preservation through glorification of a mythic past, is seen by Desai to have this negative, evil side as well. This is perhaps why Hugo's life in India, where he goes to escape the tentacles of Nazism, is presented in such realistic, down-to-earth fashion—with Hugo himself adopting an antimythic, antipast stance.

The only connection he has with his German past is the letters and postcards he receives from his mother until the middle of the war: 1941. After that, even the cryptic postcards stop, and Hugo never finds out what happened to his mother—thus all links with the past are severed.

During his first years in India, spent in Calcutta, Hugo meets another German, a cabaret dancer named Lotte. What binds them most strongly together is that neither of them wants to remember the past, not even with all of its positive mythic aspects of poetry, love, and emotional and spiritual sustenance.

Thus it is that upon Hugo's death, reading through his collection of postcards from his mother, Lotte is reminded of that very past she has tried so hard to escape:

> Lotte pressed her fingers to her lips, to her eyes, to her ears, trying to prevent those words, that language, from entering her, invading her. Its sweetness, the assault of sweetness cramming her mouth, her ears, drowning her in its sugar. The language she wanted not to hear or speak. It was pummeling her, pushing against and into her, and with her mouth stuffed she moaned, "Nein, nein, nein, Hugo, no." Her teeth bit on the crystals and her nerves screamed at their sweetness. All the marzipan, all the barley sugar, the chocolates and toffees of her childhood descended on her with their soft, sticking, suffocating sweetness . . . sugary, treacly, warm, oozing love, childhood love, little mice and bunny rabbits of love—sweet, warm, choking, childish love. Lotte wept and drowned. (Desai, *Bombay*, 5)

Here, the past being remembered in spite of itself is a pre-Nazi childhood that was Edenic. However, since it ultimately turned into something horrific for all Germans, and since clinging to it therefore symbolized a nonrealistic attitude to the evil atmosphere developing around them, both Hugo and Lotte chose to dispense with the mythic mode of the "glorious past" altogether. And clearly, since the body of the novel deals with describing the lives of Hugo and Lotte from a realistic standpoint, showing their daily struggles to maintain a balance between individual needs and their sense of duty toward each other and to others they come across (including Hugo's family of cats), so it would seem that Desai is endorsing the realistic approach to life.

However, the fact remains that life lived totally within the bounds of realism, without the counterbalancing effects of myth, becomes a very lonely and ultimately unbalanced existence. Neither Lotte nor Hugo is able to achieve the ideal goal of critical realism: a balance between the needs of man as individual entity and man as social phenomenon. It would seem that to achieve such a balance even within the realm of critical realism requires some input, some connection with the mythic realm. In order to remain firmly rooted within the present, one has to understand and acknowledge the past, even though one may argue with it. But one cannot pretend it never happened, never existed. Both Lotte and Hugo try to do this, with unhappy results. Hugo ends up meeting the very fate he has tried to escape—being murdered in India at the hands of an Aryan German, Kurt, who, in a fashion, serves as Hugo's alter ego. The failure to deal with the past and its myths historically and realistically, has resulted in the horror of a Kurt:

> Kurt's playing fast and loose with material reality, transforming his life into a series of fictions, independent of truth or history, initiates a process of destructive fantasy which culminates in the murder of Baumgartner, appropriately in pursuit of the latter's racing trophies, the symbols of his own past magical desires, in order to procure fresh supplies of illusion-producing substances. The title of the novel, therefore, with its echoes of travelogue . . . is deeply ironic. Baumgartner's Bombay has not been very different from his Berlin after all. He is murdered by an alter-ego deeply enclosed within fictions, much as his earlier self had been. Fairy stories and nursery rhymes have yielded to travelers' tales and thence to a horror story. Fictions appear to have triumphed over fact, and the reader is left with an image of history as textual repetition, and of repetition as horror. (Newman, 44)

Lotte, at the end, is also left alone to contemplate the ruins of her life and the absence of all meaning in an existence that has tried to sever all connectedness with the past.

It seems, then, that Desai is saying in this novel that the evil of the mythic mode of thought and being can be counterbalanced only by acknowledging, simultaneously, the power of good in it. If the communal mentality or the impulse toward a collective identification intrinsic to myth can be used for evil purposes, as it was by the Nazis in Germany, surely it can also be used for the good of a community, for the preservation of memory, of shared love and customs that link individuals together to form a shared history different from other groups. After all, why do Lotte and Hugo come together in India? Surely, in part at least, because as nationless wanderers they share a common heritage that—though neither wishes to acknowledge it—nevertheless links them together.[18]

Thus, by the end of the novel, Desai is stating a similar message as in the rest of her oeuvre: clearly the call of realism, both as an attitude toward life and as a genre of fiction, is the call of responsibility and moral strength; however, to reap its full benefits, it must be tempered with some of the aesthetic and emotional underpinnings of myth. Yet, the caution against myth in the service of the social state is great: we must never allow ourselves, as nations, to be swayed by the seductive power of evil inherent in all mythmaking. By extension, the mythic mode in literature too must be used critically and judiciously. As Newman points out astutely, "Without minimizing the real horrors of the past, Desai emphasizes the need not to be complicit with those forces that would erase historical truth, reducing events to myth, fantasy or silence" (Newman, 45).

Anita Desai's position as a postcolonial writer, then, is clear: she has opted to remain within history, despite its ravages and cruelties. She has shown in novel after novel her moral disapproval of a stance that refuses to shoulder responsibility for the past and present and chooses to withdraw from a painful present reality into a romantic or mythicized past. Yet the lure of myth is great, especially as an aesthetic form, and Desai deals with this dilemma by letting her writing and many of her characters take on the formal qualities of mythic fiction (for example, the poetic lyricism of her prose, the proneness to solitude and to the extraordinary in her characters). In matters of message, however, Desai is clearly on the side of realism, so she chooses to view myth and its attractions from, and ultimately to subordinate it (or at least balance it) within, the critical realist perspective.

18. It must be noted that Judie Newman does not share my belief in the "power of good" that coexists with the will to evil inherent in the fantastic aspect of Myth. She reads *Baumgartner's Bombay* as a novel in which myth is entirely debunked by Desai in favor of an approach that endorses historical responsibility (realism).

# 3

# Kamala Markandaya

## Myth Versus Realism or East Versus West

Kamala Markandaya, the third of the four novelists under consideration, like her other three Indian contemporaries, is also concerned with the issue of colonial imagery in Western "Orientalist" literature. She feels the same need as the others, to come up with some fictive strategies that will liberate her and her people from the denigrating and confining images of "other" as depicted in this body of literature. In the opening paragraph of her paper "On Images," presented during a seminar in socioliterature at the East-West Center for Cultural Interchange, Honolulu, in August 1973, Markandaya states quite clearly her concern with the imagery of colonialism and the need she feels, as a Third World novelist, to address and rectify such imagery:

> During the colonial and imperial eras there were certain concep-
> tions widespread throughout Europe, regarding the inhabitants of
> Asia and Africa. These conceptions or images, were held and
> cherished, largely by the white world of the non-white world. . . .

If we examine them [the images] we find they were usually formed
on the slightest acquaintance. And they were fairly exhaustive: that
is to say, they covered social, moral and physical aspects. Some
were paternalistic and nearly all were derogatory. . . . Each image
carried a counterpart: that is to say the image of the other man, in
the colonial mind, was balanced by one of himself: a study in
contrast, if you like. . . . The counterpart image was of the white
man of superior intellect and attainment. The second image was to
regard the non-white as a heathen . . . as a worshiper of false gods
. . . companion-piece to this piece of crudity was of the European
as the upright and enlightened Christian, the only caste to which
God had cared to reveal himself.[1]

Having described the "exhaustiveness" and pervasive influence of such
pernicious imagery, how then does Markandaya propose to counter it? She
proposes to do this by calling for "a clean-out of the entire clutter of
distorted and distorting imagery with which we have lumbered ourselves."
Such a "clean-out and confessional," she feels, "will come most fruitfully
. . . from the literature of concern." By such literature she means that
which brings home "the elementary truths" of human commonality so that
the reader finds he or she has "an instant neighbor," rather than strange
characters "marked THEM" (Shimer, 358).

Thus, Markandaya will try to portray her native people in her novels in
all their human glory and frailty, not as the prejudged "exotica" of Western
novels. In order to be able to do this, she will have to choose the appropriate
genre that will best convey, in both moral and aesthetic terms, the lives of
her characters in all their complexity; a genre that will help restore the
dignity of her people, so that they no longer appear "inferior" either in
intellectual or spiritual terms when compared to their European counterparts. The choice of such a genre, however, is not easy.

Kamala Markandaya's novels can be divided into two groups according
to subject matter: those dealing primarily with native Indian (mostly rural
or small-town) life, such as *Nectar in a Sieve* (1954), *A Silence of Desire*
(1960), *A Handful of Rice* (1966), and *Two Virgins* (1973); and those set
either in India or in England and India that deal primarily with the
interrelationships between the two peoples and cultures, namely, *Some*

---

1. Dorothy Blair Shimer, "Sociological Imagery in the Novels of Kamala Markandaya," *World
Literature Written in English* 14 (November 1975): 358. All subsequent references to this work will be
cited parenthetically in the text as Shimer.

*Inner Fury* (1956), *Possession* (1963), *The Coffer Dams* (1969), *The Nowhere Man* (1972), *The Golden Honeycomb* (1977), and *Shalimar* (1982).

Formally, however, both sets of novels depict the same concern shared by the previous two writers: that is, which genre, morally and aesthetically, is appropriate to convey the subject matter at hand, a subject matter always rooted in the historicity of colonialism and its aftermath. For Markandaya, as for Anita Desai, choosing a generic mode that is both morally and aesthetically valid poses a conflict that often results in a confusing or mixed "message" for the reader; and whether or not this is construed as a defect in the writing, in the final analysis, it is a symptom of the confusing situation in which the postcolonial Indian writer of English finds himself or herself.

Thus, although morally Markandaya often (though not always) seems to favor those characters who ultimately choose to respond to life's crises and problems within the mode of realism rather than that of myth (such as Mirabai in *Some Inner Fury*, or Rabi and Usha in *The Golden Honeycomb*), aesthetically (and in some cases even morally) her attraction to characters conceived within the mythic mode counterbalances and outweighs her attraction to those characters who endorse the realistic mode. In this category fall Rukmani and her husband Nathan of *Nectar in a Sieve*, Valmiki and the Swami of *Possession*, Saroja of *The Two Virgins*. At other times, Markandaya seems equally disillusioned with both modes and their ability to lend dignity and stature to her characters; this is truest of Ravi's fate in *A Handful of Rice*. And yet, there are times when she seems simultaneously attracted to both modes, optimistic that a fusion might create fresh possibilities for her characters to lead more enriched, compassionate lives. This is true, for example, of Dandekar and Sarojini in *Silence of Desire*, of Helen, Mackendrick, and Bashiam in *The Coffer Dams*, and of Rikki and Tully in *Shalimar*.

With reference to Kamala Markandaya, realism means not only the form of critical realism referred to thus far, but realism in the more fundamental sense of a mode that forces one to face up to the crude reality of a particular situation. In this sense, realism is often equated in Markandaya's work with rationalism and materialism and the forces of change that are seen primarily as Western modes of thought and belief, whereas the mythic mode is usually the Eastern mode of being, which encompasses notions of spirituality, mysticism, and fateful resignation that are in direct conflict with the goals and beliefs of realism.

In *Nectar in a Sieve*, Markandaya's earliest published novel (1954) and probably her best known, the conflict between myth and realism is quite evident. The protagonists, Rukmani the narrator and her husband Nathan, are simple, landless peasants whose struggle for survival on the land makes them assume the heroic proportions of characters of the mythic/epic mode. As S. C. Harrex notes, Kamala Markandaya establishes the peasants as heroic figures of the mythic mode by showing how their sense of identity, linked to a traditional intimacy with the earth, helps them survive nature's calamities, just as it helps them coexist with nature's cycles of creation and preservation:

> The calamities of the land belong to it alone, born of wind and rain and weather immensities not to be tempered by man or his crea-tions. To those who lived by the land there must always come times of hardship, of fear and hunger, even as there are years of plenty. This is one of the truths of our existence as those who live by the land know: that sometimes we eat and sometimes we starve . . . still while there was land, there was hope.[2]

They are mythic characters also in that "*the peasant roles are archetypal* and clearly defined: Rukmani as childbearer, Nathan as provider."[3] Fur-thermore, Rukmani's character is clearly drawn according to "the tradi-tional image of the Pativrata in the silently suffering, sacrificial role," as Meena Shirwadker points out. She goes on to say that women like Rukmani "are the daughters of the soil and have inherited age-old traditions which they do not question. Their courage lies in meek or at times cheerful ways of facing poverty or calamity" (49). That Markandaya chooses such a heroine for her first novel puts her quite clearly in a different camp from Anita Desai, whose first heroine, Maya, rebels against just such a definition of "ideal womanhood."

What Rukmani and Nathan must survive are not simply the misfortunes common to farming, such as failed harvests due to too much or too little rain; they also have to contend against the encroaching materialism of city industry, represented by the tannery that is built and run on the outskirts of their village by Western contractors and bosses. This, however, is

---

2. Kamala Markandaya, *Nectar in a Sieve* (New York: John Day, 1954), 136. All subsequent references to this work will be cited parenthetically in the text as Markandaya, *Nectar*.

3. S. C. Harrex, "A Sense of Identity: The Novels of Kamala Markandaya," *Journal of Common-wealth Literature* 6, no. 1 (1971): 73, emphasis added. All subsequent references to this work will be cited parenthetically in the text as Harrex.

"reality" and the way of the future. Yet, the narrator cannot bring herself to accept it.

A neighbor, whose sons are among the first to earn good wages at the tannery, says, "The tannery is a boon to us. Have I not said so before? Ours is no longer a village either, but a growing town. Does it not do you good just to think of it?" To which the narrator's response is clearly in favor of stasis over change, a desire to remain rooted in the myths of the land:

> "Indeed no," said I, "for it is even as I said, and our money buys less and less. As for living in a town, there is nothing I would fly from sooner if I could go back to the sweet quiet of village life. Now it is all noise and crowd everywhere, and no man thinks of another but schemes only for his money." (Markandaya, *Nectar*, 50)

And clearly, by making Rukmani the narrator and heroine of the novel, Markandaya is setting the reader up to endorse and prefer her response.

Despite her desire to remain rooted in the old way of life, Rukmani has to face the fact that things are changing. She first loses her sons to the tannery, and then to a corporation that sends them overseas to Ceylon to work on a tea plantation. She then lives to see the city entrap her only daughter in its vicious grip, as she turns to prostitution (even though she does so to help feed her family, which the land, despite its mythic qualities, cannot always sustain). Yet, through all this, including the trauma of her youngest son's death by starvation during a period of drought, the narrator and her husband still cling stubbornly to a belief in the old ways and in the power of the land to sustain its people.

It is this stubborn belief, leading to a fatal resignation, that so irks Kenny, the British philanthropist/medicine man who has made it his life's work to live among and to help these ill-starred peasants. In the climactic exchange that takes place between Kenny (who has earlier helped cure the narrator of infertility) and Rukmani, the clash between the two modes of Western realism/rationalism and Eastern myth/spiritualism is made clear. Kenny is telling the narrator of his plans to build a hospital for her village and others surrounding it, with money collected in England. When the narrator expresses her naive surprise that "people who have not seen us and who know us not should do this for us," Kenny angrily lashes out:

> Because they have learnt of your need. Do not the sick die because there is no hospital for them? . . . I have told you before . . . you

must cry out if you want help. It is no use whatever to suffer in
silence. . . .

"It is said—" I began.

"Never mind what is said or what you have been told. There is
no grandeur in want or in endurance. . . ." Privately I thought,
well, and what if we gave in to our troubles at every step! We would
be pitiable creatures indeed to be so weak, *for is not a man's spirit
given to him to rise above his misfortunes?* As for wants, they are
many and unfulfilled, for who is so rich or compassionate as to
supply them? . . . *What profit to bewail that which has always been
and cannot change?*

His eyes narrowed: . . . he always knew the heart of the matter.
"Acquiescent imbeciles," he said scornfully . . . "do you think
spiritual grace comes from being in want, or from suffering?" . . .
"Yet our priests fast and inflict on themselves severe punishments,
and we are taught to bear our sorrows in silence and all this so that
the soul may be cleansed." He struck his forehead. "My God" he
cried. "I do not understand you. I never will. Go, before I am too
entangled in your philosophies." (Markandaya, *Nectar*, 115–16;
emphasis added)

This long excerpt underscores that the Western realist mode, here represented at its best and most generous by Kenny, despite its eminent
rationality and moral virtuousness, is nevertheless a foreign mode; Kenny,
for all his genuine caring, still comes across as bearing the white man's
burden and, ultimately, is no match for the heroically mythic stature that
the narrator assumes.

Thus, in the native rural setting of this book, the mythic mode wins out,
even though to follow the realist mode would make so much more "sense."
For ultimately, despite (or perhaps because of) the material advantage
associated with this realism, it is this mode that allows for a greater
communal good, for achieving some balance between what is good for the
self and what is good for the community. Only if one has money can one
do things both for oneself and for others (Kenny's message). In the mythic
mode, on the other hand, one not only sacrifices individual desires and
needs (as the narrator and her husband do constantly, in order to provide
for the children), but when things are bad (as they often are), even others'
needs remain unsatisfied.

As Kenny cynically says to the narrator, "What thoughts have you when your belly is empty or your body is sick? Tell me they are noble ones and I will call you a liar" (116). And yet, not all the rationalistic thinking in the world can help undermine the power of myth that operates in this book and through its protagonists. Perhaps, according to Markandaya, the traditional, mythic attitude is needed to survive the tremendous hardships of life faced by the common peasant in rural India—an India that is beyond the understanding of its Western colonizers and their offspring. And yet, what is ironic here (as elsewhere in her oeuvre) is the fact that the influences on Markandaya's choice of language and genre are clearly those of nineteenth-century English romanticism rather than any authentically Indian literary tradition. As one critic points out, in Kamala Markandaya's early work:

> English romantic influences (especially in regard to diction) are clearly visible. When the heroine of *Nectar in a Sieve* . . . describes her garden, she does so in unmistakably romantic terms:
>
> > "with each tender seedling that unfurled its small green leaf to my eager gaze, my excitement would rise and mount; winged, wondrous."
>
> The marked emphasis laid here, and in the novel generally, on the cultural wholeness of rural life; the romantic, even Shelleyan aura created by the evocation of nature's fragility and generative power in such words as "winged," "wondrous," . . . and the building up of Rukmani herself as an archetypal, earth-mother figure who suffers and transcends all, are features that relate Miss Markandaya to an English romantic, rather than to an Indian rural, literary tradition.[4]

However, it is important to note that Markandaya, despite her use of a foreign (Western) literary idiom and mode to convey indigenous reality, succeeds through "her sense of the tragic dignity of Indian rural life in creating a heroine who is a convincing symbol of it" (Gooneratne, 127). Thus, she succeeds (as do our other writers) in using a foreign, colonial mode as a liberating strategy for herself and her people in her fiction.

---

4. Yasmine Gooneratne, "Traditional Elements in the Fiction of Kamala Markandaya, R. K. Narayan, and Ruth Prawer Jhabvala," *World Literature Written in English* 5, no. 1 (1975): 125. All subsequent references to this work will be cited parenthetically in the text as Gooneratne.

The theme of conflict between the materialist and spiritualist modes, between a Western-derived rationalism and an Eastern-based mysticism, between the real and the mythic, is continued in Markandaya's next novel about Indian village life, *A Silence of Desire* (1960).

Dandekar, the male protagonist, is the "modernist," whereas his wife, Sarojini, is the "traditionalist," and the reader realizes from the first page that the conflict that is to ensue will be between husband and wife, between their two ways of viewing the world. As one critic describes it, such a conflict is essentially between Eastern and Western, past and present modes of thought and belief:

> The chief thematic tensions in *A Silence of Desire* issue from a conflict between deeply held faith and that insistence on what is broadly described as rational explanation and behavior. Each represents a view of life, one drawing deeply from the past, the other relatively new and chiefly initiated by a skepticism mainly Western in propagation.[5]

In the very first paragraph, Dandekar, the narrator, presents himself as more rational than, and therefore in some sense superior to, his wife (who is consequently in need of his "guidance"):

> The six rooms that they rented were built around a courtyard, a square of about eight feet with an uneven cement floor in the middle of which stood the divine tulasi that his wife worshiped. . . . Dandekar did not pray to it, he was always careful to say; it was a plant—one did not worship plants—but it was a symbol of God, when one worshiped. He had been at pains to bring up his children with a correct understanding of these matters, and to educate his wife. Not that she did not understand . . . it was just that sometimes she seemed to forget, tending the tulasi with a reverence it did not merit.[6]

Despite Dandekar's sense of "knowing better" and of his desire to guide and control his wife, he soon finds events unfolding in a way that his

5. Edwin Thumboo, "Kamala Markandaya's *A Silence of Desire*," *Journal of Indian Writing in English* 8 (January–July 1980): 109.

6. Kamala Markandaya, *A Silence of Desire* (New York: John Day, 1961), 8. All subsequent references to this work will be cited parenthetically in the text as Markandaya, *Silence*.

"reason" is unable to deal with; his wife seems to be slipping out of his control rapidly, for she is now frequently absent from home when he returns from the office where he works as a junior clerk. After snooping around in her trunk one day, Dandekar discovers a photograph of a strange man, and now suspects the worst. Despite his belief in the powers of reason and rationality (passed on to him by his British "superiors"), Dandekar finds himself caught in the grip of an irrational jealousy ("irrational" because as yet unfounded and because he won't ask his wife for an explanation as a rational person might), which destroys his peace both at home and in the office. Finding himself incapable of following any reasonable course of action (such as talking to his wife, which hitherto he has always been able to do), Dandekar takes to hiding around street corners, waiting for his wife to leave their house, and then following her in the hope of "catching her red-handed" with her "lover."

And indeed, one day he does see Sarojini with "a man." He follows her to a small whitewashed house and sees her enter, and looking through the screen of a door, he sees that she has sat to the right of a man who is surrounded by a small group of men and women, all of whom seem terribly engrossed in whatever he is saying. Unable to grasp the true meaning of the scene, Dandekar stumbles home in a daze, there to await his wife's return.

When she comes home, Dandekar informs her that he has followed her and self-righteously demands to be told what she, "a married woman," was doing "with this man in his house." And then, very quietly, she tells him, "I go to be healed. So do the others whom you saw. I have a growth in my womb" (Markandaya, *Silence*, 97). Shocked and embarrassed by the implications of his wife's "confession," Dandekar is further belittled by her justifiable recriminations:

> "So now you know," she said harshly. "For a month now you've been snooping and sniffing at my heels because you suspected something very different. I've watched you, I'm not blind. You listened to every poisonous word of every petty clerk in your office and you believed it." (98)

To which Dandekar's only reply is, "I was mad. I went mad because I loved you. Is that a crime? Is it possible to love without jealousy?" The problem was, Sarojini replies, "you would have stopped me going to be healed." Although poor Dandekar is shocked and hurt by her reply, her subsequent

explanation clarifies that it is not a lack of caring but a fundamental
conflict of beliefs that would have prevented him from complying with her
wishes: "You would have sent me to a hospital instead. Called me supersti-
tious, a fool, because I have beliefs you cannot share. . . . You would have
*reasoned* with me until I lost my faith, *because faith and reason don't go
together, and without faith I shall not be healed.* Do you understand that?"
(99; emphasis added).

Quite out of his depth, Dandekar stammers, "Is he a—a faith healer?"
To which his wife, now completely in command, replies:

> Yes. You can call it healing by faith, or healing by the grace of
> God, if you understand what that means. But I do not expect you to
> understand—*you with your western notions,* your superior talk of
> ignorance and superstition when *all it means is that you don't know
> what lies beyond reason and you prefer not to find out.* To you the
> Tulasi is a plant that grows in the earth like the rest—an ordinary
> common plant. And mine is a disease to be cured so you would
> have sent me to the hospital and I would have died there. (99–100;
> emphasis added)

Sarojini's self-expression here has authority because she has acquired a
dignity that Dandekar, by his somewhat ignoble behavior, has lost. Thus,
Markandaya is clearly weighing the scales in favor of her response.

Yet, after exposing the limits of Western rationalism, Sarojini also
realizes the limits of Indian mysticism, which mistrusts anything related to
the former, including modern medicine and hospitals. And indeed, the
rest of the book proceeds to expose the limitations, as well as to examine
the benefits, of adhering to either of these two modes of belief, facets of
the modes of realism and myth. For example, Dandekar, despite his
blindness to and nonunderstanding of the mode of his wife, is in fact the
person who cares most to preserve the balance between fulfilling individual
desires or needs and those of the larger family circle. It is he who comforts
the children during the absences of Sarojini and tries to keep an eye on
their pubescent daughters. And, when he discovers that Sarojini has been
steadily giving away the small store of silver cups and gold chains they had
saved and put aside for their daughters' marriages, he decides to get them
back from the Swami. Although his concern for material goods may seem
crass compared to the spiritual motives that inspired Sarojini to give away

these things, he is firmly grounded within the realist mode of existence, which insists that he fulfill his responsibility toward his dependents:

> It's all very well, he reflected a few days later, well and good for those who can, but who will replenish my chests and coffers? And I have a sick wife, and two daughters whose dowries I have yet to provide, and a son to be settled in life. . . . They danced across his ledgers, his wife, his daughters, his responsibilities, and he thought, desperately trying to put sense into the figures before him. I must try to get Sarojini away from him [the Swami] because our worlds do not mix. It is disastrous to try to make them. (179)

This then becomes Dandekar's mission—to try and wean his wife away from the Swami, the faith healer, because the mythic mode he represents is making his wife lose all sense of her responsibility to her own flesh and blood. Equally important, of course, is the fact that Dandekar believes in modern medicine, whereas faith healing is a concept he essentially mistrusts.

Thus begins a series of visits Dandekar pays to the Swami in the hopes of convincing him to persuade Sarojini to undergo medical treatment and to leave his care. The Swami, however, informs Dandekar that his wife must leave him, the Swami, of her own free will—he does not believe in imposing his will on others. So, Dandekar's mission does not succeed; and though afterward he feels frustrated and tries another avenue of attack, while in the presence of the guru he feels curiously reassured and comes to believe that the Swami is "authentic" in his own way—thus developing a better understanding of his wife's beliefs: "Dandekar knew, now, what Sarojini had meant. When you were with the Swami, actually there, nothing material or physical mattered. You saw them for the worthless trumperies they were, rose above your body, knew for a while the meaning of peace" (179). Of course, such "peace" does not last, at least not for Dandekar. He now sets official wheels in motion to try and get the Swami ousted from the town, on the basis that he is defrauding poor people of whatever little they possess. What he has not realized, however, is that these poor people will fight to keep their guru, for he fulfills an intrinsic spiritual need in them—he gives them faith. When it seems as though Dandekar's efforts are doomed to failure, the Swami suddenly decides to leave of his own accord, saying to his disciples that he does not wish to stir discord in the community.

Dandekar now is overcome with guilt, especially as he fears that his wife may be heartbroken over the Swami's departure and refuse to be treated in the hospital. His wonder and respect for the guru are therefore complete when he realizes the guru has cured his wife of her fears of Western-style hospitals:

> "I'm not afraid now of knives or doctors, or what they may do. All will be well. He said so."
> Her face was confident, serene. He's achieved the impossible, Dandekar thought, sponged away those fears . . . driven out her devils. He has done what I couldn't do. So I am to be humbled, beholden once more to this man of all others. Well, if I am, he thought, so be it. It was less tiring than to rebel; and after a while, it became touched with something like peace, like a homecoming. (246)

By the end of the novel, Dandekar the realist has "won" his battle, but only after recognizing the power of, and accepting help from, the supreme symbol of the mythic/mystical mode. Dandekar's acceptance of the mythic mode is finally realized when, at the very end, he is able to reject the material objects he had gone to reclaim from the Swami's old haunt and is able to say to the attendant of the Swami, "I shall remember all my life those who are here, derelict" (253).

In other words, Dandekar is now a humbled rationalist who will remember that there are people for whom the mythic and spiritual modes have a meaning (as they now have a meaning for himself) that cannot be simply scoffed at or mistrusted. At the same time, Sarojini has realized the necessity of sometimes relying on practical action and having a more pragmatic approach to life. To quote S. C. Harrex once again:

> At the end both husband and wife have enlarged their understanding of human experience by becoming aware of the limitations of their respective approaches to life: Sarojini because she recognizes that the fulfillment of faith may be dependent on practical action, and Dandekar because he is forced to acknowledge his debt to the Swami and the Swami's spiritual psychology. (Harrex, 68)

The real and the mythic both fulfill a need in contemporary Indian society, it seems, and "in the parable of Dandekar and Sarojini united in a new way, *A Silence of Desire* offers the hope of a new realization of self, reconciling past and present in a better future" (Harrex, 69).

Markandaya's next book, *A Handful of Rice* (1966), is, as the title implies, about the struggle to survive, a struggle that usually overpowers the poverty-stricken, teeming masses of India. This novel demonstrates the failure of the realistic mode to sustain its practitioners, but neither does the mythic mode seem capable of providing a soothing alternative. For the poor man, it seems, neither myth nor realism can provide any answers or solutions to the problems of life—leading to a truly depressing vision.

The story revolves around Ravi, a young man who leaves his ancestral village to try his fortune in the city. He falls in first with a band of petty criminals, led by a man named Damodar, who live by looting and pillaging the townspeople. Then, after falling in love with Nalini, daughter of a local tailor, Ravi tries to reenter the mode of respectability by becoming an apprentice to Nalini's father, Apu. Soon thereafter, Ravi succeeds in winning Nalini's hand in marriage, moves into the joint family household of Apu, and begins to contribute his share to the family income. He thus becomes firmly ensconced within the critical realist mode: "Since his marriage, he thought . . . he had become a responsible householder, a decent citizen with a decent job and a wife to support."[7] Yet, despite his initial success at town life, Ravi cannot completely forget the pastoral bliss of life in the village, the quality of reassurance and wholeness that only tradition can provide in the face of stress and loneliness. Thus, when his wife is undergoing her first labor and Ravi is hustled outdoors with no words of reassurance, he immediately thinks of how, in the village, things would have been different:

> Here there were no fields to lose oneself in, as the men of his village had done: and as he waited he could not help remember-ing—stress having eaten away his defenses—that there was some-thing about the land, mortgaged though it was to the last inch, that gave one peace, a kind of inner calm, that he was acutely conscious of lacking as he gazed at the narrow, hard, bustling and indifferent street. (Markandaya, *Handful*, 153)

7. Kamala Markandaya, *A Handful of Rice* (New York: John Day, 1966), 133. All subsequent references to this work will be cited parenthetically in the text as Markandaya, *Handful*.

But rhapsodizing of this sort is often followed by a return to harsh reality, for Ravi, at bottom a Realist, cannot for long overlook the bitter underside of village life, the misery and squalor that had made him flee it in the first place:

> It still sickened him, that life: the misery and the squalor, the ailing babies who cried all night long, the way one was always poor and everyone one knew was always poor too, the desire—the constant nibbling desire—to have a second helping of food . . . a shirt without holes . . . and to know that one never would. They always knew: knew that things would never be any better. . . . It was this knowing the worst, the hopelessness of it, plus *the way people accepted their lot and event thanked God it was no worse—thanked God!—that sickened him.* (58; emphasis added)

Thus, like Kenny before him in *Nectar in a Sieve,* Ravi is rebelling against the fatal resignation, the tendency toward stasis that is inherent to the mythic mode. Ravi wants to change his way of life, since he believes he can make things better for himself and his wife and kids.

But alas, through the course of the rest of the book, he is steadily disillusioned and finally comes to realize that even faithful adherence to the realist mode cannot change much when the odds of society are heavily against you. As long as Apu is alive, he is able to aid Ravi in securing clientele. He has been a good tailor, and therefore his old customers are willing to give orders to his young assistant as long as they know Apu is supervising. And even Ravi realizes that he is not really a very talented tailor; it is only with Apu's constant help and guidance that he is able to accomplish his daily tasks.

Yet, despite his diligence and obvious competence at his trade, Apu does not command much of a price for his handiwork. When Ravi finds out that the beaded jackets they sell at Rs 80/- a dozen are sold at a fancy store for Rs 125/- per jacket, he is stunned. When he confronts Apu with this fact, the latter takes it very calmly, for, as he sees it, "that's the way it is" (83). Infuriated, Ravi clamors for change and derides the old man for not refusing to sell so cheap. Apu, the true realist, is amazed at this outburst and, controlling his shaking voice, finally tells Ravi, "You go on like this, my lad, and see where it gets you. Just wait and see, that's all" (84).

Later, when he calms down, Ravi realizes what the old man had meant.

Even realism has its limitations, just like the mythic mode. And to be a critical realist (as Ravi has tried so hard to be, but not quite succeeded), one has responsibilities to others, and to oneself, that must be fulfilled, and fulfilled in a respectable fashion. And that leaves no room for idealism:

> But what could he do, within the narrow frame of respectability he had slung around his neck like a penance? Rebel, and a contract might be lost, the steady wage would be lost, and then what of Nalini? He had to think of her, he had to think of himself for that matter. There seemed to be no answer. (84)

Indeed, there seems to be no answer. Things only go from bad to worse when Apu suffers a stroke and then ultimately dies. Ravi, trying to keep up the tailoring business, discovers now the ruthlessness of customers (mostly foreign "memsahibs"), who withdraw their patronage the minute Ravi makes his first mistake. Reduced to living hand to mouth, with so many family members to feed, Ravi's relationship with his wife suffers a serious decline, and his only son eventually dies due to lack of proper care and nourishment.

Toward the end of the novel, Ravi is increasingly attracted once again to the criminal mode represented by Damodar, who is now a rich man. Yet, when it comes to the crunch, Ravi cannot perform the criminal acts Damodar requires of him; his realism has left him unfit for any action that does not fall within the realm of civically responsible behavior.

When there is a severe rice shortage at the end of the novel and the deprived masses decide to raid the granaries (for they believe the shortage is being artificially created by grain merchants), Ravi decides to participate in the raid. He feels himself to be the victim of a large conspiracy, between the "memsahibs" (remnants of the ruling British class) and the rich store owners (new breed of colonizers), who sell items they obtain dirt-cheap from poor laborers like Ravi and Apu at exorbitant prices to these upper-class people. Having worked himself into a righteous rage, Ravi is about to hurl a brick at one of these fancy stores (which to him symbolize all the indignity heaped on him and his like by the ruling elite), when, all of a sudden, he finds he cannot indulge in such an act of anarchistic violence, not only because he is overcome by physical lassitude but because he "is caught up in an existential moment of soul-searching," which forces him, as a realist, to choose the response of "conscience" over that of "violence."[8]

8. Shiv K. Kumar, "Tradition and Change in the Novels of Kamala Markandaya," *Books Abroad* 43

Ravi took aim, posing the jagged brick level at his shoulder. But suddenly he could not. The strength that had inflamed him, the strength of a suppressed, laminated anger ebbed as quickly as it had risen. His hand dropped. "Go on brother, go on! What is the matter with you?"

"I don't feel in the mood today," he answered, a great weakness settling upon him. "But tomorrow, yes, tomorrow . . ." (Markandaya, *Handful*, 297)

But of course, "tomorrow" will never come. The fatal resignation of the mythic, and the commitment to responsible behavior associated with realism are both equally ineffective ways of dealing with the tremendous burdens and difficulties that are the heritage for the majority of postindependence Indians. Whether one blames the colonialists or their legacy, a native ruling elite, or a propensity for myth in the people themselves, the conclusion remains the same: there seems to be no way out of the present depressing reality of life, and fictive strategies or modes themselves seem a very inadequate response at such a critical juncture of Indian history.

In the last book of the first group, *Two Virgins* (1973), the conflict between old and new, the mythic and the real, is once again reenacted; and again, there seem to be no easy answers. Yet here the balance seems distinctly tilted in favor of the ancient pastoral/mythic mode, even though, by the end of the novel, the reader is made to realize that such a mode cannot endure in the face of encroaching materialistic individualism.

The story centers around two adolescent sisters, Lalitha and Saroja, who live with their parents and widowed aunt in a typical Indian village. The story is told through the eyes of Saroja, the younger sister. From her perspective, Lalitha is the more beautiful, ambitious, and prone to Western influences of the two, whereas Saroja is quite happy and content in the old established mode of village life.

In this respect, Lalitha is more like her father, Appa, who believes in a Western, rational way of life, whereas Saroja is more like her mother, Amma, and Aunt Alamelu, doyens of the ancient, mythic code of life. This contrast is pointed up when Miss Mendoza, headmistress of the Christian missionary school Lalitha attends, comes to visit the family:

(Autumn 1969): 510. All subsequent references to this work will be cited parenthetically in the text as Kumar.

[Aunt Alamelu] was quite caustic, the truth of the matter was she disapproved of Miss Mendoza's ways, which were modern. Cosmopolitan, said Lalitha, who knew a lot of words like that, used them when she was in the mood to disparage village life, which was often. Westernized, Appa backed her up, he liked Indians to be westernized, which advanced them into the big world instead of remaining static in a backwater.[9]

Thus, the contrast between old and new, East and West, stasis and change, is clearly established here. What is interesting is that Markandaya is able to see, and show, the good and bad in both modes. For instance, when the washerman's donkey dies of starvation, and his carcass rots for days in the local river into which it had crawled before its death, Appa blames such an unhygienic state of affairs on the lack of an efficient sanitation system, a lack that is due to "the country being so behind the times." Amma and Aunt Alamelu defend the system, saying it is the pariahs' job to dispose of such waste, and when Appa reminds them of Gandhi's teachings—that all men are children of God and therefore no one caste should have to do all the dirty work—Aunt Alamelu's traditional response is, "It is their karma, their fate, brother" (Markandaya, *Two Virgins*, 39).

In this instance, Markandaya highlights the drawbacks of clinging to old, traditional beliefs, rooted in the ancient mythic consciousness of India. Yet, at later instances, she shows the strengths of the old way of life and its ancient values, rooted in a sense of community and mutual caring. This old code insists that a widowed woman like Alamelu be taken care of within a joint family system by her relatives, no matter how well-off or poor they be. Of course, individual self-actualization is rarely possible in such a mode, as is evident in the case of Appa, whose modern, westernized notions of individual success can never be realized within the ancient, communal, mythic code of village life.

And yet, what is the alternative? The realist Western mode, associated with city life, with a chance for growth and change, material well-being and an opportunity for self-actualization, can also be a deadly trap. Although the aim of the critical realist mode is to achieve a balance between fulfilling one's individual needs and desires and fulfilling one's responsibilities toward others, one can easily be led into excesses in the

9. Kamala Markandaya, *Two Virgins* (New York: John Day, 1973), 57. All subsequent references to this work will be cited parenthetically in the text as Markandaya, *Two Virgins*.

name of individual freedom. Thus, Appa shows his insensitivity to the plight of a woman in Aunt Alamelu's position by constantly railing against the joint family system. Believing wholeheartedly in "progress" and "change," Appa and his city-educated sons are all for the introduction of machines into the village, oblivious to the fact that this would deprive thousands, like Chingleput the sweet vendor, of their livelihoods.

It takes Saroja, with her mythic mentality, to see that such a gloriously "realistic" course of action would be unwise in the context of the villagers' pastoral way of life: "She always said a prayer . . . asked God not to allow machines into their village that would destroy Chingleput and his skills. She kept her prayers secret, however, because of Appa and the boys who were progressives [realists]. They often said machines were the answers to the country's problems" (86). Saroja indeed has powers associated with the pastoral, mythic mode, as is evident from the way she relates to animals: "The buffalo followed where she led, it would even heave itself out of the river though it loved water. But it turned stubborn with Lalitha, stood with its horns lowered, and nothing would shift it" (69).

Lalitha, it is obvious, has no such talent as her sister, nor has she any love for the rural way of life. To her, the buffalo shed, their house itself, is nothing but "a dump," a "hole" (71). No wonder then, that as soon as she gets the chance, she leaves the dumpy village for the infinitely more promising city. She has been lured there by the promise of movie stardom held out to her by one Mr. Gupta, filmmaker, who had seen her in the village and had even made a documentary on village life with Lalitha in it, with her parents' permission, of course (much to Aunt Alamelu's disgust). After he returns to the city, Lalitha decides to join him, and so disappears one day without informing any of her family (undoubtedly her parents would never have permitted her to go off on her own).

The rest of the story follows a fairly common pattern—the young village lass is seduced by the corrupt city man, promises of stardom come to nothing, she returns to the village carrying the shameful burden of a child conceived out of wedlock. Naturally, the first reaction is shock, and Aunt Alamelu, the traditionalist, now feels justified in saying "I told you so" to Appa, the modernist:

> Have I not said from the beginning that no good would come of it? Allowing her to . . . simper with young men and flaunting them-selves in films and such like, is there any propriety in it, no, it is shame-shame, totally contrary to our code of Hindu decorum which

has safeguarded the virtue of our youth for a thousand years . . . it is not for us puny denizens of this immoral age to question the wisdom of our ancient mentors. (176)

Yet of course, as Appa angrily points out and the reader also realizes, such an advocation to escape present reality by adhering to an ancient code of beliefs and values rooted in a mythic, pastoral way of life, is not the answer in the face of increasing westernization and urbanization. Then what is the answer? Unfortunately, there doesn't seem to be one. If the mythic mode is unable to cope with the complexities of modern urban life, is the realist mode a better alternative? From the choice Lalitha makes, that would seem to be the case (despite its being depicted, in some sense, as a sign of self-betrayal), for after her abortion, she chooses to remain in the city and take her chances there, rather than return to the "wholeness" of the old village life. For in the city she has some chance to develop her individual talent, achieve some measure of self-recognition, whereas she would be crushed under the communal weight of the old pastoral mode if she returned to the village.

Yet, one can only wonder if indeed this is the right choice, for the very last image of the book is one of Saroja crying for a way of life that she knows, in her heart of hearts, is ended. "She could hardly see for the tears that were cascading down her face, she couldn't have told for whom they were falling, for her, or for Chingleput, or for what was ended" (250). Having seen the vagaries of the city life (she had accompanied her sister there), Saroja has returned with her parents to the village, but she knows that despite all her wishes to the contrary, the path Lalitha has taken is, in fact, the path of the future. Tradition will have to give way to modern reality, and though neither mode is exalted in this novel, the reader cannot help but shed a tear, along with Saroja, for the old myths, the old pastoral mode that will soon be no more (if it is not already). In fact, by having Saroja lovingly say of the village (while she is in the city and feeling lonely) that "no one could ever be lost [there]," that "you knew who you were," Markandaya, according to the critic Alice Drum, is siding "with the many Third World writers who stress the importance of a nation's maintaining its own cultural identity, dancing its own dances, in the face of encroaching westernization."[10] And this, despite what the reader senses as a certain

10. Alice Drum, "Kamala Markandaya's Modern Quest Tale," *World Literature Written in English* 22 (Autumn 1983): 327.

authorial resignation to the inevitable path of the future in India (which will be, as the novel suggests, one of increased westernization and urban materialism).

The second "group" of novels into which I have divided Markandaya's works, whether set in India or abroad, deal essentially with the relationship between Indians and their former colonizers, the British. *Some Inner Fury* (1956) is set around the time of India's independence and so becomes the perfect place to examine the ramifications of relationships between the races as Markandaya understands them.

The central relationship of the book is between Mira, the young Indian narrator, and the Englishman she falls in love with, Richard. She first meets Richard through her brother Kit, who, on his return to India from Oxford, has Richard in tow. The latter, on his way to take up a government post, stays on for a month's vacation with Kit and Mira's family, and it is then that the seeds of a long-term relationship between him and Mira are planted.

From the beginning, their budding relationship is bathed in the colors of myth, of the "unreal": Mira, who, in her own words, "for three years, since leaving childhood . . . had not known the sweetness of walking alone,"[11] is now allowed to accompany Richard alone as tour guide. This happens not only because of her brother Kit's westernized influence on her mother but also because, despite her fears, Mira's mother can't really conceive of any "real" relationship springing up between members of two alien races. And indeed, Richard and Mira's activities seem to occur on a quite different plane from that of other people's. Their trips into the countryside, atop hills and caves, have nothing to do with the everyday reality lived by other people. In fact, when they do encounter "reality" in the shape of an official "leech" (guide) on one of their visits to some caves, it spoils the "magical" quality of their trip, which can only exist in a vacuum. "At the top, the cave we had come to see, and at its mouth, intruding, a figure in a turban, with the metal tab of office exacting dues, leechlike, *but when we had shaken him off, the magic returned*" (Markandaya, *Fury*, 33; emphasis added).

As romantics, Mira and Richard are blind to reality in not realizing that this man, whom they see as an "intrusion" on the mythic landscape (and

11. Kamala Markandaya, *Some Inner Fury* (New York: John Day, 1956), 32. All subsequent references to this work will be cited parenthetically in the text as Markandaya, *Fury*.

to their pleasure in it), is in fact only trying to earn his living by selling postcards and plaster casts of the carvings inside the caves to the few tourists who happen to chance his way. For, as he informs the couple, begging them to buy his artifacts, usually "no one comes here." Richard asks Mira if this is true, and she concurs, explaining that very few people come there, since they are put off by the climb, as well as the heat during the summer months. To this, Richard replies that in any other country there would be "lifts or railways or something," and Mira agrees it is a shame they, in India, have nothing of the sort. But Richard has not been angling for her agreement; rather, he shows his disdain for commercializing these places, even though that would create income for many poor people like "the leech": "More guides, more people filing in, and a rupee for a candle?" (34). Richard here has shown how cut off he is from the very "real" struggle for survival faced by the teeming masses of India. As a well-paid official of the British government, he has no idea of the everyday life of the majority of Indians, and for that matter, neither do westernized Indians like his friend Kit or, to a lesser extent, Mira.

In fact, when Mira moves to the city where her brother Kit is stationed and begins an affair with Richard, their relationship once again isolates them from the rest of the community, making them blind to the political reality of India at that time. Although Mira has started to work for a local newspaper and so knows what the political situation is leaning toward, she nevertheless remains blissfully (perhaps willfully) blind to the seriousness of the situation. And so off she trots on an idyllic tour of India with Richard, on which trip they finally become lovers. Her relationship with Richard again assumes a romantic, remote quality, in that it exists on a plane that is totally removed from the reality of the present situation of India, where the majority of Indians are clamoring for independence, and the British are punishing all those suspected of "seditious" activities. In other words, this is a time of mutual hatred between the two races, not a time when a relationship such as Richard and Mira's can survive in the "real" world.

No wonder, then, that when Mira and Richard return to the city, they are rudely jolted out of their magical, mythical dreamworld by the vision of a city whose walls are painted with obscene messages that, as even Mira is forced to recognize, "had been written with a hate such as only an occupied country can generate" (190). And as Mira and Richard stand gazing around dumbfoundedly, there is "a splintering crash, heavy, with glass in it" (191); somebody, seeing the "white man," has thrown a bottle or something to register the community's feelings. Dazed, Richard says to Mira, "It is a terrible thing to feel unwanted. To be hated." Mira hastens to reassure him: "Richard—this feeling isn't for you—or for people like you. You must believe me." But they both finally realize that at a time like this "you belong to one side—if you don't, you belong to the other. It is as simple as that" (195).

And this, of course, is the beginning of the end. Events take a turn for the worse, and after a missionary school is burned down in a village by a group of pro-independence revolutionaries, in which act Mira's stepbrother is implicated, Mira and Richard are forced to choose sides in a way that finally strips away the mythical illusion that there can be any kind of rapprochement between the colonizer and the colonized.

Realism in this novel demands that one see the situation in its totality, from a communal point of view, not merely an individual one. In other words, the "balance" to be struck here is one in which the scales are tipped more in favor of society than of the self. At a critical moment of history (as independence was for the Indians—and for the British, for that matter), it seems that the only responsible way to act is within the realist mode, but in such a way that allegiance to community takes precedence over individual desire. And indeed, it is such a direction that Mira ultimately chooses:

> Go? Leave the man I loved to go with these people? What did they mean to me, what could they mean, more than the man I loved? They were my people—those others were his . . . they are nothing to you, cried my heart. . . . If you go now, there will be no meaning in anything, evermore. But that stark, illuminated moment—of madness? of sanity?—when, I knew I would follow these people even as I knew Richard must stay [with his]. (253)

Once again, the demands of political realism win out over those of personal romance, despite the attractiveness of the latter.

*Possession* (1963), set partly in India and partly in England during the 1950s, is very much about the struggle for supremacy between two modes of thought and being: the Indian mythic/spiritual mode, and the Western realistic/materialistic, aggressive mode. The symbol of the former mode is the Swami, spiritual guru of Valmiki, the artistic goatherd. The symbol of the Western mode is Lady Caroline, a rich British divorcée who, having "discovered" Valmiki's artistic talent, wishes (in her imperialist fashion) to take "possession" of him. As S. C. Harrex observes:

> In *Possession* . . . the frames of reference are traditional contemplative India and the active possessive West. *Possession* is a drama of de-Indianization in which the central character, Valmiki, is not only culturally and psychologically conditioned by the West, but also "possessed" by it. The presentation of this theme is complex because the possession is literal and symbolic at the same time; for while the substance of the novel's action is the taking over of Valmiki by an Englishwoman, Lady Caroline Bell, Kamala Markandaya interprets it as symbolic of the historic relations between Britain and India. (Harrex, 69)

The story (which seems to be patterned after the fiction of Rudyard Kipling and Isak Dinesen, showing once again Markandaya's fascination with Orientalist literature, which she is obviously revising here) begins with the narrator, an Indian woman writer by the name of Anusuya, or "Suya" being introduced to Lady Caroline Bell at a party in Madras. The latter doesn't waste time in asking the former to take her to a local village where some "arak" (a potent local brew) could be found. Despite her better judgment, Anusuya is somehow persuaded to take Caroline to a village, and here Caroline "discovers" her artist-goatherd. The young peasant boy has been painting in the wilderness, using mud walls for canvas and mixtures of flower and herb pastes for paints. Caroline, convinced of his talent, immediately wishes to take him out of his "primitive" surroundings, where no one appreciates his art (he is, in fact, treated as an outcast by his family), back to England with her, where she can introduce him to the "real" world of art and artists.

Although Suya at first refuses to help Caroline in her endeavors, she later relents when she sees that this is what Valmiki also wants. She helps negotiate his "release" from his parents, but just as she and Caroline think everything is settled and prepare to take Valmiki back to the city with them (whence Caroline will arrange to take him to England with her), the goatherd springs a surprise on them: "We had meant to leave first thing in the morning; but when morning came the boy had other plans. There was the Swami, whom he must see before leaving the village; he could not possibly leave before this had been done."[12] Caroline is angry at this

---

12. Kamala Markandaya, *Possession* (New York: John Day, 1963), 23. All subsequent references to this work will be cited parenthetically in the text as Markandaya, *Possession*.

sudden development, since going to see the Swami will completely upset their schedule for departure. So she insists that the boy drop his plans, and when he remains adamant, she angrily asks Suya to "remind him that I am his guardian now and he is to do as I say." However, the struggle for "possession" will not be so easy, for the boy replies scornfully, "She has not bought me. She has only compensated my family for the loss of a laborer" (Markandaya, *Possession*, 25). The Swami (and all that he stands for) indeed proves to be a formidable adversary of Caroline's mode, for the boy gets his way and they all go up the mountainside to see him, as well as to see the "gods" the boy has painted on the walls of some caves in the mountainside.

From the way in which Valmiki looks to the Swami for guidance, and from the fact that the gods and goddesses, emblems of spiritual belief, have been painted with material help from the Swami, it becomes clear that the Swami represents the spiritual and mythic tradition. And when Valmiki asks the Swami whether or not he should go with Caroline, the Swami's reply indicates how well established he is within the mythic mode, for his answer to Valmiki is the advice of one who has no personal stake in the outcome—it is not rooted in the struggle of realism, which leads one to desire something that will both serve the self and fulfill the responsibility one has taken on for another. The Swami tells Valmiki, "if you did not [go with Lady Caroline], you would have no peace yourself. . . . And once you have gone, and looked and found in yourself the answer, then you will know whether to stay or return." This kind of thinking is representative of exactly the mode that is anathema to Caroline, for she stands for the opposite system. No wonder, then, that the narrator senses "from the very beginning, he [the Swami] was the only human being with whom she was ill at ease" (33).

Once in England with Caroline, Valmiki enters the realist mode of living, in which Caroline reigns supreme. At the same time, Caroline also represents a rather "fantastic" mode of being, with her outlandish life-style and her imperialistic desire to "possess" another human being. Fantasy, as an ignoble facet of the mythic mode, is also clearly opposed to the spiritual aspects of myth. "Under Caroline's intimate patronage Valmiki achieves success in the western sense, which the author defines in terms of money, public acclaim, and exhibitionism" (Harrex, 70).

It is interesting to note, however, that in order to enter this mode of "real" living, of painting for money and recognition in the eyes of men rather than God, Valmiki needs his mythic prop, the Swami. For, when

Suya visits the pair in London two years after their departure from India, she discovers that Valmiki has not produced a single worthwhile painting in all that time—in fact, he has hardly painted at all. Guilt-ridden at his failure, Valmiki immediately demands to know of Suya whether she had known of this before she came to England, and, if so, whether she had told the Swami. When Suya replies in the negative to both questions, Valmiki appears considerably relieved. Caroline, who had been listening to the conversation (Valmiki now speaks broken English) sits up at the mention of the Swami and asks Valmiki, "The Swami means a great deal to you, doesn't he?" To which Val replies unhesitatingly, "Yes. He was like father and mother and friend. Always good. Always help" (Markandaya, *Posses-sion*, 55). When asked how the Swami actually helped him, Valmiki replies that the help was never monetary (like Caroline's) but instead spiritual, magical, that his "help" inspired Val to work: "He say good, I feel good. He say work for God, I work for God. He say you paint well, I paint well." Caroline realizes now the strength of her adversary: "It's not the same, is it, if I say you paint well. It doesn't work, *there's no magic in it*" (56; emphasis added). But Caroline, never one to be defeated, uses the knowledge of the Swami's influence over Valmiki to serve her purposes, the purposes of realism. She now commences to dictate to the Indian cook, who can write in Tamil, phony letters from the Swami to Valmiki. In these letters, the Swami keeps repeating the same thing: that he is always near Valmiki in spirit, if not in body. And this has the desired effect: Val starts to paint once more.

Why is Caroline doing all this? Simply out of some crazed imperialistic impulse for power and domination over another? Although this is to a large extent the reason behind her actions, her actions toward Valmiki are not motivated only by a selfish desire to fulfill some need in herself; she is doing what she does, because, at one level, she genuinely believes in Valmiki's talent, and in bringing him over from India, she believes she has provided the kind of environment and support he needs to advance that talent and become appreciated. There is thus a genuine element of caring and doing something for the good of another in this relationship, as Suya is quick to remind Valmiki when he becomes angry at Caroline's arrogant attitude and refuses to return to her:

> You have forgotten what it was like in the beginning—who it was that praised you, showering you with sweet words you had never heard before which made you feel like a god whose feet are washed

in money; who had faith in you though the whole village laughed; *who cared enough to insist you were never alone*—not even one single night in all that dreadful time when nobody would take you both in. (60; emphasis added)

Thus, Caroline fits well into the realist mode, in the sense of its materialist, commercial values (she is, after all, interested in Valmiki earning good money for his paintings and herself lives surrounded by material comfort) as well as its humanist ideal of achieving some kind of balance between gratification of the self's desires and doing something for one's fellow beings.

However, as the novel progresses, the realist ideal of balance is quite lost in the Caroline-Valmiki relationship. In fact, Caroline's obsession to possess Valmiki begins to override any real concern for him as a human being with needs and desires of his own that may not coincide with hers. It is the element of fantasy, associated with dreams of empire, that now takes over her "relationship" with Valmiki. As Caroline herself admits to Suya one day, apropos of her relationship with Valmiki, "It's a sort of love-hate relationship. . . . Like the kind Britain and India used to have" (75). And Suya thinks:

I wouldn't have called it that, I thought; it would have been difficult, with majestic exceptions, to have found much love lurking in the old relationship. Perhaps, indeed, relationship was not the word to describe a forcible possessing which had established nothing so clearly as that there could be no reasonable relationship—merely a straddling of one stranger by another with little out of it for either. (75)

And indeed, this insightful analysis of the old colonial relationship between the two countries becomes the paradigm for the Caroline-Valmiki relationship. The more Val begins to "flower"—that is, to paint better and more, to speak English properly, and to dress well (under Caroline's tutelage of course), the more Caroline wants to "possess" him absolutely. For now the desire for possession takes on a physical dimension as well. When Valmiki becomes involved with Ellie, the immigrant maid who is a survivor of the Holocaust, Caroline is clearly miffed: "It's beyond me why Val should have thought her worth putting on canvas," she says rather unguardedly one evening to Suya. Later, after Caroline and Valmiki have become lovers, Ellie very conveniently disappears from the household one day, despite the fact that she is carrying Valmiki's child and has no place to go and no one to turn to. What is worse is that no one seems to care what has become of Ellie, or why she left in the first place. Valmiki, too, under Caroline's expert guidance, has learned to shrug off responsibility for another when it interferes too much with selfish desires. Thus, he too has begun to acquire all the negative qualities of the realist mode, and it is not until the Swami visits him in London that Valmiki realizes the trap he is falling into. When, at the end of the Swami's visit to London, Valmiki thanks him for the many letters he has written, and the Swami tells him he has never written any (it being against the mythic ideal of detachment to do so), Valmiki realizes the web of deceit in which Caroline has ensnared him. He rants and raves at her, but she only responds coolly that it was all done for "his own good." At this point Valmiki realizes the powerful force Caroline exerts over him and is not surprised when she tells him she would stop at nothing to hold on to him.

Their complex relationship continues even after this major altercation, but it is obvious that things are drawing to a head. Even though Valmiki returns to living with Caroline, to touring Europe and America with her, Suya, astute observer that she is, understands that "power, of the kind that Caroline held and used with so little hesitation, to a man with Valmiki's foundations was evil. Whatever its manifestations—however excusable its manipulations or well-favored the end—it would never be other than evil" (198). That Valmiki will try and escape from the influence of such power sooner or later seems a foregone conclusion.

At the end of the novel, Valmiki finally leaves for India and returns to the spiritual/mythic mode of the Swami. Even then, Caroline does not give up, but later follows him to India to try and win him back; but, for the present at least, that is not to be. As Caroline is quick to observe, the cheques she had sent Valmiki adorn the cave wall, uncashed. Certainly the materialist ethos of the Western realist mode seems to have lost its hold over Valmiki. Even so, Caroline refuses to acknowledge defeat and ends her visit by telling the Swami, "Valmiki is yours now, but he has been mine. One day he will want to be mine again, I shall take care to make him want me again: and one day I shall be back to claim him" (249). But, of course, for the present at any rate, the spiritualist mode has won out over both the materialist and the fantastic. In this novel, it is clear, the only way for the native to retain his integrity in a postcolonial situation is to return to his own mythic and mystical traditions, even if it means giving up material progress. As one critic puts it in a nutshell:

> That despite her [Caroline's] glamour, her wealth and her seductions, Valmiki has left her for the bleak cave of the Swami, speaks of the defeat of all that Caroline and her society had represented: clever talk, sensuous living, material comforts, and career opportunities. In establishing the triumph of Indian values, Markandaya has also demonstrated the spiritual poverty of western living.[13]

*The Coffer Dams* (1969), in some ways a revision of Kipling's "The Bridge-Builders," once again explores the possibility of bridging the gap between the two modes and cultures, and once again comes up with a primarily negative response. The story, set in newly independent India, is about the building of a "great dam" across a wild river in the Indian highlands. The chief engineer for this project is an Englishman named Howard Clinton, whose company, Clinton-Mackendrick Inc., won the contract for the construction. He has working for him both English and Indian technicians and a host of Indian workmen. As the story opens, the project has reached a crucial stage at which work on the coffer dams (the two protective dams for the great dam) must be completed before the monsoon begins.

From the start, Howard Clinton is an arch realist and pragmatist, who has no sympathy for the mythic, spiritual propensities of the local people. As he later confesses to his partner, Mackendrick, he had come "within an ace of walking out" at the time of submitting tender, because of the interminable and passionate (if somewhat guilt-ridden) appeal of the Indian authorities to the builders to be sensitive to the mythic beliefs of the natives who were going to be displaced due to the building of the dam:

> The people who lived by its [the river's] waters . . . propitiated it with sacrifice and ceremony, and strengthened the banks with clay when the water levels rose. Sometimes when the rains failed, there was no river at all. . . . At other times the land was inundated. They saw their crops drowned . . . their mud huts dissolved . . . and carried away on the flood tide. At both times they prayed to God; they never blamed him. It was their fate.

---

13. P. S. Chauhan, "Kamala Markandaya: Sense and Sensibility," *Literary Criterion* 12, Nos. 2–3 (1976): 140. All subsequent references to this work will be cited parenthetically in the text as Chauhan.

All this the planners of the new India, flanked by their technical advisers, had passionately expounded. Clinton listened with a vast boredom. It did not really interest him, this dreary saga of a hapless peasantry. . . . Then it was over. They turned from the woes of the people to a discussion of the project. Clinton returned to earth, abruptly disconcerting anew his alienated hosts; and suddenly they were speaking the same language.[14]

From his reactions, it is quite obvious that Clinton is not at all drawn to the emotional and mythic propensities of the Indians, but only to the rational, scientific work mode. That he operates within the realist framework is made clear by the following passage, where his aspirations are articulated, both for achieving personal glory and glory for the group and country he represents, as well as for reaping the commercial benefits:

There was something about the project that had begun to inflame Clinton. Partly because it was a testing of strengths: his own, his men's, their joint accumulated power against the formidable natural hazards of the scheme. Partly because others wanted it. The country was full of foreigners—Americans, West Germans, Russians . . . all of them eager . . . to gain a foothold in an expanding subcontinent of vast commercial potential. Both aspects of the power struggle excited Clinton. (Markandaya, *Coffer Dams*, 12)

However, it becomes increasingly clear as the novel progresses (if it isn't already) that Clinton's concern for the material well-being of others extends only to his own countrymen and not to the Indians in his employ. His mentality, thus, functions very much along the old imperialist racial lines, which divide the world into "them" and "us." In this, he is no different from most of the other Britishers working there, the only notable exceptions being his wife, Helen, and to some extent his partner, Mackendrick.

It is no wonder, then, that several incidents and crises involving Anglo-Indian relations put Clinton and Helen on opposing sides, initiating a rift between husband and wife that comes to symbolize the ever-widening gulf between the British and the natives (with Helen as defender of the natives' rights) that, in the end, threatens to destroy the very project itself. The

14. Kamala Markandaya, *The Coffer Dams* (New York: John Day, 1969), 12. All subsequent references to this work will be cited parenthetically in the text as Markandaya, *Coffer Dams*.

essential difference between Clinton's and Helen's attitudes toward the natives can be summed up in the way each views them. Clinton is dumbfounded by the native psyche: "What went on behind those black, depthless eyes? He could not ask, there was simply no communication." Whereas, as even Clinton can perceive, his wife's attitude toward the natives is entirely at odds with his:

> Helen, his wife, had no such blocks. Was it, he wondered, because she was half his age? When he asked her, she laughed. "It's nothing to do with age. I just think of them as human beings, that's all." He frowned at the equivocal statement, and she added seriously, trying to help. "You've got to get beyond their skins darling. It's a bit of a hurdle, but it is an essential one." (15)

Helen's real sympathy for the natives, coupled with her genuine desire to understand their way of life, leads her to establish contact with the tribes living on the mountainsides and to learn their language. Through this contact she is shocked to find out how one of these tribes was forced to move from the site now serving as the British residential enclave. When she confronts her husband with this piece of information and asks why they were "persuaded" to move, he replies, irritably (from the other side of the racial divide), "Because they occupied a site we needed." "Were there no other sites?" asks Helen. To which she receives the rational answer, "Not suitable ones." And when she asks how many people were "persuaded" to move in order to give up this "suitable" site to the British, she receives the coldly nonchalant reply: "I don't know how many people . . . I didn't count heads. There was an encampment of sorts and it had to be moved and it was. It doesn't matter, does it?" (34).

But of course, it does matter, at least to Helen. After this first altercation with her husband, the gulf between them only continues to widen, as Helen becomes increasingly more involved with the native tribespeople and grows close to the old village chief of the tribe who had been moved. She comes to understand and respect their beliefs and customs, their mythic/spiritual mode of existence, so different from the Western rationalist and materialist mode of which her husband is the supreme avatar.

At the next major crisis, she and Clinton again find themselves on opposing sides. Two local men have been killed by machines while working on the dam, and it is the recovery of their bodies from the dam site that becomes the bone of contention between native labor and ruling company.

The natives want the bodies dug up and returned to them in order that they be given the proper funeral rites; otherwise they will go on strike. Clinton and company, however, view this as merely an added impediment to continuing the work on the dams, an obstacle in the way of their achieving the desired goal before the monsoon arrives. The following exchange between Helen and Clinton on the subject underscores the differences between their two modes of perception and warns the reader that despite exceptions like Helen, there is little chance for bridging the gap between the races, little chance of understanding each other. More importantly, the exchange shows up the limitations of the rationalist mode, its inability to cope with whatever lies outside the scope of a cold logic:

> "It is not the dying," she said. "Lives have been lost before. They are used to death, it is everyday and they see it, having no hospitals to cover up. It is not that. . . ."
>
> "If it is not that," he said, to whom death was an end, "then I do not know what it can be."
>
> "The bodies," she answered "which are to be incorporated into the dam." "Bones," he said, and thought of calcium. . . . "They are not so easily reduced," she said, "by some people. Not always by us. Never by them. Who believe the spirit will not be freed, until its body has been reverenced."
>
> "Are these same beliefs," he said, shaking . . . , "beliefs of sanity, to which I am asked to pander?" "They are beliefs," she said. "One does not walk over graves wearing jackboots." (204)

As the crisis prolongs and threatens to destroy the very project itself (for the workers refuse to come back and the monsoons are due any day), Clinton, forced to acknowledge the perceptiveness of his wife's remarks, has to come up with some way of recovering the two bodies. Since any method other than lifting the main boulder intact with a crane and replacing it after the bodies have been recovered would mean a fatal delay for the project, Clinton decides to take up Bashiam's offer to attempt the feat. Bashiam, "jungly wallah" or jungle man as he is called by his colleagues, is a self-taught mechanical engineer who belongs to the primitive tribe of the area. Enamored as he is of Western machines and of the Western mode of realism, he has chosen to cut himself off from his tribe and their mythic, spiritual base. He is thus doubly an outcast, both from his tribe as well as from the people he works for, but his competence at his job commands the respect and trust of his employers. Therefore, Clinton knows that Bashiam, master crane operator that he is, is the best bet for the difficult job at hand and asks him to go ahead with it. What he doesn't tell Bashiam, however, is that the crane is defective, and Bashiam, in doing his job, ends up breaking his spine.

Once again, Clinton the realist has shown that his caring extends only to his own kind (he did not ask one of "his" men to do the job) and that he (like Caroline in *Possession*) will stop at nothing that stands in the way of his personal glory and power and the glory of his company.

When the rains begin, they come down with such force and continue so unabatedly that it appears to everyone, including Mackendrick, that if they do not stop soon, the coffer dams will have to go, for the people in the tribal basin to be saved. When Mackendrick hints of this to Clinton, the latter's egocentrism is revealed at its extreme, for he won't hear of any scheme that might spell destruction for his beloved dams. Mackendrick and Helen, knowing then the futility of arguing with Clinton, leave to visit the old chief, who is lying on his death bed in his hut on the mountainside. Once there, Mackendrick loses control of all his "rational" beliefs and begs the chief for a mythic sign that would indicate the end of the rains, so that the lives of so many people may be saved and the project salvaged. And lo and behold, the chief, just before dying, does indeed manage to say, "When the ridges rise clear" (259), which they are already beginning to do, he knows; but this latter part of the message he is unable to convey, as the death rattle is upon him.

As Mackendrick and Helen leave the hut, the former asks Helen (and his question reveals his skeptical acceptance of the mythic, which, as a Western realist, he has thus far shunned), "Do you think that the ridges are clear of rain? Because if they are . . . it will mean, if the old man was right, that the rains are ending" (255).

And indeed, as it turns out, the old chief was right, for the ridges are clear and the rains do stop. Disaster is averted and the balance restored, but it is the spirituality of the mythic mode, embodied in the old chief, that is needed at the end to restore the balance of life. For realism, here seen to serve only the ends of the Westerners, has failed as a mode to embrace the totality of different cultures. As P. S. Chauhan puts it:

> *Symbolically, the novel sets up one worldview against the other: the mechanical against the mystical.* . . . The prophecy of the chief, no more unambiguous than Delphi's oracle, is proved to be true,

and the dam is saved. Such a denouement suggests that the technology [of the West] may possess the tools to build a dam, but it does not have the wisdom to ensure its preservation. (143; emphasis added)

In conveying such a message, the novel sets itself up in direct opposition to Kipling's short story "The Bridge-Builders," in which the authorial scales are weighted quite clearly in favor of Western pragmatism and mechanical expertise rather than Indian mysticism. In Kipling the mythic beliefs of the Indian people are shown to be of no real value, since their gods are ultimately exposed as somewhat ridiculous figures who appear to the people only in states of hallucination. The values that help the British engineers, Findlayson and Hitchcock, survive and ultimately win the battle against the Indian elements are the values of Western technical prowess and honest hard work. Peroo, the one intelligent native worker in the story, is also convinced, at the end, of the fallibility of believing in the Indian (Hindu) gods and in their earthly surrogates, the gurus (priests). The closing paragraph of the story clearly suggests that Peroo no longer holds the local guru in any esteem; in fact, he wishes to punish him for his useless beliefs:

Peroo . . . had possessed himself of the inlaid wheel and was taking the launch craftily upstream. But while he steered he was in his mind, handling two feet of partially untwisted wire-rope; and the back upon which he beat was the back of his guru.[15]

Thus, by revising the Orientalist message of Kipling's story, Markandaya is clearly carrying out her design of clearing out the "entire clutter of distorted and distorting imagery" that she feels has been created by Western Orientalist literature.

Her next novel, *The Nowhere Man* (1972), set in post–World War II London, recounts the life and trials of the Indian immigrant Srinivas, again to probe the possibilities of love and reconciliation between the West and the East. The novel follows Srinivas from his early years in India after World War I, when he briefly participated in revolutionary politics, to his death some

15. Rudyard Kipling, "The Bridge-Builders," in *The Day's Work* (New York: Doubleday and McClure, 1894), 47.

forty years or so later, at the hands of a racist hoodlum who sets fire to Srinivas's house and, fittingly, is himself consumed by it. Between these bracketing events the story traces Srinivas's departure for England with his wife, Vasantha; his purchase of a three-story house in South London, where he and his wife raise two sons; the death of his wife and one son during World War II; the inevitable rift between the second son (who marries an Englishwoman) and himself; and, finally, his friendship with Mrs. Pickering, a genuinely humane and empathic Englishwoman who comes to live with him and takes care of him till his death, nursing him through the final stages of leprosy.

Although the novel charts the steady increase in racial hostility after World War II, giving the lie to the early years of tranquility that had led Srinivas to accept England as his home, the novel's tone and message is not one of bitterness and despair. The reason for hope and reconciliation lies, I believe, in the relationship that develops between the middle-aged, grieving widower Srinivas and the tough, unsentimental middle-aged English divorcée Mrs. Pickering. It is the bond of mutual caring and respect forged between these two individuals in the best tradition of critical realism that counters and prevails spiritually over the fantastic, ignoble aspects of myth symbolized by the crassly racist Fred Fletcher, who is responsible for the gentle old man's death by fire. In the following description of their living together, Markandaya paints a deeply moving picture of two individuals from vastly different backgrounds coming together in a spirit of mutual forbearance born of human sympathy and caring:

> He gargled and washed and spat, for hours on end it sometimes seemed to Mrs. Pickering as she waited to use the bathroom; and performed delicate balancing feats on the lavatory pan as he cleansed himself with water; and bathed under a shower he installed himself, an inept affair . . . so that when he finished, the walls dripped water. . . . If Mrs. Pickering noticed—she could hardly fail to—she did not comment. She restrained herself. . . .
>
> There were restraints he exercised too. He could not bear the smell of meat being cooked. When she cooked these items . . . he had to go out, or retreat into the basement . . . although he took care not to do so ostentatiously. Consequently, she did not realize the extent of his aversion to flesh, though she knew he did not eat it. [16]

16. Kamala Markandaya, *The Nowhere Man* (New York: John Day, 1972), 61–63. All subsequent references to this work will be cited parenthetically in the text as Markandaya, *Nowhere Man*.

Thus, despite obstacles to mutual understanding and acceptance imposed by differences in cultural upbringing and values, Markandaya shows two individuals, set in the ways of middle age, struggling nevertheless to live and let live, and even to love. Srinivas's overcoming of nausea at the sight of a lamb's heart Mrs. Pickering has brought home to cook, then, acquires a deeply empathic significance:

> Srinivas opened his eyes, which had involuntarily closed. They do not see it, he said to himself, as feverishly forgiving as any missionary. . . . As she does not, he told himself, because, of course, she is one of them. It saddened him a little to think like this, since they were after all so close, in so many ways; but having given it recognition, he would not allow the gap to grow. Live and let live, he said, as indeed Mrs. Pickering also often had occasion to say. On this note of mutual forbearance they continued to enhance and advance their living. (Markandaya, *Nowhere Man*, 63)

And indeed, the key to the success of this unexpected relationship is the ability, on the part of both people, to recognize their differences but not to dwell on them, to focus, rather, on the universal human need for love and tolerance that all human beings share, regardless of race, color, or creed.

It is precisely the inability to see human connections that feeds the racist fantasies of people like Fred Fletcher, fetishizing difference into the proportions of myth as fantasy. For Fred—an unschooled, working-class young man without a job, forced to live with his mother (a neighbor of Srinivas)—immigrants like Srinivas become the targets of a rage at the unfairness of life. The fantasy that can fuel this rage and condone it is, of course, the myth of empire. Small wonder, then, that as Fred fantasizes about annihilating the "others" in their midst, he does so by deploying colonialist imagery:

> Pod's about to burst, he said to himself, though the picture that formed was rather of buckshot flying, spinning pellets sprayed from the exploding capsule to pepper the flesh. . . . He enjoyed dreaming too: not the night variety, which he could not control, but day-dreams, which could be made to fit. In these dreams . . . he was always the top man. The Governor. Governor-General. His Excellency the Viceroy. In cockaded hat, erect on a dais, one arm over

which gold braid fell in thick loops, raised stiffly in salute, acknowledging the homage of dark millions. . . . He could see himself. He could hear. Boss, baas, bwana, sahib. Fred allowed some top names that he knew to slide over his tongue. They tasted ambrosial. He closed his eyes, and went higher, if shakily. Your Honor. Your Excellency. In dazzling duck, with a retinue. (245)

It is significant that just prior to burning down Srinivas's house, Fred buys a coat that can cloak him in the mythic glory of empire, further fueling his grotesque fantasy of wreaking righteous revenge on "those blackies" who are displacing the "true" Britons, that is, the "whites":

He kept going, his mind full of foreigners, until he was lost in the depths of Soho. And there, on a barrow, in an open-air market, so casually flung he instantly knew it came within the housekeeping, was what he had dreamed of. Scarlet, and gold, with loops, and lanyards, and braid, and a broad white buckskin crossbelt.

It could have been the regimentals of a trooper, touched up by a fanciful theatrical costumer.

Or the livery of some faithful, obsolete retainer.

Or it could well have been the vestments laid, somewhere, sometime, on proud, viceregal shoulders, or so Fred, who had seen pictures and saw visions, became convinced.

It was a bursting, riproaring representative of the Queen that rode home on the bus. But purposeful, and determined, and dedicated solely and totally to the welfare of his people. (288)

Clearly, Markandaya is warning the reader here against just those excesses that Cassirer had pointed out that the mythic mentality, in its ignoble mode, is capable of committing (see the Introduction). It is the characters operating within the realm of critical realism, like Srinivas and Mrs. Pickering, who offer the despairing reader any hope for the redemption of humankind, any chance of reconciliation between East and West. Summing up the conclusion of the novel, David Rubin confirms my viewpoint:

But curiously, despite these horrors, the impression the novel makes is not one of bitterness. The wonderfully drawn Mrs. Pickering, both eccentric and competent, and equally a victim of prejudice through sharing her life with Srinivas, holds a promise of hope, of reconciliation, with neither condescension nor sentimentality. (Rubin, 165)

When, at the very end, one of the Philistine neighbors, Mrs. Glass, offers Mrs. Pickering hollow comfort, the latter refuses to cry. The dignity and depth of her response underscore the social and moral commitment that she had brought to her relationship with Srinivas; and, in the final analysis, that is all that counts:

> "Don't take it too hard," said Mrs. Glass, nervously. Is that possible? wondered Mrs. Pickering, whose mind was crammed with images, of the fallen, weak and helpless, and of their sons, and sons' sons, who would not be content as Srinivas had been but could be trusted to raise Cain—if Cain had not already been raised.
> "You mustn't blame yourself," said Mrs. Glass, sweating. "Blame myself," said Mrs. Pickering. "Why should I? I cared for him."
> And, indeed, that seemed to her to be the core of it. (Markandaya *Nowhere Man,* 312)

In her ninth novel, *The Golden Honeycomb* (1977), Kamala Markandaya chooses for her setting not the contemporary India or Britain of her previous novels, but the glittering court of a Maharajah at the turn of the century, some decades before India achieved independence. Like her previous work, *The Golden Honeycomb* once again explores human relationships caught in the web of confrontation between East and West, the tussle between the two modes of myth and realism. However, myth, here, is no longer associated with the spirituality of the East, but rather with courtly traditions that are essentially materialist in nature, emphasizing as they do the rich splendor and luxury of the nawabi lifestyle. Thus, the mythic mode in this novel takes on largely the aspect of fantasy, which is appropriate given that it is also being used to represent the entire British imperial system, which propped up native Maharajahs in order to maintain the mythic stature of the English as godlike rulers of a colonized, inferior India. It is not surprising, then, that the myths and legends that native rulers like Bawajiraj grow up with are favorable to the British, espousing British heroism in the face of native (Indian) treachery. The mythic mode, in this novel, is then clearly seen to be serving the needs of empire.

Realism, therefore, becomes the mode to counter the pernicious effects of myth, even if it is only concerned with the material well-being of others. In this novel, what is needed is a mode that will take into account and provide for the needs of the common masses of India, which happen to be material. The mythic mode here, in its function as fantasy, is an essentially isolationist, rather than a communal, mode, and here it isolates the privileged rulers (both native and foreign) from the real problems of the majority whom they rule. Critical realism alone can bridge that gap between ruler and ruled by striking the balance between self and other. Eric Stokes, in an article written for the *Times Literary Supplement,* more or less confirms this hypothesis:

> Lady Copeland, the Resident's wife, creates a world of ordered beauty in house and garden to enable her to cope with the bitterness of exile and lend her courage against neurotic fears of a racial massacre. The Maharajah and Resident revel in subtle traditions of civility and ceremony which permit them to form a restrained friendship and screen the naked facts of power. Yet the historical theme of the book is the recovery of reality and the overcoming of estrangement, hypocrisy and alienation. This is the function of Rabi, the heir-apparent born out of wedlock. [17]

Thus the task of bridging the gap between rulers and ruled, between myth and reality, devolves upon the shoulders of the young Rabi, illegitimate son of Bawajiraj (or Waji, as he is known to friends), Maharajah of Devapur. Rabi, born of the tempestuous union between the easygoing, pleasure-loving Waji and his fiery concubine, the commoner Mohini, has inherited his father's love of the good life as well as his mother's sensitivity to the needs of the common people, from whom she hails. No wonder, then, that as a child and adolescent he has for his two best friends Sophie, the charming little daughter of the British Resident of Devapur, and Janaki, the common servant girl who sweeps the palace grounds.

It is being with Janaki and observing the squalor of her life that starts little Rabi thinking about the problems of the common people. Coupled with instruction from the two prime realists of the novel, his grandmother and Mohini, he begins to realize that life may not be as rosy and splendid as the mythic mode makes out. In fact, both his grandmother and mother

---

17. Eric Stokes, "Generally Ravishing," review of *The Golden Honeycomb,* by Kamala Markandaya, *Times Literary Supplement,* 19 April 1977, 307. All subsequent references to this work will be cited parenthetically in the text as Stokes.

often circumvent the effects of myths and legends celebrating the glory of the British in India, which are taught the young heir-apparent by the English tutors appointed for his schooling.

Often, the grandmother will take the young Rabi in her lap and recount tales of the bravery and courage of native rulers in the face of British treachery and military might. When Bawajiraj, trained as he is in the mythic mode of the British, questions his mother's "traitorous" behavior, the heated exchange between mother and son that follows reveals the importance of myths in shaping ideology; and it becomes clear that if Rabi is truly to become a leader of the people (unlike his father, who is totally cut off from them), he will need the support of an indigenous mythic mode, not the foreign one imposed on rulers like Bawajiraj.

> "Why do you tell him these stories?" Bawajiraj is none too pleased with his mother, who he feels interferes with the proper education of his son. . . .
> "Why shouldn't I tell him these stories?"
> [says the grandmother].
> "They're so half-baked! They're only legends!"
> "Legends are the blood history of a country."
> "He'll learn history properly, when the time comes for it."
> "Your kind of history."
> "My kind of history! History is facts!"
> "How can you be so naive?"
> "Me—naive? It's you! You've believed every story your nursemaid ever told you."
> "Nursemaids are as truthful as tutors."
> "Do you mean my tutors were liars?"
> "They saw the truth differently."
> "Facts are facts."
> "They can be slanted."[18]

Thus, the mythic mode, though used in the book primarily as a means of ensuring the material well-being of a native privileged elite by tutoring it in the ideology of the real rulers (that is, the British) can also be used for the opposite end. By associating myth not with the tradition of wealth

18. Kamala Markandaya, *The Golden Honeycomb* (New York: Thomas Crowell, 1977), 48. All subsequent references to this work will be cited parenthetically in the text as Markandaya, *Honeycomb*.

and privilege concentrated in the hands of a few, but with the tradition of
a rich native history in which commoners and rulers alike fought for their
sovereign integrity, the old grandmother hopes to inculcate in Rabi something she was unable to in his father: a sense of pride and belonging to his
own people and past, rather than a past concocted by the British. She
hopes that Rabi, strengthened by a belief in his own mythic tradition and
history, will be able to address the very real problems of poverty and
hunger faced by the people of his land, overtaxed as they are by the British
Indian government.

And indeed, one day Rabi, now on the brink of adulthood, finally comes
face to face with the reality outside the palace; from this point on, he
becomes committed to doing what is required of him within the realist
mode: working for the material betterment of his people while still maintaining his status as heir-apparent.

The incident that sets off this train of action is the mill-workers' strike
in Bombay, going on while Rabi and his parents are in Bombay. At a time
of great political unease, when the poor laborers are demanding an increase
in their wages, Bawajiraj shows up in a town seething with their anger to,
of all things, collect some Rolls-Royces he has just imported. He is clearly
oblivious to the charged atmosphere around him and takes his son and
mistress to stay, as usual, in the fanciest hotel in town. While Rabi is in
his room, surrounded by the most extravagant luxury, he finally begins to
sense the "unreality" of his existence:

> It began to grate upon him, the gilding, the pearly floors, these
> bland shining surfaces that would never reflect, he felt, the cruder
> compositions of substance, the bowels, bones and grimaces stitched
> up inside a reality that he knew existed. Only he did not know
> where he could go to find out, or how, or from whom. (Markandaya,
> *Golden Honeycomb*, 245)

As it turns out, Rabi doesn't have to go far to search for the "bowels,
bones and grimaces" of "real" life. Having witnessed the rebellious mood
of the people (who had attacked his father's car at the docks where he and
Rabi had gone to pick up the Rolls-Royces), Rabi is determined to find out
the causes of their grievances, to see for himself how these people live. So,
one night he slips out from the hotel and "enters areas where livings are
unlined" (265). He finds a motley crowd headed toward Chaupati Beach
and joins in with them, although he "has been steered away from this

insalubrious and plebian meeting-place" by his father and retinue. It is at this meeting-place that leaders of the mill-workers gather to speak out against the injustices of the government. But before they can say much, the police descend on them, employing their breakup tactics to scatter the meeting. Both the crowd and Rabi are stunned:

> If this kind of action was new to the crowd, most of whom spend their days humped over looms and levers rather than tangling with the *"sircar,"* for Rabi it was a revelation to observe the limbs of government so deployed.
>
> He has never seen policemen like this before. There is no connection between the benign and courteous paladins of his experience and this punitive horde pouring onto the beach. These men are *mad,* they are *rampaging.* They have unstrapped their *lathis* and are using these berserk clubs to strike down unarmed people. The scene has manic overtones. (270)

Rabi too is struck down by a lathi and wakes up to find himself in a lowly hovel, home of a woman laborer who has taken him there to let him recover from his injuries. During his period of recovery Rabi closely observes the hardships endured by people of the lower classes. He observes how powerless they are and is ashamed to think that the likes of his father are in league with a government that can treat people in such a dishonorable manner.

When Rabi returns to Devapur, he is a changed man. Although the mill-workers' strike achieved nothing in terms of getting any changes instituted, Rabi learned a very important lesson from it: that one day, when the time was right and the groundwork firm, "his" people would be able to demand change from a position of strength rather than weakness. He decides that as a future ruler of the people of his state, he will commence to do his duty by them, which his father has so long neglected. Thus, with the help of the Dewan (Bawajiraj's native chief minister, whose sympathies lie with the common people), Rabi embarks on his first major scheme, that of constructing a dam and irrigation project that would control the flow of water so desperately needed by the people (who are mostly farmers) of his state. Because of his involvement with such a scheme, the people come to identify him as one who truly sympathizes with their woes, and take their troubles to him rather than to his father, who, in their minds, is associated with measures like the increased salt taxes levied by the ruling government.

When World War II breaks out, Bawajiraj, loyal servant of the British that
he is, upholder of the old mythic ideals of chivalric honor, leaves to
participate in the fighting, whereas Rabi chooses to stay behind in order to
take care of what he perceives as the more pressing daily concerns of his
own people. When the war ends, the British, in a drive to restore some of
the reserves depleted in the war, call upon Bawajiraj (and other rulers like
him) to raise yet again the salt levies on the people. As usual, Bawajiraj,
convinced this is for the best, complies with the request. But finally the
time of the people has come. The Gandhian movement for independence
from Britain has already gained a steady momentum, and now, with Rabi
on their side, the people of Devapur amass outside the Palace and the
Residency to demand their rights, using the tactics of nonviolence so
successfully employed by Gandhian followers in other parts of India:

> The crowd that had assembled to challenge the Palace and the
> Residency and beyond these two an untenable order was, certainly,
> different from those that had gone before.
> These people have not come here for justice. . . . They have
> learnt it is window dressing, for display purposes. . . .
> No. They have done with justice, and have come instead to claim
> their natural rights. . . .
> This crowd is not going to make the mistake of the mill crowd,
> or any other crowd. . . . It has discovered muscle. Further, it has
> found out that muscle is a mesh of physical and mental fibre. It
> intends to use this strength, which is founded even more basically
> on its human spirit.
> It intends to stay. It, or if not, its heirs and successors. Time is
> on its side.
> This is the force against which, somewhat halfheartedly, and
> with a dismal conviction of bullying, they [the government] are
> attempting to pit the tinny might of soldiers. (463)

And of course "they" ultimately realize the time has come for them to
give in to the legitimate demands of the people. Thus, Bawajiraj is advised
to do so by Sir Arthur Copeland, and, as the novel ends on the optimistic
note of a beginning of a new era, Mohini, Waji's beloved concubine,
celebrates the victory of the realist mode:

> "But what is there to grump about?" Mohini wanted to know. "For
> once in your life you're behaving like a father to your people. You're

actually letting them keep a fraction of what's theirs, instead of grabbing the whole lot for yourself and your bania British friends. You ought to be pleased for their sake." (465)

And the Maharajah, basically lovable fellow that he is, concurs with Mohini's sentiments, so long as she still loves him.

Thus, in a sense, realism has won the day, but, as Eric Stokes points out, the victory is qualified by Markandaya's ambivalence toward both modes:

> Reality is to be found in the people, in the harsh actuality of their poverty. . . . But in the novel it is kept in the wings and never possesses the stage: the author's own aesthetic sense is too strong for her to get close. She cannot manipulate stench, filth and violence or transmit other than an ordered and tidy image. No blood is spilt, the gathering personal and political tension is readily dissipated by British concessions. (Stokes, 507)

Therefore, neither the British Resident nor the Maharajah is ever presented in a really bad light, and in fact, the mythic mode they represent does hold the reader's interest and fascination for the length of the novel (more so than the people's troubles!). Thus, although morally Markandaya allies herself with realism in this novel, aesthetically she is more attracted to myth.

*Shalimar* (1982), Markandaya's last novel to date, takes up the theme of East-West confrontation once again, but with a difference. For once, the "confrontation" has positive overtones, since the possibility of friendship based on true mutual understanding and respect between individuals of the two races is seen to exist.

The confrontation in generic terms is still one between myth and realism. The myths and ancient traditions of an isolated little fishing village in India are threatened by the realism of modern technology that arrives in the shape of a British construction company (AIDCORP) invited by the host country (India) to build and develop a tourist resort in the area. The arrival of these men and women threatens the small fishing community because their project "Shalimar" holds out the lure of good steady material compensation for native labor, something that the vagaries of the fishing profession can never promise.

With the building of the international resort, the feelings and behavior of the men that come with the high-tech machinery are once again brought into contrast with the ancient myths and modern aspirations of the isolated little fishing village.

In this old grouping, however, many of the men and women who represent the overspill of empire are a new breed, as are many of the local people (especially the younger ones) who are attuned to the jet age and its benefits. Of course, there are a great number still living in India as they always had, and who resist change, just as several Westerners are imperialists in a new guise. But the emphasis in the book is on the hope for rapprochement provided by the new kind of people on both sides of the racial divide.

Thus, Tully, descendant of the British consuls, clearly represents the best that the modern West has to offer: he is effective in his work, humane, and sensitive to the beauties of India. And then there is Rikki, the sixteen-year-old fisherboy, who was introduced in early childhood to a world beyond his village by an old English missionary couple. Both Tully and Rikki are open to companionship and to the new world the other represents, and it is the relationship they develop in the course of the book that holds out a promise of release from colonial dilemmas.

From the start, there is an unmistakable rapport between the two. On the very first day that AIDCORP officials are out on the site near the village, recruiting local labor, Tully notices Rikki as the one who speaks fluent English. The next day, when Tully is out swimming, it is Rikki who swims out to warn him of the dangerous currents beyond the reefs. An amicable relationship is thus established from the outset, and through the course of the novel it just grows stronger. Although Rikki abandons his old way of life, his trade as a fisherman, for the steady employment he finds at Shalimar (first as tea-boy, then as lifeguard), it is Tully who helps him keep in touch with his traditions by commissioning him to build a sturdy yacht that could be used as a fishing boat. At the end of the novel, just before he departs for England, Tully even offers Rikki the boat as a gift, should he choose to return to his old way of life.

But of course, it is too late for Rikki to do that. He has learned to enjoy the freedom from material worries that having a steady income has provided him with. Although his father, Apu, and brother, Muthu, are sad to see the decline of the old ways, Rikki's outside income has meant more food and better shelter for them all. Thus, the realist, modern mode is shown to have its advantages. And in this novel, it is seen in its best light because it does not totally displace the mythic. In fact, what brings Tully and Rikki closer is their realization of the common mythic ground between them, between their civilizations. When, for instance, Tully tells Rikki that he does what he does (that is, build tourist resorts like Shalimar where, in all conscience, he feels the place should be left untouched) because he feels compelled to, as though he were tied to a juggernaut, Rikki immediately recalls a myth from his childhood, the myth of Jagganath's Chariot. As he recounts the myth, it is amazing to note how subtly Rikki is able to interpret Tully's thoughts and emotions, and vice versa. When he finishes his tale, Tully feels moved to say, "What I love about you is the labyrinth you invite me to enter."[19] "Labyrinth" is a new word for Rikki, so Tully tells him the old Hellenic myth to explain that concept.

As Tully tells the story, "Rikki listen[s], now and then exclaiming over resemblances to certain tales in his own repertory. *Myths reaffirming a common ancestry, sailed around the world and connected*" (Markandaya, *Shalimar*, 160; emphasis added).

Thus, on a mythic and symbolic level, as well as a realistic one, Tully the Englishman, descendent of imperialists, connects with Rikki, a native Indian of humble origins. And on both levels, it is an equal relationship: they trade myth for myth, material favor for material favor (Rikki builds Tully's boat, Tully pays him for it), and, most important, true caring each for the other.

Unsurprisingly, when Tully leaves at the end of the novel, both men are overwhelmed by emotion, and the last thing that Rikki does (he hurries to Prospect Point to watch the sunrise) reminds him of the countless things that "he and Tully had often agreed" on (341). (In this case, the thing agreed upon being the opinion that views from this particular vantage point were "matchless.")

What the novel seems to be suggesting, then, is that if, on the individual level, some true understanding and appreciation is reached of one another's traditions and way of life, and a give-and-take relationship established in which each can imbibe the best of the other's world or mode, then everything is not lost; one can then find some cause for hope in the peaceful coexistence of races and nations that, till yesterday, were embroiled in deep hatreds and conflicts.

Integrity is retained by each side in such a symbiotic relationship, for Rikki, having adopted and learned all that is useful from the Western

19. *Shalimar* (New York: Harper and Row, 1982), 160. All subsequent references to this work will be cited parenthetically in the text as Markandaya, *Shalimar*.

realist mode, nevertheless remains attached to his past, his myths, his family and village. Tully, for his part, returns to the country where he belongs (despite the attractions of living out a neo-imperialist fantasy in the renovated Avalon, haunt of former colonialists). He returns enriched with the knowledge that there is a deeper, a mythic bedrock that unites people so different from each other on the surface—a bond much stronger and more meaningful than the commercial ties of commercial enterprise. For once, then, myth and realism come together in mutual harmony. How much faith one is to put in such an optimistic resolution, however, remains a dubious issue, in light of the rest of Markandaya's oeuvre.

Her work to date, indeed, does not seem to present any one response to the question, Which generic strategy is an ideologically liberating choice, in both moral and aesthetic terms? For her, much more so than for Narayan and Desai, it seems, the postcolonial situation is fraught with ambiguities and confusion. Although Markandaya's stance is not as radical as Rushdie's, it is nevertheless clear that, like him, she too does not see any one genre inherited from the Western novelistic tradition to be quite capable of sustaining the postcolonial burden of impoverished Third World societies, which are the victims of a culture clash that has left in its wake a deep spiritual and material malaise.

# 4

## Salman Rushdie

## The Debunking of Myth

In this final chapter, I would like to suggest that Salman Rushdie, the most "modern" and youngest of the four contemporary Indian novelists discussed here, has used the genre of myth both as a "strategy of liberation" and as an ideological form that avoids historical petrification, something that none of the other three novelists has accomplished so far: all three of them have had to enlist the help of the genre of realism to offset the petrifying effects of myth. Rushdie too uses other generic forms besides myth, such as realism, the comic epic, even science fiction, but his aim is not so much to strive for a wholeness born of a pleasing commingling of genres as it is to mirror the state of confusion and alienation that defines postcolonial societies and individuals. It must be said, however, that Rushdie's refusal to "mythologize" history in his books *Grimus, Midnight's Children, Shame,* and *The Satanic Verses* must ultimately be seen as a failure to construct a viable alternative ideology for himself or for postcolonial society in general.[1]

1. Timothy Brennan, in his book *Salman Rushdie and the Third World: Myths of the Nation* (New York: St. Martin's Press, 1989), constructs a slightly different argument. Although he too sees

If *Midnight's Children, Shame,* and *The Satanic Verses* are difficult to
define in generic terms, then *Grimus* (1975), Rushdie's first published
"novel," is even more so. The book is a mishmash of myth, fantasy, and
science fiction. Although the subject matter is very different from the three
later books, in that *Grimus* is about the life quest of an Axona Amerindian
rather than an "Indian Indian," thematically and generically Grimus begins
to sound out the concerns that will be paramount in the two later books.

Flapping Eagle, like Omar Khayyam in *Shame,* is a "peripheral" hero,
since he is marginalized by his own tribe for the inauspicious circumstances of his birth (his mother died shortly after bearing him), as well as
for the pale color of his skin—which, to the dark-skinned Axona, denotes
foreignness. In this latter aspect, Flapping Eagle (a self-given name)
foreshadows Saleem Sinai, the protagonist of *Midnight's Children,* who is
an outcast from the rest of his native society too (because he is literally the
offspring of a genetic mismatch between Methwold, the white foreigner,
and a native woman):

> As for my coloring: the Axona are a dark-skinned race and shortish.
> As I grew, it became apparent that I was, inexplicably, to be fair-
> skinned and tallish. This further genetic aberration—whiteness—
> means they were frightened of me and shied away from contact.[2]

When his aggressive older sister, Bird-Dog, meets a man called Sispy,
drinks the elixir of eternal life he gives her, and then vanishes with him,

---

Rushdie's oeuvre in terms of a failure of ideology, he locates the reason for this failure elsewhere—
not, as I see it, in an inability to mythologize history (while always remaining rooted in history, of
course), but rather in his inclusion in a particular class: that of the "cosmopolitan elite." In Brennan's
view, this class of writers/thinkers is unable to effect a true decolonization, because such a class of
people is too sophisticated, too much a co-opted part of the elite of the West, to be committed to a
concept of any "national struggle." That is the crucial point of difference between, in Brennan's
opinion, a Frantz Fanon or an Amilcar Cabral and a Salman Rushdie. Referring to the former "type,"
Brennan writes: "What they did know, and insist on, was the necessity of national struggle. That is a
point of view Rushdie shares in theory, but which he cannot bring himself to fictionalise. . . .
'Discipline,' 'organisation,' 'people,'—these are words that the cosmopolitan sensibility [such as
Rushdie's] refuses to take seriously" (166). Brennan goes on to suggest that in the works of writers like
Rushdie one finds a sense of "protest but not affirmation, except in the most abstractly 'human' sense."
Yet, what I am interested in charting in my book are precisely these voices of protest. Rushdie's is one
such voice, which even Brennan admits is "something, and it is perhaps even necessary as a mediation."
The need for such voices, regardless of class, is what I argue for in my book. And Brennan concludes
by essentially concurring with such a view, when he remarks that "the greatest problem is still being
unable to conceive of the colonial as even having a voice that matters" (166). From this perspective,
clearly Rushdie's is a "voice that matters."

2. Salman Rushdie, *Grimus* (1975; reprint, New York: Overlook Press, 1982), 10. All subsequent
references to this work will be cited parenthetically in the text as Rushdie, *Grimus.*

Flapping Eagle, unable to continue facing life as an outcast by himself, also drinks the same potion (after its antidote has been destroyed by Bird-Dog) and leaves Axona to travel in unknown places in search of companionship; he becomes an eternal voyager, forever homeless, rootless:

> Stripped of his past, forsaking the languages of his ancestors for the languages of the archipelagoes of the world, forsaking the ways of his ancestors for those of the places he drifted to, forsaking any hope of ideals in the face of the changing and contradicting ideals he encountered, he lived, doing what he was given to do, thinking what he was instructed to think. (Rushdie, *Grimus*, 36)

Living out such an uncentered, meaningless existence, century after century, becomes in the end quite unbearable for the perennially young hero. His only hope is that a place exists for the likes of him where he can finally grow old and shake off the burden of immortality: a place that he can finally call "home." Nicholas Deggle, a man Flapping Eagle meets on his travels, confirms for him the existence of such a place and says it is called Calf Island. Eagle sets off for the "promised land," convinced this is the place he has been destined for, even though Deggle warns him that others who have drunk the elixir of life repair to this place to enjoy their immortality, rather than end it: "they chose immortality. Whereas you are after something quite different: old age, physical decay, and presumably, death. You should set the cat among the pigeons, pretty-face" (42).

And indeed, Flapping Eagle's arrival at the town of K in Calf Island (after much help from his guide, Virgil Jones) does cause havoc and leads, ultimately, to the destruction of the entire place and most of its inhabitants. The reason for this is, as Deggle had correctly pointed out, Eagle's desire for change and growth (which certainly involves facing up to and accepting the unpleasant side of life, that is, death). Such a desire can only bring chaos to K, since the town's survival rests solely on the fact of its being a "petrified," changeless society. As Virgil Jones explains to Eagle:

> That's what they're like in K. . . . Petrified. And why? . . . Why, because of the damned dimensions (he frowned). You remember my saying you should fix your mind on one thing, like Bird-Dog. It's the only defense. The effect is much stronger in K you know. Much nearer to Grimus. It drove them out of their wits. They found the only way to keep the bloody thing at bay was to be single-minded.

To a fault. Obsessive. That's the word. *Obsessions close the mind to the dimensions.* (99; emphasis added)

The "dimensions" are everything that is foreign to the self of those who live in K, which is, in fact, a "colony" created by the Gorfs, and "ruled" for them by Grimus (also known as Sispy). The Gorfs are an alien life-form whose penchant for "Ordering" has led them to devise the "Divine Game of Order," which gives them the chance "of measuring the extent of their brilliance or mediocrity against other civilizations" (79).

Like any other colonizing power, the Gorfs feel they must have "a measure of control over their new idea," and to this effect they "conceptualize" an "object," contact with which will be the only means for any movement between the different "Endimions," or realms.

The "object" in the case of the realm of earth is the Stone Rose, and the person who wields ultimate control over it is Grimus. Thus, Grimus/Sispy becomes the prototype of the native-turned-neocolonizer, for he starts to rule Calf Island and its inhabitants in the way of the Gorfs.

The only way for the inhabitants of K to resist the Grimus "effect," to hold on to a sense of their indigenous past, their "self," is to become obsessive. As Jones says quite explicitly:

Often they [the inhabitants of K] fix themselves a time in their lives to mull over. Live the same day over and over again. Displaced persons are like that, you know. Always counterfeiting roots. Still. If a false growth's thick enough, it serves. To Protect. (100)

The reference to displaced persons is very pertinent, because a colonized person is a displaced person, for he has, in a sense, been cut off from his own indigenous past, culture, and values. The desire to create the myth of an "authentic" past and live in it, then, is understandable in the people of K who, like Eagle, sold themselves into eternal bondage to the man who gave them the promise of eternal life, and who himself is but a pawn in the Gorfs' Divine Game of Order. Yet, the only defense against the "effect" is "obsessionalism, single-mindedness, the process of turning human beings into the petrified, simplified men of K" (186).

No wonder, then, that the book ends on such a depressing note. If the only way to resist the deleterious effects of colonization is to create an obsessive mythical world to exist in—in other words, to live in a world that is historically petrified—then clearly, this is a world that neither author nor hero can live in. In fact, Flapping Eagle, who has chosen action over stasis, change and decay over stagnant life, can do only one thing: destroy K. For such a petrified society only perpetuates the rule of the oppressor by refusing to step out of the dialectic of oppression-resistance.

Thus, Eagle realizes that in order to destroy the Grimus "effect" altogether, he must destroy not only Grimus but also the Stone Rose, the "object" devised by the Gorfs to keep one man (in this case, Grimus) master over the rest of his people. To achieve this end, he leaves K and journeys to the top of Calf Mountain, where Grimus is supposed to reside. On the way, he encounters his long-lost sister, Bird-Dog, sent by Grimus himself to bring Eagle to him. Wondering why Grimus should deign to send for him, Flapping Eagle nevertheless accompanies his sister. Brought into the presence of Grimus, he realizes with a shock that his once-independent, spirited sister has become a subservient, "colonized" object:

> Bird-Dog stopped and lowered her head . . . to Flapping Eagle, the sight of this servile Bird-Dog . . . a totally subservient menial, was a shock and an upset. This was not the sister who has foraged for his food, who has raised and protected him. This was a shadow of the Bird-Dog he had known. What had Grimus done to her? (279)

What he "had done to her," Flapping Eagle soon finds out, is precisely what Grimus has in store for him: that is, he has turned Bird-Dog into a servile "object," someone who is willing to serve him, Grimus, and through him, the Gorfs. And, knowing that Eagle wishes to destroy him, Grimus offers the latter an alternative that will help perpetuate, rather than end, the rule of the Gorfs. He tells Eagle:

> When I became Grimus, I took the name from a respect for the philosophy contained in the myth of the Simurg [of which "Grimus" is an anagram], *the myth of the Great Bird which contains all other birds and in turn is contained by them.* The similarity with the Phoenix myth is self-apparent. Through death: the annihilation of self, the Phoenix passes its selfhood on to its successor. *That is what I hope to do with you.* Flapping Eagle. Named for the king of earthly birds. *You are to be the next stage of the cycle,* the next bearer of the flag, Hercules succeeding Atlas. (292–93; emphasis added)

In other words, what Grimus wants to do is to "contain" Flapping Eagle, as he himself has been contained by the myth of Simurg. Such containment has led Grimus to fulfill his role as neocolonizer, which is what he hopes now is the role that Flapping Eagle will adopt.

Eagle, however, surprises him by asking, "What if I refuse?" To which Grimus, after a pause, gives this interesting response:

> How can you refuse? . . . Consider your life: you will see that I have shaped it to this express purpose. In a sense, Flapping Eagle, I created you, conceptualizing you as you are. Just as I created the island and its dwellers with all the selectivity of any artist. (293)

Grimus, as a mouthpiece for the colonial ideology of containment, thinks (mistakenly) that he has "created" everything in the colony he rules and, therefore, that he is in complete control over it and its inhabitants, who are thus reduced to being mere "objects." Flapping Eagle, however, refuses to submit to such "object-hood," and thus answers Grimus fearlessly, "We existed before you found us" (293).

Faced with such a rebellious stance, Grimus nevertheless continues trying to induce Flapping Eagle to give up his grand design of destroying both himself (Grimus) as well as the Stone Rose. In fact, he is willing, even eager, to let Flapping Eagle destroy him, as long as Eagle will agree to keep and preserve the Rose. For if Eagle can be induced to keep the Rose, then he can become a replacement for Grimus and continue to rule K and the rest of Calf Island for the pleasure of the Gorfs. If, on the other hand, he breaks the Rose, then all is lost, for, as Grimus cries out, "The Gorfs made the Rose to link the Dimensions. Break it and you break us" (316).

A conflict now ensues in Flapping Eagle's mind between that part of him that is truly Eagle, the "I-Eagle" part, and that part of him to which Grimus's way is tempting, the part he calls the "I-Grimus." The I-Eagle, that is, the "true" part of Flapping Eagle, realizes that "if I chose not to destroy the Rose, I could go back to my own world" (316). Yet he has also "seen too much of the way I-Grimus has ruined lives for the sake of an idea" (317). The only "world" that I-Eagle could return to, if he agreed to Grimus's plan, would be a ruined world:

> I-Eagle saw the centuries of wretched wanderings that preceded my arrival, saw the people of K reduced to a blind philosophy of pure survival, clutching obsessively at the shreds of their individuality:

knowing within themselves that they were powerless to alter the circumstances in which they lived. (317)

The Grimus alternative is indeed a "grim" one, and Eagle finally chooses to reject it. He succeeds in destroying the Rose, and by so doing brings destruction upon himself and his world; but by the same token, he liberates himself and K from being objects of amusement in an alien power's game of order. The apocalypse at the end of Grimus ("the world of Calf Mountain was slowly unmaking itself") foreshadows the much more horrific one at the end of *Shame*. The message here, as there, seems to be: we must step out of the circle of opposition, the dialectic of power-powerlessness, oppression-rebellion, altogether, that is, destroy the old status quo, the world as we know it, entirely before the world can be made habitable for all. The only kind of narrative strategy capable of conveying the burden of such a heavy message seems to be one in which realism can be diluted, even dispensed with, through the use of mythical and surrealistic fiction, since the wholeness and balance promised by realism are no longer appropriate in a world that has become meaningless. As Elfrida, one of the characters in Grimus says, after listening to a story:

> I don't like it. . . . It's too pretty: too neat. I do not care for stories that are so, so tight. Stories should be like life, slightly frayed at the edges, full of loose ends and lives juxtaposed by accident rather than some grand design. Most of life has no meaning—so to tell tales in which every single element is meaningful . . . ? (175)

Of course, what such a "theory of the novel" calls for, ultimately, is the debunking of all representational genres of fiction (not just realism) that construct meaningful scenarios of life. Thus, in the end, even the myths of K, Calf Island, and the Gorfic Endimions must be destroyed, to avoid historical petrification and to escape the Gorfic strategy of containment.

After *Grimus*, Rushdie seems to have gone on to think about this issue of generic strategy in ever more radical, poststructuralist terms, and to begin associating "liberation" with the notion of "debunking." In his next novel, *Midnight's Children* (1981), Rushdie turns to the setting of his childhood, a pre- and postcolonial India. In an interview with the *New York Times* correspondent Michael Kaufman, Rushdie says, "It seemed to me that if you had to choose a form for that part of the world, the form you would choose would be the Comic Epic."[3] Right away, the reader should be alerted to the fact that Rushdie will be using the epic—a form with mythic, Homeric, and tragic connotations—as a parody of the form itself. Fielding's *Tom Jones*, of course, springs to mind as an earlier example of the comic epic, but Rushdie's use of the genre is more in the mode of romance or myth as described by Frye, although its "function" is different from that of the latter. That is, he is not using myth to "recreate some lost Eden," rather, he uses myth to "debunk" such a notion—in other words, to debunk itself.

*Midnight's Children,* Rushdie's second novel, is an epic that spans six decades and almost three generations of India's pre- and postcolonial twentieth-century history. It is an epic in the sense that it tries to describe, or "contain," an India whose stories are too innumerable to be contained. Throughout the book, the narrator hints at stories developing out of other stories in a never-ending cycle. For example, early on in the book the narrator states, "I paradoxically took my first tentative steps towards that involvement with mighty events and public lives from which I would never again be free . . . never [that is] . . . until the widow [Indira Gandhi, late Prime Minister of India]. . . ."[4] And so begins another story.

Thus, ends are contained in beginnings, beginnings in ends. And, because each end is the beginning of a new story, so the narrative must be circular, never-ending, an epic that must ultimately fail because no epic is large enough to contain all of the stories that are waiting to be told. But maybe that is what Rushdie intends, after all, for he is critical of the "dainty, delicate, dated" books written by countless Orientalists about a land that for Rushdie is "massive, elephantine" (Kaufman, 22) and consequently uncontainable in any one form. In fact, according to Keith Wilson:

> Basic to the conception of *Midnight's Children* is acceptance of the imperfection and partialness of the end product. The realities of public history or private experience are never reducible to the encompassing forms that the absolutist artist may wish to impose upon them. . . . The essential lifelessness of the objective and distanced ready-made-picture post cards—out of which Lifafa Das [one of the characters in *Midnight's Children*] attempts to make a

3. Michael T. Kaufman, "Author from Three Countries," *New York Times Book Review,* 13 November 1983, 22. All subsequent references to this work will be cited parenthetically in the text as Kaufman.
4. Salman Rushdie, *Midnight's Children* (1980; reprint, New York: Avon, 1982), 205. All subsequent references to this work will be cited parenthetically in the text as Rushdie, *MC.*

comprehensive yet box-enclosed world, stands as ironic comment on the worthlessness and inevitable failure of exercises in complete and contained mimesis.[5]

The epic, mythic form Rushdie uses ironically becomes, then, a "strategy of liberation"—but a "comic" one because the tragedy it masks is too painful to be otherwise expressed, though also a mythical and surreal one because realism, says Rushdie later on in *Shame*, "would break a writer's heart"; it would also be "an exercise in complete and contained mimesis" because of its emphasis on wholeness, and thus ultimately worthless.

*Midnight's Children* is an allegory of the history of modern India, which it chronicles through the magical lives of 1,001 children born within the country's first hour of independence from Great Britain on 17 August 1947. Saleem Sinai, the novel's protagonist-narrator, is one of two males born at the precise hour of India's independence—midnight—in a nursing home in Bombay. The reader learns later that he was switched with his other midnight twin, Shiva (who later becomes Saleem's formidable enemy), and brought up in an illustrious Muslim household, although he was, in reality, the illegitimate offspring of a Hindu street singer's wife and a departing British colonist. The novel begins at a point more than thirty years after the simultaneous births of Saleem and independent India. Awaiting a premature death in a pickle factory where he is employed, Saleem— prematurely aged, impotent, and mutilated by a personal history that parallels that of his country—tells his life story to Padma, an illiterate working girl who loves and looks after him. Saleem begins by relating thirty-two years of family history preceding his own arrival into the world, the tragic elements of this history unfolding from the very beginning, though told in a comic and mythic form that masks their painfulness.

Saleem begins by relating the tragedy of Aadam Aziz, his grandfather (who functions as a symbol of the colonized man), in comic, mythic, and surreal terms. The tragedy of Aadam Aziz was his loss of faith and self-identity on his return in 1915 to his native colonized India from the West. Having returned to the valley of his ancestors, Kashmir, Aadam Aziz tries to go back to the traditional customs. However, as he recites the prayer of his ancestral religion, Islam, he is barraged with memories of Heidelberg, where he had learned, along with medicine and politics, that "India—like

5. Keith Wilson, "*Midnight's Children* and Reader Responsibility," *Critical Quarterly* 26 (Autumn 1984): 25.

radium—had been 'discovered' by the Europeans" (Rushdie, *MC*, 6). As he kneels down, he recalls his friends Ilse-Oskar-Ingrid "mocking his prayer with their anti-ideologies" (5).

The description of Aadam Aziz, serious-faced but funny-nosed, bending down and being vengefully struck by a mere tussock of earth, is in the comic epic tradition: "Forward he bent, and the earth, prayer-mat covered, curved up toward him. And now it was the tussock's time . . . it smote him upon the point of the nose" (6). The tragic consequence of the accident—Aziz's loss of faith—is expressed in mythic and surreal terms:

> Three drops fell. There were rubies and diamonds . . . and my grandfather, lurching upright, made a resolve. . . . [He was] knocked forever into that middle place unable to worship a God in whose existence he could not wholly disbelieve. Permanent alteration: *a hole.* (6; emphasis added)

And so the very "real" pain of someone cut off from an authentic indigenous past—a past sensed solely as a property of its colonial masters—such pain at the loss of identity can be expressed only in comic, mythic, and surreal terms. A "whole" identity is replaced by a literal "hole," which is later transformed symbolically into a perforated sheet, by peeping through which Aadam Aziz falls in love—in order, perhaps, to fill up his own "hole." The perforated sheet functions as a discreet screen through which Aadam Aziz is allowed to observe only those parts of his female patients' bodies that require treatment. It is significant that Aziz never observes the "whole" of Naseem, and yet, by partially "piecing together" her various bodily parts in his mind, he falls in love with her: "So gradually Doctor Aziz came to have a picture in his mind, a badly-fitting collage of her severally-inspected parts. This phantasm of a partitioned woman began to haunt him, and not only in his dreams" (23).

Obviously, what is being implied here is that Dr. Aziz, himself a "fragmented" man, becomes obsessed with the woman whom he sees only in fragmented form, and in his desire to somehow unify these pieces, to possess the whole woman, he decides to marry her. Unfortunately, the hole is too insidious—it devours and destroys everyone it touches. Naseem, once she becomes Aadam Aziz's wife, can only internalize the hole and become as embittered and attenuated a person as her husband. Although her response to the loss of selfhood, to the absurdity of existence in a fragmented world, is very different from Aziz's—in that she tries to hang on to any and all traditions that can give her some sense of identity ("she lived within an invisible fortress of her own making, an iron-clad citadel of traditions and certainties" [41])—it is clear that she is in the same dilemma as her husband, as in fact is every character of the novel. As Saleem observes:

> I don't know how my grandmother came to adopt the term whatsitsname as her leitmotif, but as the years passed it invaded her sentences more and more often. I like to think of it as an unconscious cry for help . . . as a seriously meant question. Reverend Mother [Naseem's nickname] was giving us a hint that, for all her presence and bulk, she was adrift in the universe. She didn't know, you see, what it was called. (42)

Her increasing bitterness at what she feels is her husband's lack of adherence to traditions and customs makes her withdraw more and more completely from him, increasing their mutual alienation.

Such "unwholeness" and fragmentation of character and existence seems to be the fate of all the innumerable characters that people the pages of *Midnight's Children*. For instance, Saleem goes on to describe the fragmented lives of his two aunts and mother-to-be, his Uncle Hanif, and the poet Nadir Khan, who is forced to go underground, literally (Dr. Aziz offers him a hiding place in his cellar) because of his refusal to support the political fragmentation of India into India and Pakistan (another result of colonialism). Characters like Nadir Khan or Uncle Hanif or the street peepshow vendor Lifafa Das, who insist on denying the reality that life is, in fact, fragmented, by their attempts to somehow "unify" and "contain" reality through realistic and mythic strategies, are shown to be failures in one way or another. Nadir Khan remains an unknown poet and is impotent to boot. Uncle Hanif is so obsessed with achieving "perfection," "completeness," and "unity" in whatever he attempts that he can't even win a hand at cards:

> My uncle Hanif played rummy dedicatedly; but he was in the thrall of a curious obsession—namely, that he was determined never to lay down a hand until he completed a thirteen-card sequence in hearts. Always hearts; all the hearts, and nothing but hearts would do. In his quest for this unattainable perfection, my uncle would discard perfectly good threes-of-a-kind and whole sequences of

spades, clubs, diamonds, to the raucous amusement of his friends. (295)

Lifafa Das's desire to somehow show the "whole" world to his audience via his peep show becomes, ultimately, a ridiculous, because impossible, obsession. As Saleem observes:

> Lifafa Das had altered his cry. . . . "See the whole world, come see everything." The hyperbolic formula began, after a time, to prey upon his mind; more and more picture postcards went into his peepshow as he tried, desperately, to deliver what he promised, to put everything into his box. (I am suddenly reminded of Nadir Khan . . . is this an Indian disease, this urge to encapsulate the whole of reality? Worse: am I infected too?) (84)

The answer to Saleem Sinai's rhetorical question, "Am I infected too?" is, as stated at the beginning of this chapter, yes. However, by repeatedly showing the failure of all such acts that are aimed at trying to "encapsulate the whole of reality," the impossibility for an individual to achieve any kind of "whole" identity, existence, or relationship with another, Rushdie (through Saleem) is able to nullify such an urge. Thus, no "whole" relationships can emerge, so Rushdie seems to imply, in a land whose people are figuratively full of "holes."

Just as no "wholeness" seems possible for the characters of fiction, neither does there seem to be a possibility in the realm of fiction for a "whole" construct of narrative realism—one that can "contain" a unified "reality." As Rushdie admits in another interview, "One of the things that has happened in the twentieth century is a colossal fragmentation of reality."[6] Therefore, the mode or genre equal to dealing with the exigencies of political fragmentation must perforce be equally fragmented. In fact, the narrative must be a mishmash of conflicting genres and modes, a narrative in which the comic and the tragic, the real, the surreal, and the mythic all "defuse" one another, so no one genre can predominate and "unify" the others.

Rushdie's defusing of genres, then, is a "strategy of liberation." As Jameson explains in "Magical Narratives," "The relationship between genres may itself play a significant and functional role within the individual

---

6. "An Interview with Salman Rushdie," *Justice* 1 (May 1985), 15.

work itself . . . [thus] one mode can be used to de-fuse the other for an explicitly ideological purpose" (MN, 154).

The character of Tai the boat man (a person of some importance in Dr. Aziz's childhood and youth) is a figure conceived in both the mythic and the realist modes. In "reality" he is a "simple ferryman [who] despite all rumors of wealth, take[s] hay and goats and vegetables and wood across the lakes for cash" (10). At the same time, he is mythical in that "nobody could remember when Tai had been young. He had been plying the same boat, standing in the same hunched position, across the Dal and Nageen Lakes . . . forever" (9). The narrator tells us that "the boy Aadam, my grandfather-to-be, fell in love with the boatman Tai precisely because of the endless verbiage which made others think him cracked. *It was magical talk*" (Rushdie, *MC*, 10; emphasis added)

The "magical" talk, however, foretells events that turn out to be only too historically "real" and painful to be consigned to an imaginary realm. Dr. Aziz, adult, red-bearded, "slanting towards the future," remembers the day he, as a young boy, asked Tai the "unaskable" question, "But how old are you really, Taiji?" To which he received the mythical response, "I have watched mountains being born; I have watched Emperors die. I saw that Isa, that Christ, when he came to Kashmir" (11). Of course, the reference to Christ should alert the reader that this is a possible reference to Christian missionaries—the first wave of colonizers. The rest of the description, followed by the narrator's comments, only serves to confirm this suspicion. So, Tai continues:

> Yara, you should have seen that Isa when he came, beard down to his balls, bald as an egg on his head. And what an appetite! Such a hunger, I would catch my ears in fright. Saint or devil, I swear he could eat a whole kid in one go. And so what? I told him eat, *fill your hole*. (11; emphasis added)

Christ's "hole-of-hunger," of course, prefigures the hole-that-must-be-filled at the center of both the colonizer's and the colonized's being. At the end of this little story, the narrator interpolates: "In the brandy bottle of the boatman Tai I see, foretold, my own father's possession by djinns . . . *and there will be another bald foreigner*" (12; emphasis added)

The "other bald foreigner" turns out to be Methwold, symbol of the colonizer and of his ominous "Tick-Tock," the "real" father of the narrator Saleem. At the end of book 1, the reader learns that Saleem is the son of

Methwold, departing British colonist, and Vanita, the Indian wife of a poor Indian accordionist and singer named Wee Willie Winkie. Saleem, who is thus conceived in an unholy alliance between colonizer and colonized and born on the night of India's independence, can only live out the most schizophrenic of existences, having been literally and figuratively disfigured by the awful ravages of history. As he himself says, "I was not a beautiful baby. Baby snaps reveal that my large moon-face was too large; too perfectly round. . . . Fair skin curved across my features—but birthmarks disfigured it; *dark stains spread down my western hairline, a dark patch colored my eastern ear*" (144). It should be clear from the foregoing description that the "disfiguring birthmarks" on Saleem's face are a symbol of his politically fragmented heritage. As the turbulent history of postindependence, postpartition India unfolds, so the visage and psyche of Saleem Sinai become more and more battered and disfigured.

Saleem witnesses the language riots of Bombay in 1956; in West Pakistan he sees the awful effects of the two Indo-Pakistan wars of 1965 and 1971 on the psyches of the local population. The latter war proves so devastating that Saleem consciously secedes from history by developing amnesia, thus paralleling the secession of East from West Pakistan, which occurred as a result of this war.

Amnesia, like myth, serves to protect the narrator from facing up to the cruel reality of history. When history becomes too painful to bear, a desire to escape it through some means is only natural. As Saleem says, "What I hope to immortalize in pickles as well as words: that condition of the spirit in which the consequences of acceptance could not be denied, in which an overdose of reality gave birth to a miasmic longing for flight into the safety of dreams" (431). And it is fortunate indeed that Saleem, victim of history, has been endowed with the mythical, magical powers that have been the birthright of all the children born on the midnight of independence. It is the exercise of these powers, as well as communication with his other "midnight siblings," that helps relieve some of the burdens Saleem has to bear in "real" life.

The reference to "pickles" is also important here, for Rushdie constantly refers to the "pickling," or "chutnification," of history as one of the processes whereby the painfulness of history can be transmuted into something else, thus making it bearable. In other words, "pickling" becomes a metaphor for the act of writing itself, and according to Rushdie's theory of narrative, there can be no complete or perfect version of history, because facts are inevitably distorted, mythified, changed in the course of writing; therefore, no narrative can presume to contain, or encapsulate, the whole of reality.

That the narrator waits out the end of his days in a pickle factory signifies that he has at least learned to face up to the imperfection of his own art. And of course, the acknowledgment of the imperfection of art is itself a refutation of all those Orientalist texts that seek to contain other peoples and cultures:

> Every pickle-jar . . . contains . . . the most exalted of possibilities: the feasibility of the chutnification of history; the grand hope of the pickling of time! Tonight, by screwing the lid firmly onto a jar bearing the legend Special Formula No. 30: "Abracadabra," I reach the end of my long-winded autobiography; in words and pickles, I have immortalized my memories, although distortions are inevitable in both methods. We must live, I'm afraid, with the shadows of imperfection. (548)

The real pain of history, then, can only be dealt with in mythical, magical fashion—realism must be diluted by myth. But despite the attractiveness of the mythic mode, myth itself is ultimately no solution and can never replace history. Therefore it, too, must be defused, debunked. Thus, Saleem first receives knowledge of his magical powers while hidden in, of all places, a washing chest! On the one hand, it is of course appropriate that Saleem should receive an inkling of his magical powers in a place that symbolizes for him a mythic retreat from reality and history, a "place which civilization has put outside itself, beyond the pale; this makes it the finest of hiding-places. In the washing-chest I was . . . safe from all pressures *concealed from the demands of parents and history*" (184; emphasis added). On the other hand, that the "mythic" retreat itself should be a washing chest is a rather ludicrous notion. The reader is forced to ask at this point whether magic and myth born in a basket of dirty laundry is going to have much potency. The reader is further confirmed in this skepticism when the narrator says that the way in which he is able to contact the other "magical" children of independence is by becoming a sort of all-India radio! By insisting, too emphatically, that "it is entirely without a sense of shame [that I reiterate] my unbelievable claim: after a curious accident in a washing-chest, I became a sort of a radio" (197)— Rushdie in fact underscores the rather shameful ludicrousness of such a "claim." By disappointing the reader, who has been led to expect a truly magical, mythological reunion of the children of midnight, Rushdie is, in a sense, using myth to debunk itself. Clearly, myth is an inadequate and even foolish response, so Rushdie seems to be asserting, to the very complex reality of postcolonial independence.

Any doubts left about Rushdie's ideological stance in *Midnight's Children* should be put to rest by the conclusion of the novel. The children of independence, adults by now, are literally and figuratively sterilized by the "widow" (Indira Gandhi) during the Emergency period (which followed the 1974 elections in which she and her party lost)—obviously one of the darkest periods (for Rushdie) in postindependence India. As Saleem puts it, in his uniquely surreal style:

> Influence of hair-styles on the course of history: there's another ticklish business . . . if the Mother of the Nation had had a coiffure of uniform pigment, the Emergency she spawned might easily have lacked a darker side. But she had white hair on one side and black on the other; the Emergency too had a white part—public, visible . . . a matter for historians—and a black part which, being secret macabre untold, must be a matter for us. (501)

The fact that their magical powers can do nothing to save the "children" from such a horrendous end (just as the actual people forcefully sterilized and otherwise debilitated during the Emergency could not be saved) points directly to their fallibility and to the fallibility of a response that mythicizes some kind of magical, romantic retreat from history. In the end, says Rushdie, we have to accept the burden of history, no matter how painful the past and present, or how sterile the future may appear. That the future of postcolonial India and Pakistan does indeed appear bleak to Rushdie is born out by the final events of the book.

Saleem's hope for some kind of reconciliation with his midnight twin, Shiva, who, as noted earlier, was his simultaneous birthmate, is completely shattered. For Shiva, having grown up with bitterness and hatred for Saleem (because of the latter's good fortune in being placed in a well-to-do family that Shiva realizes was his birthright), has no wish to be reconciled with the latter. On the contrary, Shiva, now a major in Indira Gandhi's army and a righthand man of hers, becomes, to Saleem and the reader's horror, the instrument of Saleem's destruction (he is responsible for carrying out Indira's orders of sterilization). If Saleem and Shiva are viewed as the two halves of India partitioned at birth (independence), then it is quite clear that Rushdie sees no hope for friendship or reconciliation between these two countries. Neither does Rushdie see any hopeful future for the new generation that is born in India and Pakistan to take over from the bruised and battered generation of Saleem Sinai and his midnight siblings. The child born of Shiva's union with Parvati (another of the magical children of midnight) and brought up, in a continuing paradox, by Saleem (who has married Parvati), is described in terms that recall Oskar, the arrested child-hero of Gunter Grass's *Tin Drum:*

> Aadam Sinai was in many respects the exact opposite of Saleem. I, at my beginning, grew, with vertiginous speed; Aadam, wrestling with the serpents of disease, scarcely grew at all. . . . And while Saleem had been so determined to absorb the universe that he had been, for a time, unable to blink, *Aadam preferred to keep his eyes firmly closed.* (507; emphasis added)

The optimism that had marked at least the beginning to Saleem Sinai's life is totally denied to Aadam, his "son." There seems to be no possibility for optimism in the cruelly ravaged world that is being passed on by Saleem's generation to the next. The novel ends then, with the narrator apologizing to the children of the next generation for his and his generation's failure to pass on to them a less painful heritage. Listening to his "son" formulate his very first words, Saleem is tempted to hope that the solution of myth and magic works for his son's generation:

> And Aadam, very carefully: "Abba." Father. He is calling me father. But no, he has not finished, there is strain on his face, and finally my son, who will have to be a magician to cope with the world I'm leaving him, completes his awesome first word: ". . . cadabba." (547)

Saleem's hope is short-lived, however, for he realizes immediately that such a magical incantation is powerless to change reality: "Abracadabra! But nothing happens, we do not turn into toads, angels do not fly in through the window: the lad is just flexing his muscles. I shall not see his miracles" (547). And indeed, Saleem will not see these miracles because, in fact, they will not happen.

So, in the case of Rushdie's narrative, ideology gives rise to a peculiar use of genre, in which each genre defuses the other, and the mythic/

romance mode defuses, or debunks, itself. Rushdie's use of myth liberates his people from Western hegemonic strategies of containment; at the same time, by using the comic/surreal mode to defuse myth, Rushdie is able to avoid historical petrification.

This debunking of the mythic mode is continued by Rushdie in his third novel, *Shame* (1983), which

> blends history, myth, politics and fantasy in a novel at once serious and comic. "A sort of modern fairy tale," describes the author, "the novel is set in a country that is not Pakistan, or not quite," and it explores such issues as the uses and abuses of power and the relationship between shame and violence. [7]

Describing a "not-quite Pakistan" thirty-seven years after its independence from colonial rule, Rushdie sees it still caught up in the subject-object dialectic imposed on Third World people by a Manichean imperialism.

Pakistani people, according to him, still view themselves as objects because they have been unable to shake off the sense of shame and denigration heaped on them during colonial rule. This sense of shame arising out of one's "quasi-ontological experience of objectness" (Fanon, 110) results ultimately in its converse: shamelessness. "Humiliate people long enough," writes Rushdie "and a wildness bursts out of them."[8] This cycle of shame leading to shamelessness, which was set in motion because of the humiliation experienced by the natives under colonial rule, exists, in Rushdie's opinion, to the present day (chapter 7). It is this vicious cycle, which reinforces our "objectness" (because we see others and ourselves only from the perspective of shame), that Rushdie feels must be destroyed if colonized peoples are ever to succeed in throwing off the colonial heritage.

In *Shame* Rushdie uses myth to point out that the natives were never anything other than objects in their own esteem and never will be unless they step outside the circle of shame; outside the subject-object dialectic. The novel, which spans three generations, centers on the lives and families of two men—Raza Hyder, a celebrated general, and Iskander Harappa, a millionaire playboy, both of whom are based on real-life characters:

---

7. Hal May, ed., *Contemporary Authors* (Detroit: Gale Research, 1984), 3:413.

8. Salman Rushdie, *Shame* (London: Jonathan Cape, 1983), 117. All subsequent references to this work will be cited parenthetically in the text as Rushdie, *Shame*.

Pakistani President Zia-ul-Haq, and former Prime Minister Zulfikar Ali Bhutto. Their life-and-death struggle, played out against the political backdrop of their country, is based on recent Pakistani history—Bhutto was deposed by Zia in a military coup in 1977 and ultimately executed.

Because, in Rushdie's view, the sense of "objectness" is so deeply embedded in the people of Pakistan, it has led to an extremely shameful political and social history for the country (he obviously views Bhutto's execution and the establishment of a military dictatorship with deep abhorrence). The result is that such a painful history can be discussed only through a "fairy tale," or mythic/romance mode. Realism under such conditions, says Rushdie, "would break a writer's heart" (*Shame*, 70).

Rushdie begins his "myth" by describing the mythic hero, Omar Khayyam, as a "peripheral hero," one who was afflicted from his earliest days by "a fear that he was living at the edge of the world, so close that he might fall off at any moment." He experiences such a sense of marginality, of "objectness," because he was conceived out of his mother's sense of "objectness," a sense shared by the family in their cloistered world, significantly situated right across from the Palladian Hotel, where the "suited and booted" imperial "angrez" (British) officers gathered nightly to dance but from which they (by virtue of being natives) were naturally excluded. So, after the death of their father, they invite the white officers to a gala celebration, and then choose one of them to conceive a baby by!

Omar Khayyam, born out of three sisters' "shameless" gesture of defiance against the "shameful" existence they had been forced to lead, ends up, however, being an object himself, entrapped in a world that is itself a dead object because created in reaction against the subject-object dialectic. In other words, despite, or perhaps because of, their shameless reaction, the sisters are unable to transcend their "objectness":

> Omar Khayyam passed twelve long years, the most crucial years of his development, trapped inside that reclusive mansion, *that third world that was neither material nor spiritual, but a sort of concentrated decrepitude made up of decomposing remnants.* . . . The finely-calculated gesture with which his three mothers had sealed themselves off from the world had created *a sweltering entropical zone in which, despite all the rotting down of the past, nothing new seemed capable of growth.* (30; emphasis added)

This decaying "third world" of his mothers' mansion becomes, then, the paradigm for all Third World countries, which, as Rushdie implies, have become enmeshed in an endless objecthood of shame and shamelessness.

The three mothers also come to symbolize the three countries that ultimately came into being after India's independence from Britain: India, Pakistan, and Bangladesh (the latter at first the eastern wing of Pakistan). And from Rushdie's description of the relationship between Omar Khayyam and his three mothers, it becomes clear that the relationship is an unhealthy one, for the three women are portrayed as close-minded, dictatorial, and repressive; their treatment of Omar turns him into the shameless, marginalized, circumscribed creature that he is:

> He was not free. His roving freedom-of-the-house was only the pseudo-liberty of a zoo animal and his mothers were his loving, caring Keepers. His three mothers; who else implanted in his heart the conviction of being a sidelines personality, a watcher from the wings of his own life? He watched them for a dozen years, and yes, it must be said, hated them for their closeness . . . [their] three-in-oneness . . . [which] redoubled that sense of exclusion of being, in the midst of objects, out of things. (35)

As soon as he gets the chance, then, Omar Khayyam Shakil makes his escape from the cloistered world of his mothers, from the very town of Q itself, where he had lived for twelve years. However, he takes with him the legacy of his mothers: shamelessness. For knowing that in the outside world Omar would become the object of others' hostility (on account of his "shameful" origins), the mothers have made sure to wipe out any tendencies toward shame and honor in their son:

> It was not only shame that his mothers forbade Omar Khayyam to feel: but also embarrassment, discomfiture, decency, modesty, shyness: the sense of having an ordained place in the world. . . . Can it be doubted that Omar Khayyam . . . having been barred from feeling shame . . . at an early age, continued to be affected by that remarkable ban throughout his later years, yes, long after his escape from his mothers' zone of influence? (39)

Thus, Omar Khayyam becomes one of those characters in the book who behaves shamelessly toward others, engendering a shamefulness in them, which shame then ultimately turns on its head and vents itself on the perpetrators of shameful humiliation through acts of shameless violence.

The clearest example of this dialectical process in the book is seen in the development of the character of Sufiya Zenobia, retarded daughter of Raza Hyder. From the moment of her birth, she is the object of her parents', especially her father's, shame. For in wanting a son, Raza Hyder shamelessly refused to believe that the female child could be his, thus engendering a deep sense of shame in the daughter for not being what she is not:

> And at this point . . . when her parents had to admit the immutability of her gender, to submit, as faith demands, to God; at this very instant the extremely new and soporific being in Raza's arms began—it's true!—to blush. . . . *Then, even then, she was too easily shamed.* (90; emphasis added)

As if to confirm her own status as a shameful "object," Sufiya Zenobia, two months after her birth, develops a brain fever that turns her into an idiot—a literal "object." Her mother, Bilquis Hyder, seals her idiot daughter's fate as an object of shame when she admits to her friend, Rani Harappa (Iskander Harappa's wife), that she feels her daughter to be

> a judgment, what else? He [Raza] wanted a hero of a son: I gave him an idiot female instead. That's the truth, excuse me, I cant help it. Rani, a simpleton, a goof! Nothing upstairs. . . . Empty in the breadbin. To be done? But darling, there is nothing. That birdbrain, that mouse! I must accept it: *she is my shame.* (101; emphasis added)

That Omar Khayyam, supreme avatar of shamelessness, should end up getting married to Sufiya Zenobia, the incarnation of shame, is then not only appropriate, but necessary. For, it is just this combination of shame and shamelessness that will ultimately result in the violence that will put an end to the shamefully "objectified" Third World societies and, in this specific case, the repressive, male-dominated society of Pakistan. As Rushdie explains in book 3 of *Shame*, "Between shame and shamelessness lies the axis upon which we turn."

It is to be hoped that after the destruction of a Third World obsessed with its shameful objectness, there will be created a world that does not have to be defined through a Manichean subject-object dialectic. This is what Frantz Fanon hoped for also. Thus, once again, Rushdie has succeeded in using the mode of myth to destroy itself, in order to prove his point that ultimately we have to take responsibility for our history, that we cannot hide behind any myths, for those too will destroy us in the end.

In his novel *The Satanic Verses* Rushdie continues to promulgate his theory of generic/ideological destruction as a prerequisite to renewal. The difference here is that Rushdie has chosen to draw religion into the orbit of his critique, as yet another insidious strategy of containment. Religion has been a colonizing power too, one that has transformed men's thinking capabilities into slavish mentalities. This power to control men religion shares with the rulers of empire, and it is toward the destruction of just such power that the thrust of Rushdie's fictive strategies is aimed.

The complicated, somewhat uneven action of the novel revolves around the bizarre transformation of two men who are the sole survivors of an airplane crash, Gibreel Farishta and Saladdin Chamcha, who miraculously escape the disaster by falling leisurely through the atmosphere and landing on the shores of England, only to discover later that one of them has acquired a halo (Gibreel), while the other has sprouted horns, hair, and hooves! The classic struggle between good and evil then begins, since Farishta and Chamcha, once friends and compatriots (both are Indian by birth), now find themselves on opposing sides of the fence. The crucial question, however, is, Which is which? For from the beginning, Farishta (a Persian word meaning "angel") behaves far from angelically: he watches silently as the police come into the house where the two men are recovering from their amazing experience and proceed to whisk his "friend" off to jail. To ensure that the boundaries between the reader's concepts of good and evil remain fuzzy, Rushdie provides a fabulous description of the two men intertwined during the course of their fall from the heavens:

> Hybrid cloud-creatures pressed in upon them, gigantic flowers with human breasts dangling from fleshy stalks, winged cats, centaurs, and Chamcha in his semi-consciousness was seized by the notion that he too had acquired the quality of cloudiness, becoming metamorphic, hybrid, as if he were growing into the person (Gibreel) whose head nestled now between his legs and whose legs were wrapped around his long, patrician neck.[9]

9. Salman Rushdie, *The Satanic Verses* (London: Viking, 1988), 7. All subsequent references to this work will be cited parenthetically in the text as Rushdie, *SV*.

The quality of being "metamorphic," a "hybrid," is one that the "real" Saladdin Chamcha is very familiar with: as an Indian-born immigrant who desperately wants to be, to become, an Englishman, Chamcha smacks of the "brown Englishman," an outsider more English than the English, the Fanonian native who abandons his own race in favor of that of his oppressors. Forever metamorphosing, he remains a hybrid: neither this nor that, neither here nor there. Yet, he doesn't realize this: having alienated, and become alienated from, his past, his country, and his father, Chamcha (from an Urdu word meaning, literally, "spoon," but connoting a quality of bootlicking) quite honestly feels that he has succeeded in transforming himself from low-down Indian to high-brow Englishman. His humiliating treatment at the hands of the British police and immigration officers, then, comes as a terrible shock to him. As he is being unceremoniously dragged off by the police, who have tracked the "illegal immigrants" to one Rosa Diamond's house, Chamcha tries hard to convince them of his "British-ness," but to no avail:

> The laughing policemen got in the way, you've got to believe me, I'm a British, he was saying, with right of abode, too, but when he couldn't produce a passport . . . they began to weep with mirth. . . . Of course, don't tell me, they giggled, they fell out of your jacket during your tumble, or did the mermaids pick your pocket in the sea? Rosa couldn't see, in that laughter-heaving surge of men and dogs, what uniformed arms might be doing to Chamcha's arms, or fists to his stomach, or boots to his shins; nor could she be sure if it was his voice crying out or just the howling of the dogs. But she did, finally, hear his voice rise in a last, despairing shout: "Don't any of you watch T.V.? Don't you see? I'm Maxim. Maxim Alien." "So you are," said the popeyed officer. "And I am Kermit the Frog." (Rushdie, *SV*, 140)

Chamcha's desperate cry—"Don't you see? I'm . . . Maxim Alien"—is a reference to his former job as an actor and voice artist on British television, a reference to his authenticity as a citizen "belonging" to Britain. The irony, of course, is that even then he had played an alien, and his supplication to the police and immigration officers now hauling him off only serves to further "alienate" him from them.

Just as this episode illustrates the inhumanity of containment, by showing how falsely we judge others when we categorize them in terms of us and them, self and other, British and Indian, so the rest of the book exposes the dangers of putting vast, complex concepts such as good and evil into neat boxes, frames, categories.

Enter genus: religion; species: Islam. A central question asked frequently in the book is raised for the first time by the female "terrorist" aboard the jetliner that crashed and thus provided the occasion for the novel. She addresses the frightened passengers thus:

> "When a great idea comes into the world, a great cause, certain crucial questions are asked of it," she murmured. "History asks us: what manner of cause are we? Are we uncompromising, absolute, strong, or will we show ourselves to be time-servers, who compromise, trim and yield?" Her body had provided her answer.

Chamcha's response to this question and to the woman's answer is, I think, Rushdie's own response to the issue of what is good and what is evil within the context of Islam, which is the same issue posed by all religions and world systems generally: "The enclosed, boiling circumstances of his captivity . . . made Saladdin Chamcha want to argue with the woman, unbendingness can also be monomania, he wanted to say, it can be tyranny, and also it can be brittle, whereas what is flexible can also be humane, and strong enough to last. (81)

The controversy over good and evil in Islam begins with the fundamental question of faith: Muslims are asked unconditionally to accept the Quran as the revealed Word of God, the Archangel Gabriel (Gibreel in Arabic) as the instrument of revelation, and Mohammad as the holy prophet unto whom the Book was revealed, in an unbroken and untrammeled continuum.

To accept these tenets on faith and without doubt is, clearly, "good" within the framework of the Islamic belief system. What would be "evil" in this value system would be to raise questions or cast aspersions on the authenticity of these tenets of orthodox Islam. What Rushdie sets out to do in the sections of the novel entitled "Mahound" and "Return to Jahilia" is, then, clearly "evil" within this religious framework. Undoubtedly, Rushdie sets out to debunk the myths of Islam: not only are the epic revelations of the Archangel Gabriel reduced to the banal level of hallucinations experienced by an aging movie star on the brink of insanity, but the prophet Mohammad himself is now a Mahound: a devilish creature.

Part of what makes Mahound devilish is what one of his former disciples, Salman the Scribe, refers to as the "convenience" of his revelations, as well as the compromising nature of his beliefs, his "idea." For instance, when Mahound, businessman-turned-prophet of Jahilia, is approached, in the early founding years of his religion, by the idolatrous Grandee of Jahilia, Abu Simbel, who promises him converts in return for compromise, Mahound compromises. His three faithful disciples, of whom Salman the Scribe is one at this point, are angered and shocked by their prophet's decision to compromise on what they consider to be a fundamental tenet of belief: the monotheistic nature of God. The exchange between disciples and prophet illustrates the pragmatic motives of Mahound:

> "Or it's a different trap," Salman persists. "How long have we been reciting the creed you brought us? There is no god but God. What are we if we abandon it now? This weakens us, renders us absurd. We cease to be dangerous. Nobody will ever take us seriously again."
>
> Mahound laughs, genuinely amused. "Maybe you haven't been here long enough," he says kindly. "Haven't you noticed? The people do not take us seriously. Never more than fifty in the audience when I speak, and half of those are tourists. Don't you read the lampoons that Baal pins up all over town? . . . They mock us everywhere, and you call us dangerous," he cried. (106)

The conflicting approaches of the disciples and their prophet to the solution of a problem at hand illustrate the tensions implicit in the question, "What kind of idea are you?" raised first by the terrorist woman, later by Mahound himself, and in another episode by another "seer," a woman named Ayesha. For an idea to be "true," to be worthy of belief, does it necessarily have to be unyielding, fixed, beyond compromise? That certainly seems to be the answer the disciples want to hear. But Mahound/Mohammad holds to a different viewpoint. "Sometimes," he says, "I think I must make it easier for the people to believe" (106).

What he means, of course, is that in the face of numerous obstacles to the spread of his faith, including a strong unwillingness of a polytheistic society to accept, overnight, a monotheistic religion, why not compromise a little? What harm could it do to accept the Grandee's offer of a wholesale conversion of Jahilia in return for a declaration from the prophet that the three favorite goddesses of Jahilia be granted angelic status in Islam? As Mahound asks himself in a tormenting bout of self-questioning: "The souls of the city, of the world, surely they are worth three angels? Is Allah so unbending that he will not embrace three more to save the human race?" (111).

Needless to say, Mahound rules in favor of inclusion, rather than exclusion. However, this time his gamble does not pay off. He discovers, shortly, that he's "been had" by Simbel and his wife, Hind. As Hind puts it to him, "If you are for Allah, I am for Al-Lat. And she doesn't believe your God when he recognizes her. Her opposition to him is implacable, irrevocable, engulfing" (121).[10] So much for compromise. However, Mahound, ever the pragmatist, does manage to win back the trust and favor of his disciples by now declaring his previous declaration null and void: the work of Shaitan, verses dictated by Satan, not God.

The defection of Salman the Scribe occurs when the latter, as official scribe of the Book, realizes the convenient nature of some of the revelations. He begins to notice "how useful and well-timed the angel's revelations tended to be, so that when the faithful were disputing Mahound's views on any subject . . . the angel would turn up with an answer, and he always supported Mahound" (364). This, coupled with the fact that Mahound doesn't recognize (at least, not initially) Salman's alterations of the holy text, drives Rushdie's namesake into the camp of the nonbelievers.

Is this "blaspheming" of the central character and tenets of Islam meant to ridicule both? Should such an impulse then be seen as evil? The novelistic context would seem to suggest otherwise. For Chamcha's response to the question "What manner of cause are we?" is in favor of compromise: "Unbendingness . . . can be tyranny, . . . whereas what is flexible can also be humane, and strong enough to last" (81). Clearly, Mahound's flexibility, his willingness to compromise and to mold his needs to the situation and vice versa, as well as his demonstration of managerial skills in converting, then keeping, his sheep within the fold, attest to the strength and wisdom of a man, through whose efforts a major world religion has endured.

What emerges from the analysis so far, then, is that form and content, mirroring each other, bespeak a need for mixing up, for shattering, all neat divisions and binary oppositions such as those which exist between formal concepts like realism or myth, or between moral ones like good or evil (which have engendered the Manichean oppositions of colonialism: black and white, self and other, us and them, insider and outsider). In other words, the point of view that emerges is not anti-Islam but anticlosure,

10. For an analysis of *The Satanic Verses* that discusses it as an attempt to "locate an idiom for the feminization of Islam," see Sara Suleri, *The Rhetoric of English India* (Chicago: University of Chicago Press, 1992), 198–206.

opposed, in principle, to any dualistic, fixed way of looking at things. Framed in such a way, Rushdie's impulse toward blasphemy becomes really an impulse toward regeneration: renewal born of a destruction of old, fixed ways of seeing and understanding. The evil of blasphemy thus becomes a virtue, as lines are blurred between the sacred and the profane, between reality and illusion. Is what we are reading an enactment of "real" events from Islamic history, or merely the delusions of a crazed, aging Indian movie star? Is Mahound prophet or devil, man or saint? Must we always think in terms of such binary oppositions?

What Rushdie goes on to say in the rest of this hodgepodge, mixed-up, nonlinear novel is that it is precisely this impulse to categorize—to divide, classify, and "contain" the world, its inhabitants, and its events into a system of binary opposites—that has led to misunderstanding, exploitation, hatred, and violence. The conflict that both Chamcha and Farishta find themselves embroiled in is not just their private quarrel—a betrayal of the former by the latter, which Chamcha later tries to avenge—but a conflict between the forces of good and evil in the world; it is a universal conflict of epic dimensions that, in the world of the novel, takes the shape of an apocalyptic battle between the colonizers and the colonized, those who "belong" and those who do not, between the white Englishmen and the intruding, black immigrants.

When Chamcha is finally released from the custody of the British police and immigration officials, he finds refuge in, of all places, an Indian restaurateur's boardinghouse. The very culture and people he has spent his entire life running away from turn out, at his moment of need, to succor him. As Abu Sufyan, owner of the establishment, puts it, "Where else would you go to heal your disfigurements and recover your normal health? Where else but here, with us, among your own people, your own kind?" To which, Chamcha, alone in the attic room that becomes his abode, enunciates the following ungrateful response: "I'm not your kind. . . . You're not my people. I've spent half my life trying to get away from you" (253). Yet, if Chamcha's response is ungracious and alienated, surely the terms of Sufyan's query are just as unsettling. Within the Rushdian universe, there is surely something unhealthy, something destructive and violent, that leads to and will ensue from the conflict created by categorizing, by dividing the world into opposing camps: us against them, black against white, believers against nonbelievers, good against evil.

And this is precisely what happens.

In the chapter "The Angel Azraeel," Rushdie presents a surrealistic and horrifying picture of race relations in Great Britain. Brickhall, known for its concentration of Asian and black residents, becomes the scene of an apocalyptic "meltdown" in the wake of the race riots that break out following the death of one Dr. Uhuru Simba in jail. Dr. Simba, revolutionary symbol of the Brickhall "immigrants," conveyer of their grievances and demands for better treatment to the "powers that be," is unjustly accused of being a murderer and, while in jail, dies mysteriously. The bizarre "official" explanation of his death, that he died because of a nightmare, does not wash down well with his people. In fact, the whole atmosphere of Brickhall becomes increasingly grim, one in which a violent confrontation becomes inevitable:

> "I want you to understand," Mrs. Roberts [Simba's mother] declaimed to the sizeable crowd that had gathered angrily outside the High Street police station, "that these people are gambling with our lives. They are laying odds on our chances of survival. I want you all to consider what that means in terms of their respect for us as human beings." And Hanif Johnson, as Uhuru Simba's solicitor, added . . . that in an age of extreme overcrowding in the country's lock-ups it was unusual, to say the least, that the other bunk should have been unoccupied, ensuring that there were no witnesses . . . and that a nightmare was by no means the only possible explanation for the screams of a black man in the hands of custodial authority. In his concluding remarks, afterwards termed "inflammatory and unprofessional" by Inspector Kinch, Hanif linked the community liaison officer's words to those of the notorious racist John Kingsley Read, who had once responded to the news of a black man's death with the slogan, "One down; one million to go." The crowd murmured and bubbled. . . . "Stay hot," Simba's brother Walcott cried out to the assembly. "Don't anybody cool off. Maintain your rage." (450)

Walcott's advice, born of rage, impotence, and a desire for revenge against centuries-old discrimination, is nevertheless unsound. For hatred, once again a result of categorizing and containing others in order to maintain power over them, leads to a violence that cannot be similarly contained. The dream, the desire for revenge, must ultimately turn into a nightmare that destroys not just the object but the creating subject of hatred as well. And it is only fitting that the role of destroyer should be assigned to the "angel" of the novel, Gibreel Farishta, who goes out to purchase Azraeel, the legendary trumpet of Destruction of the World, for this express purpose. The necessity of the "cleansing mission" of destruction slowly becomes clear to Gibreel, and so to the reader:

> He is the Archangel Gibreel, the angel of Recitation, with the power of revelation in his hands. He can reach into the breasts of men and women, pick out the desires of their inmost hearts, and make them real. He is the quencher of desires, the slaker of lusts, the fulfiller of dreams. . . . What desires, what imperatives are in the midnight air? He breathes them in. And nods, so be it, yes. Let it be fire. . . . Fire, falling fire. "This is the judgment of God in his wrath," Gibreel Farishta proclaims to the riotous night, "that men be granted their hearts' desires, and that they be by them consumed." (461)

Clearly, hatred and anger, however righteous, can only lead to violence that in the end is self-destructive. Yet Rushdie seems to be resigned to the fact that this is a necessary stage in the Manichean opposition created by colonialism. Such destruction is, in fact, a tactic necessary to purge the world of the subject-object dialectic between colonizer and colonized. And this is what Farishta too, in his role as destroyer, realizes: "This is a city that has cleansed itself in flame, purged itself by burning down to the ground" (461).

In the ensuing debacle, the fire-breathing Gibreel destroys Brickhall with a vengeance. Black, brown, or white; male or female; young or old: none escapes his vengeful fury. Except Saladdin Chamcha and some young Asians he rescues, who have "assimilated" to the degree that they do not retain the old, oppositional structures of belief. In a sense, Saladdin too is spared in order to be given a chance to "begin anew." At the end of the novel, he returns to India to patch things up with his father, whom he hasn't seen, spoken to, or written in decades. In his refusal to have anything to do with his "past," Chamcha too has been guilty of thinking in terms of oppositions, of categorizing and labeling all that is English as good and worth striving after, and all that is Indian (including a demanding father) as bad and certainly unworthy of his attention and acknowledgment. By showing a Saladdin who can learn and adapt, who can go from being a Salahuddin to a Saladdin and then back to a Salahuddin again, Rushdie is once again pointing to the power of endurance inherent in flexibility; whereas an inflexible temperament, a monomaniacal fixation on any idea, is a sure recipe for madness and death.

And this is precisely what happens to the "good guy," Gibreel Farishta, who cannot shake off his obsession with retribution. He is stuck forever, it would seem, in his role as avenger, and it is this role that causes him to kill his mistress and a friend in a fit of jealousy: "I am the angel the god damned angel of god and these days it's the avenging angel Gibreel the avenger always vengeance why . . ." (544). There is no answer to the "why" except that in the end we become the roles we play, we become as contained and boxed in as the frameworks that engulf us, if we accept the conventions of definitions. Gibreel ends up destroying himself, because finally he cannot live according to the definition of himself as an angel. He tells Chamcha at the very end:

> "I told you a long time back," Gibreel Farishta quietly said, "that if I thought the sickness [of being, or thinking he is, an angel] would never leave me, that it would always return, I would not be able to bear up to it." Then, very quickly, before Salahuddin could move a finger, Gibreel put the barrel of the gun into his own mouth; and pulled the trigger; and was free. (546)

In choosing to let the "angelic" Farishta die and the "satanic" Chamcha live, Rushdie is surely challenging the conventional definitions of good and evil. He has done this, of course, throughout the novel, and ends on a note that suggests that only those who are flexible survive (hence Chamcha over Farishta, Mahound over Ayesha) and also that all old, inflexible ideologies and definitions of the world and of its peoples must die or be destroyed if there is to be any hope of renewal, of survival. This is what Chamcha himself acknowledges, as he stands alone, surveying the scenes of his childhood, of the past:

> He stood at the window of his childhood and looked out at the Arabian Sea . . . moonlight . . . created the illusion of a silver pathway, like a parting in the water's shining hair, like a road to miraculous lands. He shook his head; could no longer believe in fairy-tales. Childhood was over, and the view from this window was no more than an old and sentimental echo. To the devil with it! Let the bulldozers come. If the old refused to die, the new could not be born. (547)

All old ideologies, old forms, old oppositional structures, and rigid definitions must be done away with before regeneration can occur. This has been Rushdie's message, both in content and in form, throughout his oeuvre. It is only in *The Satanic Verses,* his most complex novel to date, however, that Rushdie draws explicit parallels between religion and colonialism as hegemonic strategies of containment. Whereas the latter has tried to contain people within racial and geographical boundaries and definitions, religion has tried to delimit and contain man's intellectual territory. Both kinds of containment are reprehensible to Rushdie, and the only way out he sees is through destruction and "blasphemy."

Rushdie's latest novel to date, *Haroun and the Sea of Stories,* published a year after the death sentence of Iran's government against him forced him to go into hiding, appears, in its celebration of the genre of myth (which takes the shape of a fairy tale), to offer an antidote (albeit a somewhat belated one) to the debunking of myth that had been Rushdie's primary fictive strategy thus far. In this novel, Rushdie handles the mythic mode playfully, and the fairy tale is replete with Arabian Nights–type characters like Iff the Genie and Butt the mechanical hoopoe, who take Haroun and his father, Rashid, to the Land of Gup (or the Land of Story in Urdu) to help them solve their dilemma. As in the Arabian Nights, the dilemma revolves around the telling of stories. Rashid, also known as the Shah of Blah, discovers one day (after his wife runs off with another man) that his magical story-telling powers have vanished. Where have they gone? demands Haroun, appalled that such a thing should happen to his father, because of course the consequences are far severer than merely a loss of livelihood for the Shah of Blah. The very world of stories is in jeopardy, because it would appear that the Arch-Enemy of stories, the tyrant Khattam-Shud (meaning "completely finished" in Urdu), has started to poison the very source of story-telling, the Sea of Stories itself. As Rashid describes Khattam-Shud to his son, it is not difficult to see the parallels with Khomeini, the silencer of Rushdie:

> "Khattam-Shud," he said slowly, "is the Arch-Enemy of all stories, even of Language itself. He is the Prince of Silence and Foe of Speech. And because everything ends, because dreams end, stories end, life ends, at the finish of everything we use his name. 'It's finished,' we tell one another, 'it's over. Khattam-Shud: The End.'"[11]

11. Salman Rushdie, *Haroun and the Sea of Stories* (London: Granta Books and Penguin, 1990), 39. All subsequent references to this work will be cited parenthetically in the text as Rushdie, *Haroun.*

The rest of the novel traces the journey of Haroun to the Lands of Gup (speech) and Chup (silence), to see if he can recover his father's story-telling powers for him. Upon arrival in Gup City, Haroun discovers that the Chupwallas (inhabitants of Chup) have abducted Princess Batcheat, Princess of Gup, and have begun to poison the Ocean of Notions, so that the Sea of Stories has become polluted and the stories have all begun to "go wrong." In order to rescue princess Batcheat and, more important, to save the Ocean, the Guppees decide to go to war with the armies of the Cultmaster of Bezaban, Khattam-Shud himself. Haroun joins them as a volunteer and, once in Chup, remarks on the strangeness of his adventure, which has brought him face to face with the Manichean dualism of life itself:

> As he watched the Shadow Warrior's martial dance, Haroun thought about this strange adventure in which he had become involved. "How many opposites are at war in this battle between Gup and Chup!" he marveled. "Gup is bright and Chup is dark. Gup is warm and Chup is freezing cold. Gup is all chattering and noise, whereas Chup is silent as a shadow. Guppees love the Ocean, Chupwalas try to poison it. Guppees love Stories, and Speech; Chupwalas, it seems, hate these things just as strongly." It was a war between Love (of the Ocean, or the Princess) and Death (which was what Cultmaster Khattam-Shud had in mind for the Ocean, and for the Princess, too). (Rushdie, *Haroun*, 125)

At this point, it would seem that the old ideological struggle between binary opposites cannot be resolved, even through a resuscitation of a mythical genre. Yet Haroun recognizes that the world cannot, or should not, be carved into such simplistic dualities:

> "But it's not as simple as that," he told himself, because the dance of the Shadow Warrior showed him that silence had its own grace and beauty (just as speech could be graceless and ugly); . . . and that creatures of darkness could be as lovely as the children of light. "If Guppees and Chupwalas didn't hate each other so," he thought, "they might actually find each other interesting. Opposites attract, as they say." (125)

Rushdie finds a way out of the dilemma of Manicheanism by allowing for a victory by the forces of Speech over those of Silence, yet in a way that suggests that the new land (world) that comes into being after such a victory will be one where such binary oppositions cease to operate: "The new government of the Land of Chup, headed by Mudra, announced its desire for a long and lasting peace with Gup, a peace in which Night and Day, Speech and Silence, would no longer be separated into Zones by Twilight Strips and Walls of Force" (191).

However, this solution becomes a strategy of petrification in the final analysis, because Rushdie does not "balance" out the historically petrifying effects of myth through the full-fledged intervention of realism, as for example, in the works of the other three writers considered in this book, a strategy that in any case is not without its own limitations, as his debunking of all genres in previous works has shown. In other words, his use of the mythic mode, despite allowing mythic parallels to Khomeini, remains essentially an ahistorical move. Even though the "hero" of the story, Haroun, operates within certain parameters recognizable as belonging to a critical realist framework (such as his willingness to suspend disbelief and enter the Sea of Stories only because he wants to save his father's source of livelihood), he becomes a "real" character, ironically, only when the mythic mode firmly takes over.

Rushdie, by refusing to mythologize history in his first three novels, successfully avoided historical petrification. However, this debunking of myth, and of the other genres used by him, could finally be construed as a failure on his part to construct a viable alternative ideology. Unlike the other three novelists whose works I have discussed, Rushdie seemed to think that no old forms or genres were capable of sustaining ideology in postcolonial societies, since there was no ideology untainted by a Manichean subject-object dialectic. With his latest novel, however, it seems that he is trying, at least, to break out of this Manichean binarism; yet, perhaps because of the surreal nature of his own predicament, he is unable to quite fully rehabilitate the genre of myth in a fashion that could provide a viable solution to the historicity of the postcolonial impasse. Maybe, for Rushdie, some new genre will emerge, after the death of all the old forms and ideologies, a genre that will be able to bear and express the burden of a "new" history. One hopes he will be allowed to continue his bold task of trying to imagine some new, more hopeful alternatives.

# Conclusion

In the work of each of the four Indian novelists writing in English examined here, genre is an important ideological tool. For Narayan, Desai, and Markandaya, a combination (in varying degrees) of myth and realism seems to provide some solution, in art, to the problem of creating an authentic, self-liberating Indian identity and history in the face of colonialist and Orientalist literary strategies of containment. For Rushdie, neither myth nor realism (with their stress on "wholeness") seems to be an appropriate fictive strategy for depicting a world that he sees as fragmented in the aftermath of colonialism. Yet his very debunking of myth (and of other genres) itself becomes a "liberating" strategy, since it reveals the ludicrousness of the Orientalist notion that Third World societies are "whole," "unified," and "simple" structures, which, once understood, can be either dismissed or placed at a safe distance and labeled other.

The danger that a native (as opposed to Orientalist) writer faces in employing myth as a generic strategy of liberation for his or her culture and people is, as stated in the introduction, that of creating a historically "petrified" society, one so rooted in the glory of its precolonial past and mythic traditions that it is unable to move into and deal with present reality (which is, by and large, that of "modern" Western-style technological "progress"). The first three writers in this study have dealt with the problem by balancing the glory of myth with the more critical mode of realism. However, it is quite true that even realism is ultimately a generic strategy of hope, for it allows the writer to construct a world that can be made whole, a world where people can achieve a harmonious balance between self and society and thus give some meaning to their existence and their culture. Realism is thus, ultimately, a "healing" fictive strategy for Third World writers, though certainly a more "progressive," less petrified one than that of myth.

One can say, therefore, that Narayan's, Desai's, and, to a lesser extent, Markandaya's moral visions of the future of their people and culture are ultimately optimistic, since they choose to write within the mythic and realist modes. To some extent, by choosing to endorse the mythic traditions of their culture, they do fall victim to the trap of petrification. Yet, by using realism to undercut and balance the mythic mode, they also succeed in pointing the way out of such petrification without yielding to the rather hopeless, ultimately pessimistic vision of Rushdie, who views both myth and realism as strategies of containment, equally so for the native writers as for the Orientalist.

I would like to point out here that Rushdie, despite his cynicism, is not writing out of self-hatred, as for instance Naipaul is (see the Introduction). As pointed out in the introductory chapter, the colonized or postcolonial writer has really only two ideological choices in the wake of the colonial aftermath: to accept the ideology of containment, by which he and his culture are represented in orientalist texts, or to refute this ideology with one of liberation. Clearly, a Third World writer who accepts and utilizes Orientalist strategies of containment can be said to be operating at some level of self-hatred.

However, as also discussed in this work, the opposite ideological choice of constructing an alternative ideology of liberation is not a path mapped with clear markers. In fact, given that the writers under discussion are really the first generation of postcolonial intellectuals, it is hardly surprising that their task appears so daunting and complex. It seems that for a "native" writer who wishes to avoid the slippage into historical petrification, as well as the risk of recreating the old simplified dichotomy between self and other, a healthy dose of self-criticism would be a necessary part of the overall strategy of liberation.

Rushdie, certainly more than the others, feels that self-critique must be a crucial component of his own liberating strategy, which in his fiction takes the form of a tendency to debunk, to demystify, and ultimately discard not just pre- and postcolonial Orientalist genres and forms, but unpalatable and unhealthy native "baggage" as well. He, therefore, in contrast to the other three writers, runs the risk of being accused of self-hatred, of re-creating Orientalist hegemonic structures and strategies in his fiction.[1]

However, it has been my contention and belief throughout this discussion that such is not the case with Rushdie. His use of myth to debunk itself is a liberating, not a containing, strategy, since its primary purpose is not to debase native mythic traditions, but rather to appropriate Western narrative fictive strategies used to contain the other, and by using them parodically and cynically, albeit self-referentially, to blast them away. For example, the authorial appropriation of the term "Mahound" in *The Satanic Verses*—which has negative connotations as an Orientalist term referring to the Prophet Mohammad—emblematizes, I think, Rushdie's stance of liberation: he uses the term in order to debunk it, not, as many of his critics would have it, because he is a self-hating Muslim out to debase Muslim traditions and beliefs. I would like to quote here an excerpt from Rushdie's recent interview with *Newsweek* magazine, where Rushdie himself makes precisely this point:

> I must have known, my accusers say, that my use of the old devil-name "Mahound," a medieval European demonization of "Mohammed," would cause offense. In fact, this is an instance in which de-contextualization has created a complete reversal of meaning. A part of the relevant context is on page 93 of the novel. "To turn insults into strengths, whigs, tories, Blacks all chose to wear with pride the names they were given in scorn; likewise, our mountain-climbing, prophet-motivated solitary is to be the medieval baby-

---

1. For an interesting account of Rushdie as an Orientalist, see Feroza Jussawalla's "Resurrecting the Prophet: The Case of Salman, the Otherwise," *Public Culture* 2 (Fall 1989): 106–17. She writes, "Among these [Orientalist] poets, novelists and philosophers, we must, of course, now number Rushdie not only as one who writes about the Orient, but as someone who writes about Oriental people, their customs, 'mind', destiny and so on, from the vantage point of a successful mainstream Westernized immigrant" (109).

frightener, the Devil's synonym: Mahound." *Central to the purposes of "The Satanic Verses" is the process of reclaiming language from one's opponents. Trotsky was Trotsky's jailer's name. By taking it for his own, he symbolically conquered his captor and set himself free. Something of the same spirit lay behind my use of the name "Mahound."* (*Newsweek*, 12 February 1990, 54; emphasis added)

Thus, in one way or another, by using some combination of myth and realism or, as in Rushdie's case, through a debunking of both, all four writers discussed herein have found a way to refute, effectively, Orientalist strategies of containment by formulating counterpart ideologies of liberation in their works. They have, symbolically at least, set themselves free.

# Bibliography

## Primary Sources

Desai, Anita. *Cry, the Peacock*. 1963. Reprint. New Delhi: Orient Paperbacks, 1983.
——. *Voices in the City*. 1965. Reprint. New Delhi: Orient Paperbacks, 1982.
——. *Where Shall We Go This Summer?* 1975. Reprint. New Delhi: Orient Paperbacks, 1982.
——. *Fire on the Mountain*. 1977. Reprint. New York: Penguin Books, 1981.
——. *Clear Light of Day*. Harmondsworth, Middlesex: Penguin Books, 1980.
——. *In Custody*. New York: Harper and Row, 1984.
——. *Bye-Bye Blackbird*. New Delhi: Orient Paperbacks, 1985.
——. *Baumgartner's Bombay*. New York: Knopf, 1989.
Forster, E. M. *A Passage to India*. 1924. Reprint. New York: Harcourt Brace Jovanovich, 1984.
Jhabvala, Ruth Prawer. *Three Continents*. New York: William Morrow, 1987.
Kipling, Rudyard. "The Bridge-Builders." In *The Day's Work*. New York: Doubleday and McClure, 1894; rpt. 1898. 3–47.
Markandaya, Kamala. *Nectar in a Sieve*. New York: John Day, 1954.
——. *Some Inner Fury*. New York: John Day, 1956.
——. *A Silence of Desire*. New York: John Day, 1961.
——. *Possession*. New York: John Day, 1963.

————. *A Handful of Rice.* New York: John Day, 1966.

————. *The Coffer Dams.* New York: John Day, 1969.

————. *The Nowhere Man.* New York: John Day, 1972.

————. *Two Virgins.* New York: John Day, 1973.

————. *The Golden Honeycomb.* New York: Thomas Y. Crowell, 1977.

————. *Shalimar.* New York: Harper and Row, 1982.

Naipaul, V. S. *The Middle Passage: The Caribbean Revisited.* New York: Macmillan, 1963.

————. *An Area of Darkness.* 1964. Reprint. New York: Vintage Books, 1981.

————. *Finding the Center: Two Narratives.* New York: Alfred A. Knopf, 1984.

Narayan, R. K. *The Bachelor of Arts.* 1937. Reprint. Chicago: University of Chicago Press, 1984.

————. *The Dark Room.* 1938. Reprint. Chicago: University of Chicago Press, 1981.

————. *The English Teacher.* 1945. Reprint. Chicago: University of Chicago Press, 1980.

————. *Mr. Sampath: The Printer of Malgudi.* 1949. Reprint. Chicago: University of Chicago Press, 1981.

————. *The Financial Expert.* 1952. Reprint. Chicago: University of Chicago Press, 1981.

————. *Waiting for the Mahatma.* 1955. Reprint. Chicago: University of Chicago Press, 1981.

————. *The Guide.* 1958. Reprint. New York: Penguin Books, 1980.

————. *The Man-Eater of Malgudi.* 1961. Reprint. Harmondsworth, Middlesex: Penguin Books, 1983.

————. *The Vendor of Sweets.* 1967. Reprint. Harmondsworth, Middlesex: Penguin Books, 1983.

————. *The Painter of Signs.* 1977. Reprint. Harmondsworth, Middlesex: Penguin Books, 1982.

————. *Talkative Man.* New York: Viking, 1987.

Rushdie, Salman. *Grimus.* 1975. Reprint. New York: Overlook Press, 1982.

————. *Midnight's Children.* 1980. Reprint. New York: Avon, 1982.

————. *Shame.* London: Jonathan Cape, 1983.

————. *The Satanic Verses.* London: Viking, 1988.

————. *Haroun and the Sea of Stories.* London: Granta Books and Penguin, 1990.

## Secondary Sources

Ahluwalia, Harsharan S. "Narayan's Sense of Audience." *Ariel* 15 (January 1984): 59–65.

Alcock, Peter. "Rope, Serpent, Fire: Recent Fiction of Anita Desai." *Journal of Indian Writing in English* 9 (January 1981): 15–34.

Amirthanayagam, Guy. *Writers in East-West Encounter: New Cultural Bearings.* London: Macmillan, 1982.

"An Interview with Salman Rushdie." *Justice* 1 (May 1985).

Appasamy, S. P. "The Golden Honeycomb: A Saga of Princely Life in India by Kamala Markandaya." *Journal of Indian Writing in English* 6, no. 2 (1978): 56–63.

Argyle, Barry. "Kamala Markandaya's *Nectar in a Sieve.*" *Ariel* 4 (January 1973): 35–45.

Asnani, Shyam M. "Anita Desai's Fiction: A New Dimension." *Indian Literature* 24 (March–April 1981): 44–54.

————. "The Theme of Loneliness and Withdrawal in Anita Desai's *Fire on the Mountain.*" *Journal of Indian Writing in English* 9 (January 1981): 81–92.

————. "Bibliography: R. K. Narayan." *Literary Endeavour* 3 (January–June 1982): 103–20.

————. "The Use of Myth in R. K. Narayan's Novels." *Literary Endeavour* 3 (January–June 1982): 19–31.

Bhatnagar, O. P. "Love, Non-Violence, and Freedom in *Waiting for the Mahatma.*" *Literary Endeavour* 3 (January–June 1982): 61–69.

Brennan, Timothy. *Salman Rushdie and the Third World: Myths of the Nation.* New York: St. Martin's Press, 1989.

Cassirer, Ernst. *Symbol, Myth, and Culture.* New Haven: Yale University Press, 1979.

Chauhan, P. S. "Kamala Markandaya: Sense and Sensibility." *Literary Criterion* 12, nos. 2–3 (1976): 135–47.

Chellapan, K. "The Apocalypse of the Ordinary: The Comic Myths of R. K. Narayan." *Literary Endeavour* 3 (January–June 1982): 32–38.

Crichton, Sarah, and Laura Shapiro. "An Interview with Salman Rushdie." *Newsweek*, 12 February 1990.

Dale, James. "Sexual Politics in the Novels of Kamala Markandaya." *World Literature Written in English* 21 (Summer 1982): 347–56.

Drum, Alice. "Kamala Markandaya's Modern Quest Tale." *World Literature Written in English* 22 (Autumn 1983): 323–32.

Dudt, Charmazel. "Past and Present: A Journey to Confrontation." *Journal of Indian Writing in English* 9 (January 1981): 93–98.

Eagleton, Terry. *Literary Theory.* Minneapolis: University of Minnesota Press, 1983.

Fanon, Frantz. *Black Skin, White Masks.* New York: Grove Press, 1967.

Frye, Northrop. *Anatomy of Criticism: Four Essays.* 1957. Reprint. New York: Atheneum, 1970.

Gadamer, Hans-Georg. *Truth and Method.* 1960. Reprint. New York: Seabury Press, 1975.

Garebian, Keith. "Strategy and Theme in the Art of R. K. Narayan." *Ariel* 5 (October 1974): 70–81.

————. "The Spirit of Place in R. K. Narayan." *World Literature Written in English* 14 (November 1975): 291–99.

Gooneratne, Yasmine. "Traditional Elements in the Fiction of Kamala Markandaya, R. K. Narayan, and Ruth Prawer Jhabvala." *World Literature Written in English* 5, no. 1 (1975): 121–30.

Green, Martin B. *Dreams of Adventure, Deeds of Empire.* New York: Basic Books, 1979.

Harrex, S. C. "A Sense of Identity: The Novels of Kamala Markandaya." *Journal of Commonwealth Literature* 6, no. 1 (1971): 65–78.

Jameson, Fredric. *The Political Unconscious: Narrative as a Socially Symbolic Act.* Ithaca: Cornell University Press, 1981.

————. "Magical Narratives: Romance as Genre." *New Literary History* 7 (Autumn 1975): 135–63.

JanMohammed, Abdul. *Manichean Aesthetics.* Amherst: University of Massachusetts Press, 1983.

Jayanta, R. A. "*The Man-Eater of Malgudi:* Some Aspects of its Narrative Strategy." *Literary Endeavour* 3 (January–June 1982): 92–101.

Jussawalla, Feroza. *Family Quarrels: Toward a Criticism of Indian Writing in English.* New York: Peter Lang, 1985.

————. "Resurrecting the Prophet: The Case of Salman, the Otherwise." *Public Culture* 2 (Fall 1989): 106–17.

Kaufman, Michael. "Author from Three Countries." *New York Times Book Review*, 13 November 1983, 22.

Kirpal, V.P.K. "An Analysis of Narayan's Technique." *Ariel* 14 (October 1983): 16–19.

Krishna, Francine E. "Anita Desai's *Fire on the Mountain.*" *Indian Literature* 25, no. 5 (1982): 158–69.

Kumar, Shiv K. "Tradition and Change in the Novels of Kamala Markandaya." *Books Abroad* 43 (Autumn 1969): 508–13.

Larson, Charles R. "A Note on R. K. Narayan." *Books Abroad* 50 (1976): 352–53.

Levy-Bruhl, Lucien. *How Natives Think*. 1926. Reprint. New York: Arno Press, 1979.

Libert, Florence. "An Interview with Anita Desai." *World Literature Written in English* 30, no. 1 (1990): 47–55.

Lukács, Georg. *The Meaning of Contemporary Realism*. London: Merlin Press, 1963.

———. *Realism in Our Time: Literature and the Class Struggle*. New York: Harper and Row, 1964.

Maini, Darshan Singh. "The Achievement of Anita Desai." In *Indo-English Literature*, ed. K. K. Sharma, 216–30. Ghaziabad: Vimal Prakashan, 1977.

Mann, Thomas. *Stories of Three Decades*. 1930. Reprint. New York: Alfred Knopf, 1966.

Markandaya, Kamala. "One Pair of Eyes: Some Random Reflections." In *The Commonwealth Writer Overseas: Themes of Exile and Re-Patriation*, ed. Alastair Niven, 23–32. Brussels: Librairie Marcel Didier, 1976.

Mathur, O. P. *"The Guide:* A Study in Cultural Ambivalence." *Literary Endeavour* 3 (January–June 1982): 70–79.

May, Hal, ed. *Contemporary Authors*. Vol. 3. Detroit: Gale Research, 1984.

Mojtabai, A. G. "The Poet in All His Squalor." *New York Times Book Review*, 3 March 1985, 7.

Mukherjee, Meenakshi. *The Twice-Born Fiction*. New Delhi: Arnold Heinemann, 1971.

Naik, M. K. "Irony as Stance and as Vision: A Comparative Study of V. S. Naipaul's *The Mystic Masseur* and R. K. Narayan's *The Guide*." *Journal of Indian Writing in English* 6, no. 1 (1978): 1–13.

———. "R. K. Narayan and 'The Spirit of Place.' " *Literary Endeavour* 3 (January–June 1982): 7–18.

———. ed. *Perspectives on Indian Prose in English*. Atlantic Highlands, N.J.: Humanities Press, 1982.

Nandakumar, Prema. "Indian Writing in English: Three Cheers!" *Indian Literature* 13, no. 4 (1970): 27–41.

Newman, Judie. "History and Letters: Anita Desai's *Baumgartner's Bombay*." *World Literature Written in English* 30, no. 1 (1990): 37–46.

Parameswaran, Uma. "On the Theme of Paternal Love in the Novels of R. K. Narayan." *International Fiction Review* 1 (July 1974): 146–48.

———. "Handcuffed to History: Salman Rushdie's Art." *Ariel* 14 (October 1983): 34–45.

Pollard, Arthur. "Kamala Markandaya's *The Golden Honeycomb*." *Journal of Indian Writing in English* 8 (January–July 1980): 22–26.

Prasad, Hari Mohan. "Sound or Sense: A Study of Anita Desai's *Bye-Bye Blackbird*." *Journal of Indian Writing in English* 9 (January 1981): 58–66.

Ram, Atma, comp. "Anita Desai: A Bibliography." *Journal of Indian Writing in English* 9 (January 1981): 93–98.

———. "A View of *Where Shall We Go This Summer*." *Journal of Indian Writing in English* 9 (January 1981): 74–80.

Ramamurti, K. S. "The Title of R. K. Narayan's *The English Teacher*." *Literary Endeavour* 3 (January–June 1982): 45–51.

Rao, K.S.N. "The Novels of Kamala Markandaya." *Literature East and West* 15 (1971): 209–18.

———. "Love, Sex, Marriage, and Morality in Kamala Markandaya's Novels." *Osmania Journal of English Studies* 10 (1973): 69–77.

———. "Religious Elements in Kamala Markandaya's Novels." *Ariel* 8 (January 1977): 35–50.

Rao, Panduranga. "Tea with R. K. Narayan." *Journal of Commonwealth Literature* 6 (1971): 79–83.

Rao, Susheela N. "A Bibliography of Kamala Markandaya." *World Literature Written in English* 20 (Autumn 1981): 344–50.

Ross, Robert, ed. *International Literature in English: The Major Writers*. New York: Garland, 1991.

Rothfork, J., "Hindu Mysticism in the Twentieth Century: R. K. Narayan's *The Guide*." *Philological Quarterly* 62 (Winter 1983): 31–43.

Rubin, David. *After the Raj: British Novels of India Since 1947*. Hanover, N.H.: University Press of New England, 1986.

Rushdie, Salman. "Outside the Whale." *American Film*, January 1985.

Said, Edward. *Orientalism*. New York: Random House, 1978.

———. *Culture and Imperialism*. New York: Alfred A. Knopf, 1993.

Sharma, K. K., ed. *Indo-English Literature*. Ghaziabad: Vimal Prakashan, 1977.

Shastri, N. R. *"Where Shall We Go This Summer?:* A Critical Study." *Osmania Journal of English Studies* 17 (1981): 83–103.

Shimer, Dorothy Blair. "Sociological Imagery in the Novels of Kamala Markandaya." *World Literature Written in English* 14 (November 1975): 357–70.

Shirwadker, Meena. *Image of Woman in the Indo-Anglian Novel*. New Delhi: Sterling Publishers, 1979.

Singh, Amritjit. "The Uses of Exile." In *Commonwealth Literature*. Ed. C. D. Narasimhaiah. Madras: Macmillan, India, 1981. 165–79.

Singh, Amritjit, Rajiva Verman, and Irene M. Joshi, eds. *Indian Literature in English, 1827–1979*. Detroit: Gale Research Company, 1981.

Singh, Satyanarain. "A Note on the World-View of R. K. Narayan." *Indian Literature* 24 (January–February 1981): 106–9.

Srinath, C. N. "R. K. Narayan's Comic Vision: Possibilities and Limitations." *World Literature Today* 55 (Summer 1981): 416–19.

Srivastava, Ramesh K. "Voices of Artists in the City." *Journal of Indian Writing in English* 9 (January 1981): 47–57.

Stokes, Eric. "Generally Ravishing." Review of *The Golden Honeycomb*, by Kamala Markandaya. *Times Literary Supplement*, 29 April 1977, 307.

Suleri, Sara. *The Rhetoric of English India*. Chicago: University of Chicago Press, 1992.

Thumboo, Edwin. "Kamala Markandaya's *A Silence of Desire*." *Journal of Indian Writing in English* 8 (January–July 1980): 108–36.

Trilling, Lionel. *Sincerity and Authenticity*. Cambridge: Harvard University Press, 1971.

Venkatachari, K. "R. K. Narayan's Novels: Acceptance of Life." *Indian Literature* 13 (March 1970): 73–86.

Verghese, Paul. *The Problems of the Indian Creative Writer in English*. Bombay: Somaiya Publications, 1971.

Vyas, Bhanushankar Odhavji. "Viscid Voices of the Inner Kingdom." *Journal of Indian Writing in English* 9 (January 1981): 1–14.

Walsh, William. *Commonwealth Literature*. London: Oxford University Press, 1973.

———. *R. K. Narayan: A Critical Appreciation*. Chicago: University of Chicago Press, 1982.

Wilson, Keith. *"Midnight's Children* and Reader Responsibility." *Critical Quarterly* 26 (Autumn 1984): 23–37.

Woodcock, George. "Two Great Commonwealth Novelists: R. K. Narayan and V. S. Naipaul." *Sewanee Review* 87 (Winter/Spring 1979): 1–28.

# Index